THE HERALD YEARS

JACK WEBSTER

THE HERALD YEARS

B&W PUBLISHING

First published 1996
by B&W Publishing Ltd., Edinburgh
First issued in paperback 1997
ISBN 1 873631 66 9 Hardback
1 873631 72 3 Paperback
Articles © The Herald
This compilation © Jack Webster 1996

British Library Cataloguing in Publication Data:
A catalogue record for this book is available
from the British Library.

Cover photograph © B&W Publishing
All other photographs
© The Herald Picture Archive

Printed by Werner Söderström

CONTENTS

CONTENTS

CONTENTS

FOREWORD

JACK WEBSTER started writing his weekly column for *The Herald*, then the *Glasgow Herald*, in the mid-1980s. At that time the paper was under some criticism for its burgeoning cadre of columnists and a bad joke doing the rounds was that the *Herald* had more columns than the Parthenon. (A tyro *Herald* journalist, on asking if he too could have his column, was duly told that the paper already had more columns than the Parthenon . . . the next morning he was heard asking his newsagent: 'Do you have a paper called *The Parthenon*?')

Anyway, a plethora of columnists there may have been, but Jack soon emerged as a firm favourite of the *Herald*'s readers, and regular market research showed that he maintained his popularity. His style was, and is, difficult to assess; it is certainly *sui generis*, very much his own. I was once chatting to a farmworker in Aberdeenshire; we were sparring in a very Scottish way. He was trying to find out more about me; I was trying to give nothing away. Eventually he managed to elicit the information that I was a journalist on the *Herald*. "Ah," he said, "ye'll ken Jack Webster?"

"Of course," I replied. "He's a good friend."

There was a long pause as the man deliberated. Then he pronounced: "Noo, there's a chiel fa's nivver forgotten faar he came frae."

It might not sound much of a compliment, but it was meant as high praise. And there indeed is the secret of Jack's success, not just as a columnist but also as a feature writer, an author, a television documentary-maker.

He has travelled the world several times, he has worked on six very different papers, he has delivered after-dinner speeches all over Britain, he has interviewed some of the greatest figures of our century, he is on Christian name terms with literally hundreds of household names in the worlds of sport, entertainment, politics and business—yet he has never forgotten whence he came. His child-hood in the Aberdeenshire village of Maud, his memories of and abiding affection for that stern but generous and characterful haunch of Scotland, the far North-east—these inform every word he writes.

Here is his touchstone for everything. He filters all his experiences and commentaries through the values of his Buchan upbringing. This gives his writing its unique quality. He has invented his own special kind of nostalgia, which is not girning or wistful or overly backward-looking, but positive and life-enhancing and somehow very much germane to the here and now. He is, in a sense, a rustic philosopher who has added more than a dash of street-savvy to his world view.

Jack certainly has his criticisms of the way we live now—and sometimes I think that his very best writing is when he allows a little anger or indignation to come through—but he is essentially a warm writer. He takes risks; he teeters on the brink of sentimentality, he flirts with hyperbole—yet the discipline and control and craft are always there. His prose is supremely readable; but I suspect that the words do not always flow from his keyboard as easily as they read. Easy reading is damned hard writing, someone once said: and although Jack makes little of the toil and sweat of journalism, and prefers to present it all as enormous fun, he has worked hard and long at his calling.

This collection of columns from *The Herald* represents the full flowering of what have perhaps been the greatest years in a long, memorable and celebrated Scottish journalistic career. And the good news is that it is proceeding apace; Jack may have reached retirement age, but he is not severing his association with *The Herald*, nor is he quitting the columnar grind. Read and enjoy these consummate columns in the safe and happy knowledge that there are many more to come.

Harry Reid
Editor, *The Herald*

INTRODUCTION

About This Book. . . .

In the mid-1980s I reached that uncertain age of fifty-five, when many people nowadays are heading for early retirement. Behind me lay an exciting career in journalism, stretching for nearly forty years, one half of which had been spent on the *Daily Express* as a feature writer, travelling far and wide and encountering some of the most fascinating characters of the 20th century.

In 1980, however, I had left the *Express* for the life of a freelance writer, which is the dream of many a wordsmith. But if that brings a sense of freedom it also calls for harder work, with a great deal less by way of security.

So had it been a foolhardy decision to give up a plum job on the *Express*? Before I had time to consider it too deeply the fates took a hand in a double-edged kind of way.

I wrote a documentary film for the BBC, based on the selling of my late father's farm at Maud in Aberdeenshire, which could be viewed as a commercial transaction or, more significantly, as a symbol of a break with the land which had bred me. As an only child who could have ensured the continuity of his heritage, I had gone away to a very different life, far from the bare land of Buchan and in search of a contrasting glamour which I would find on the distant horizons of Hollywood or Hong Kong.

There was something plain and natural about that little documentary film but it so captured public imagination that it won a television award. It was called *Webster's Roup*, filmed in one day, written in one evening and costing the BBC so little money that I became the flavour of the time, encouraged to proceed with more where that came from.

Almost at the same time, by chance, I was invited to join what was then the *Glasgow Herald* and one of the first features I was asked to write was a profile of Ian Chapman, chairman of Collins the publishers. In making the initial contact I discovered, to my surprise, that Mr Chapman's roots were within a few miles of my own in Aberdeenshire. Indeed I had known his cousins since I was a boy.

When we eventually met in London—and to remind him of that childhood scene—I gave him the video of my award-winning film, which he viewed that evening with the intention of sending it straight back. But the closing scene so choked him emotionally that he did something different.

Ever on the outlook for new titles, he tracked me down to my London hotel to insist that I write a book for Collins, all about my childhood and background in Aberdeenshire. Unknown to him, however, that book had already been written. A volume of memoirs entitled *A Grain of Truth* had been published in 1981, popular in Scotland though he would not have heard much about it in London.

But there was no stopping the persuasive Mr Chapman. He would buy that book for his Fontana paperback company and commission me to write a sequel in hardback. Before I knew what had happened he had me round to the Collins headquarters in St James's, signing a substantial contract and trying to absorb the fact that I was about to become a paperback writer.

The same Ian Chapman would play an even more significant part in my career by engaging me as the biographer of his friend and greatest discovery, the late Alistair MacLean, whose novels ranged from *HMS Ulysses* to *The Guns of Navarone* and *Where Eagles Dare*. But all that is another story.

The diversion to writing television scripts and major biographies rather masked the fact that I was now into the final decade of staff journalism, taking over the weekly column in the *Herald* made vacant by the premature death of the brilliant Colm Brogan.

As I prepared to pace myself through those years towards sixty-five, little did I know that this final phase would turn into an Indian Summer of such warmth as to add its own special chapter to a career which was already rich in memories. To discover a whole new seam of readers with such a sense of loyalty became a bonus in itself, creating a bond even with people I have yet to meet.

That final decade had covered major events in Glasgow which included the Garden Festival of 1988 and the city's Year of Culture in 1990, when everyone from Frank Sinatra to Luciano Pavarotti came to thrill the Scottish audience and put Glasgow more firmly on the map of international acceptance.

My time on *The Herald* had taken me to the beaches of Normandy for the fiftieth anniversary of D-Day, onward to the American Presidential election and eastward to that greatest of Russian cities, St Petersburg.

The response to that weekly column became a revelation, whether I was dealing with the tragedy of Dunblane or the man who phoned me about the daffodils on the day he died—or discovering the strange phenomenon that Aberdonians tend to dry between their toes whereas Glaswegians don't!

As that final year drew to a close in the summer of 1996, I stepped up to receive the award as Columnist of the Year, rounding off nearly half a century of journalism in a most agreeable manner.

The publishers decided that this was as good a time as any to produce a selection of those weekly columns in the more permanent form of a book. They had followed a similar course with *The Express Years*, published in 1994, and now it was time to address a more recent audience with *The Herald Years*—well over a hundred columns which appeared in Scotland's national newspaper from the mid-eighties to the mid-nineties.

As with the *Express* volume, I have left the articles exactly as they were written on the day, with whatever spontaneity or imperfection —and with the inevitable overlapping of topics. I hope they stir memories of the times in which we have lived, as filtered through the heart and soul of one Scottish journalist who cannot believe his luck in having led such a rewarding life.

Jack Webster
Glasgow, October 1996

For My Grandchildren
JACK, SINEAD AND FRASER

MY FRIEND WALTER—LOCAL HERO

I HAVE never doubted that Walter, my friend and neighbour, fought a good war as a bomber pilot of the 1940s.

Like many another veteran of Hitler's holocaust, he fights it still in the repository of his mind and would fain regale us from time to time with tales of the drama that was engraven on young lives as they dropped their bombs amid flashing searchlights and cracking anti-aircraft guns.

How could he forget? They came home on a wing and a prayer, these lads, spared for a continuation of life by the random chance of where the German shellfire might land.

Such wartime recollection, however, wears thin to a succeeding generation and many a genuine hero has had to endure the doubting laughter of his children as they sought to fit the picture of a dashing young pilot into the greater girth of the bumbling geriatric that most of us become to an ungrateful offspring.

Walter has taken it all with high good humour, cackling out a hearty laugh as a circle of friends have chaffed him about his wartime heroics. Even his wife would come back from motoring holidays on the Continent with tales of an embarrassing moment when Walter, standing high on some German vantage point, would spread an arm across a landscape now rid of Nazi marshalling yards which he had destroyed in a night.

No taut-faced Teuton within earshot was going to divert him from his moment of rekindled glory. His wife would smile apologetically at the host nation in a spirit of forgive and forget.

Back home, Walter was leaving my house one evening when he slipped on the top step and took an alarming tumble to the ground. Our dash to help him was met with a smiling face which reassured us that he was really all right.

1

What raised the look of positive glee was the fact that, after all those years, he had saved himself with an instinctive application of the old parachute roll. Bravo! It still worked.

Those wartime memories, we thought, were at last receding into suitable perspective when the phone rang in Walter's home last Armistice weekend. In the current mood of ex-service reunion, his old bomber squadron were planning a get-together in the spring. They would gather at Cosford, where a large museum still houses the aircraft relics of the Second World War. Wives would be welcome.

New life sprung into Walter the Wing. Here at least he would have a sympathetic audience of people who would not only believe his stories but were a part of them.

As the great day approached, he was out in his driveway, polishing the cockpit of his Vauxhall Cavalier in readiness for take-off. The old pride was blossoming once more.

A few loafers among us, with nothing better to do, leaned over the garden fence and treated him to some scurrilous banter.

Where were his goggles? When "Biggles Goes to War" in 1984, should we perhaps alert all marshalling yards between Glasgow and Cheshire?

On the appointed morning it was "Chocks Away!" as Walter took off from the runway of his suburban semi on the South Side and disappeared in a cloud of dust with only a navigating wife for crew.

With him he took a typical story of the young Scot of his generation, still at school when war broke out in 1939 but soon to be whisked off from his early studies at Glasgow University, no more than a lad of 18 but fit for training as a pilot.

By the age of 19 Walter was guiding massive Lancasters and Liberators towards German targets, dicing with death by the minute, a Glasgow boy growing into a man in the night.

If his wife had ever any doubts about the authenticity of his stories, she was soon to have a flea in her ear to match the lump in her throat. For there was Walter with his wartime pals, in assorted stages of preservation, re-living the days when they went through hell together and formed bonds of trust and admiration which no galloping time could diminish.

Older men came up to tell her of their admiration for the young Glasgow lad who had kept his head in the heat of battle. They remembered the emergency of his take-off when engine failure plunged him into high-tension wires and he brought his plane to a safe and skilful landing with a potentially explosive load of bombs and fuel.

Out in the museum hangar at Cosford, Walter suddenly disappeared in the direction of the surviving Liberator. By the time his wife caught up, he had already clambered in through the bomb-bay and was waving to her from the cockpit, filled with the joy of a kid who has found an old toy.

Memories came flooding back. Like the time his bomb-aimer was going through the golden-shot routine of "Left a little, right a little" and came up with the sudden outburst: "Oh Christ, skipper, BACK a little!"

When the war was over, the mature young man returned to complete his university studies and to teach at Eastbank Academy. He now heads his department at Springburn College.

Walter was recalled as a reservist during the Korean War, gained a taste for those new-fangled jets and considered making a career out of the RAF.

Clearly, flying was in his blood. Now, since the Vauxhall Cavalier came in to land from that memorable reunion the other day, the lady navigator has been giving us a fresh picture of that pilot she has been living with all those years.

The familiar stories of his bombing raids on Germany were certainly not pie in the sky. In fact, good old Walter hadn't told us a half of it.

Maybe next time that old codger in your local pub starts telling you about how he sorted out Hitler, you should pay a little more attention.

Whatever beer he drinks, there is just the chance that he, like my courageous friend Walter, is a very genuine local hero.

HARRY BENSON—LORD OF THE LENS

IN the ribbing that runs between writing journalists and their photographic colleagues, there is an assertion that, if the latter can push that button often enough, they should surely come up with at least one decent picture, perhaps even an award-winning one by chance.

But if we scribblers harboured any serious doubts about the art of photo-journalism they would be dispelled by the recent television programme on that king of the camera, lord of the lens, Glasgow's own Harry Benson, the freelance photographer who bases himself in New York and beats the best in the world.

Some of the tales about Harry are legend, many of his pictures classics. Through 20 years on the American scene, he has covered every major drama and scooped the world by catching the uncatchable Garbo in one of her rare off-guard moments.

He so gained the confidence of the Beatles that he was privileged to snap their more private occasions, not least the famous pillow fight.

He does it, I would say, by a combination of instinct, perseverance and what the world now calls charisma. Even at 54, he is brimful of a boyish enthusiasm which I was able to witness at first hand when I worked with him in the wild days of the sixties.

As *Daily Express* men we had gone to the United Nations building in New York to cover the meeting of King Constantine of Greece and U. Thant, the Secretary-General. That glamorous film star, Melina Mercouri (now in political power but then in exile) was trying to hand a petition to her king, protesting about the military junta in Greece. The photographers were running after her to record a poignant moment.

In the rugby scrum of tough American snappers, it was Harry Benson who emerged next day with the picture to cap them all.

Back in Glasgow, I was telling a mutual friend of the way he had elbowed his way to the front and captured the historic frame.

He laughed heartily and said in reminiscence: "Oh that's just Harry. I remember him as a young lad on the *Hamilton Advertiser*, taking wedding pictures outside Hamilton Old Parish Church. He was elbowing his way to the front of two photographers even then!"

The irrepressible Harry found his way to London and then to Manhattan, where I would drop in for a drink at his apartment on East 63rd Street and we would indulge in great blethers about Glasgow.

I was not the only visitor during those bewildering, exciting days of the sixties. Another of Harry's callers was Bobby Kennedy, who lived round the corner by the East River.

Not long after I left New York, he was accompanying Kennedy on a visit to Los Angeles, somehow sensing that he should be there. He was passing through the kitchen of the Ambassador Hotel, heading towards a back exit, when suddenly there were shots and the second Kennedy lay dying at the hands of an assassin.

Harry was just feet away. Instinctively he jumped on to the kitchen hotplate and caught that memorable picture of Ethel Kennedy leaning over her dying husband, with a hand of disproportionate size reaching up towards the camera.

What the recent television programme failed to get into focus, presumably because it was too short to do the subject justice, was the Scottish end of Harry Benson's story.

It would have interested viewers to learn, for example, that he is the son of the late Sidney Benson, who founded and ran Calderpark Zoo and whose widow still lives in Newton Mearns. Harry never fails to phone his mother or to stop off for a fleeting call on his frequent flights around the world.

If son Harry has notched up some high dramas in the land of Uncle Sam, his father once told me a story to match most of them.

With the same adventurous spirit as his son, Sidney Benson left Glasgow for the Brooklyn district of New York in 1929 and soon found himself playing football for the Scottish team in the local ethnic league.

The match against the German team took on a special excitement when it was learned that the great Max Schmelling, in New York for a big fight and about to become the heavyweight champion of the world, was coming along to cheer on the Germans.

In the course of the match, a Scot who had been fouled by a German got up in retaliation and clocked him an uppercut which would have done justice to the champ himself. As the poor fellow lay cold, Schmelling could not control an appreciative outburst and was heard to say, from the little grandstand near the touchline, that that was the best punch he had seen in years.

Sidney Benson observed it all and somehow, the name of the unfortunate German was to stick in his memory. It was Bruno Hauptmann.

A few years later the world was shocked by the first of the major kidnapping stories—that of the baby son of Charles Lindbergh, famous airman who had captured the headlines with his first-ever solo crossing of the Atlantic, from New York to Paris.

Several years later, when they eventually caught, tried and executed the man who murdered the baby, Sidney Benson was sure he knew the face in the press photographs.

It did not take long to verify that it was the same Bruno Hauptmann who had felt the full force of a Scottish fist those few years earlier.

Sidney Benson returned to Scotland to become a well-known name in zoological circles and these tales of the New World may have played some part in turning the footsteps of his son, a generation later, towards the American beat.

If young Harry had been around in his father's Brooklyn days, you could bet your bottom dollar he would have come away with a prize-winning picture of that stupendous uppercut.

HOODOO ON AMERICAN PRESIDENTS?

AS President Reagan was sworn in for his second term, the precautions of bullet-proof vest and protective shields were taken for thoroughly sound and realistic reasons, given the current climate of international terrorism.

But even without such modern madness, the President would still need all the luck and protection in the world to burst a hoodoo which has plagued the American Presidency since 1841, when William Henry Harrison became the first incumbent to die in office. (He caught a cold after a few weeks and died of pneumonia).

From that time onwards, every American President inaugurated in the following 20-year periods has also died before he left office. The facts speak for themselves.

Twenty years on . . .
   Abraham Lincoln was inaugurated in 1861. Assassinated at Ford's Theatre in Washington in 1865.

Twenty years on . . .
   James A. Garfield was inaugurated in 1881. Died from an assassin's bullet just six months later.

Twenty years on . . .
   William McKinley was inaugurated in 1901 for second time. A few months later, he was standing in a receiving line when a deranged anarchist shot him twice. He died eight days later.

Twenty years on . . .
   Warren G. Harding was inaugurated in 1921. He died of a heart attack in San Francisco in 1923.

7

Twenty years on . . .

Franklin D. Roosevelt continued in office in 1941, with the emergency of the Second World War. Already stricken with polio, he died of a cerebral haemorrhage while still in office towards the end of that war.

Twenty years on . . .

John F. Kennedy was inaugurated in 1961. Killed by an assassin's bullet as his motorcade drove through Dallas, Texas, in November 1963.

Twenty years on . . .

Ronald Reagan was inaugurated in 1981. He later survived an assassin's bullet and now embarks upon a second term.

Thus the hoodoo has applied to all seven of the Presidents inaugurated on the 20-year mark since 1841. All but one of the other 31 Presidents, from George Washington nearly 200 years ago, have survived to resume a life beyond the Presidency.

Let us hope that Ronald Reagan is not given too strongly to superstition—and that his reputation as a survivor will defeat all the omens and stand him in good stead over the next four years.

DINING AT THE CARLTON CLUB

I WENT to a dinner the other evening in London's Carlton Club, that bastion of British Conservatism which sits in the heart of St James's, where else?

Within these portals the fates of Prime Ministers have been decided, major political issues thrashed out. On the majestic stairway, pride of place among a multitude of portraits goes to the Iron Lady herself, relegating the more widely accepted royal personage to a position of lesser prominence.

Whatever the lady was doing in the prime position, she was there to stay for the duration of her tenancy at No. 10, admitted with honorary status to an establishment where women are normally permitted as guests and no more.

I sampled their sense of inferiority the moment I presented myself to the hall porter, having been granted a room for the night on the strength of my host's good name at the Carlton.

"To which club do you personally belong, sir?" was the question which put me in an immediate quandary. Unless Clydesdale Cricket Club or Aberdeen Football Club were acceptable then I was lost without trace of breeding.

Reclining his head to view me all the better along the double-barrel of his nose, the lofty fellow said: "You mean you belong to no club at all, sir?"

Such an unthinkable species was worthy of closer scientific study, in the company of his colleague, with whom he conferred in hushed tones about the possible contaminative risks of my presence.

Serious deliberation gave way to compassion and I was finally allowed, under sufferance, to stay. After all the fuss, the room charge for the night at £25 was no more than you would pay in a cheap hotel.

9

By the transport of an old iron-cage lift I reached the room, which turned out to be plain and serviceable but far from fancy.

There was no TV or radio, not even a telephone, just a solid wooden wardrobe and one of those old-fashioned chanty-cabinets by the bedside—but no chanty. Still, the bathroom was near enough.

Having regained composure, I thought I would venture down the grand staircase to console myself with a lunchtime drink in the spacious lounge before taking a stroll along the Mall.

A dozen or so pin-striped gents were already spread around the room, discussing politics or reading the *Financial Times*. Choosing what I thought was a strategically-placed settee by the window, I awaited the arrival of the manservant to receive my drink order. The choice of drink had better be strategic as well.

If this was no place for a quenching lager then I had better follow the example of Downing Street's Denis and order myself a gin-and-tonic.

As the butler glided towards me, cool and aloof, I was ready to say my piece when, suddenly, he was launching upon some point of etiquette that had escaped me.

"I'm sorry sir but you cannot sit here with your overcoat on," he said. "Would you kindly deposit it downstairs?"

A dozen disapproving heads turned slowly in my direction as I walked the plank towards the exit and down to meet my original hall porter. Peeling off my respectable camel, I realised I was still in my travelling corduroys, a fact which was already under scrutiny from the superior flunky, with ill-concealed disdain.

"All right," I said, by now impatient with the nonsense, "am I not properly dressed to be here at all?" Inflating his lungs while measuring me from top to toe, he replied: "At least you have a tie and jacket sir."

Thus reprieved, I returned to the lounge for my gin-and-tonic and to peruse a history of the Carlton Club, which turned out to be rather interesting. An earlier Carlton lay round the corner in Pall Mall, one of many gentlemen's clubs in that well-heeled neuk of London which replaced the old coffee houses. There it stood until the evening of October 14, 1940, when Hitler took a hand in its demolition.

As his bombs scored a direct hit on the home of British Conservatism, with ceilings collapsing like thunder and clouds of black smoke invading every corner, the people in the morning-room who escaped miraculously included the young Quintin Hogg (now Lord Hailsham) and Harold Macmillan who, on that occasion at least, had never had it so bad.

So they moved round to St James's Street, taking over the former premises of another famous London club, Arthur's, where they remain to this day.

Just as I was sampling my G-and-T and accepting that my rural background had not prepared me for this kind of life, I was suddenly comforted by a passage in the Carlton history, in which the author wrote: "One of the most frightening experiences in ordinary life is the first visit to a club . . . the apologetic explanation of who you are to the hall porter, the haunting fear that you have unwittingly taken the chair of an outstanding figure . . . above all, the suspicion that, by your behaviour, you are confirming the servants in their belief that the type of member now being elected is very different from what used to be the case. . . ."

I was not alone! Yet, for all their concern about rules, it did strike me they might have paid more attention to the contents of my travelling bag. After all, there is recent history to show that Mrs Thatcher and other symbols of Conservatism are targets for terrorist attack—and I was a stranger who might have had connections.

There is no nameplate on the door, not even a letterbox, so the thought must have occurred to them. In the Carlton's position, wouldn't you be more concerned about that kind of risk than bothering about a man's etiquette or the texture of his trousers?

Postscript.

Five years after that visit, the Carlton Club was indeed blown up by a terrorist bomb. The hall porter was seriously injured.

SO I TAKE MY FAREWELL
OF HONEYNEUK

FOR most of his lifetime, my father bestrode the broad acres of Buchan, as auctioneer at Maud Mart, in the very heart of the Aberdeenshire cattle country.

Everybody knew John Webster, a rugged, rumbustious character of great good humour who called a spade "a bloody shovel" and would offend you only with the truth. You took him as he was or not at all.

From the twenties to the seventies he sold the beef cattle of Buchan through the sale-ring every Wednesday, measured land, valued crops, conducted displenish sales and came to know every farm and farmer in a radius of 20 miles and beyond, the yield potential of the land and the nature and trustworthiness of its master.

His sturdy independence was born of a testing childhood, after his own father, tenant of a small place, contracted the animal disease of anthrax from one of his cattle and died.

At the age of nine, my father was mucking out the byre and protecting the livelihood of his widowed mother and small brother. Neighbours lent a hand and marvelled at the industriousness of the wee lad. In time he became a cattle drover, then a clerk at the mart before reaching his ambition to be an auctioneer.

During those years as a salaried employee, however, there was another ambition—to run his own farm and, if there was a choice in the matter, the picturesque holding of Honeyneuk, on the edge of Maud village.

It came on the market in 1952, when he was 47, and it must go down as a tribute to his solid worth that he could borrow every penny of the purchase price with very little to show for collateral.

And there he farmed for the rest of his life, hoping that the natural succession of the land would apply, while knowing that his only child had gone off to another career, which seemed to him like a worthless way of earning a living.

Yet there were times when my mother would catch him basking in some reflected glory as a farmer commented on my despatches from Washington or Moscow or Hong Kong. With thoughts that were not confined to agriculture, she would argue the case for people going their own way and not feeling obliged to follow in the footsteps of the father. Such logic was met with a grunt.

When his day was over, however, I did not have the heart to dispose of his life's work immediately and kept it going, with work for his two employees. It was never intended as a long-term arrangement but one year led to another till nearly a decade had passed since last my father was running his farm.

It was just the other week that I brought myself to selling Honeyneuk, certain pangs of conscience intruding upon the knowledge that long-distance farming is not a sensible proposition.

Suspicious of large combines and speculators, my father believed that the farm should be a home and a way of life for the people who own it. Indeed he sought always to encourage good farm servants to become small farmers.

So he would have approved of the new owners of Honeyneuk, Jim and Belinda Muir, who left their place on the Orkney island of Shapinsay last week, crossed to Kirkwall then to the Scottish mainland, driving themselves and their belongings, together with their two children, a dog, two cats, a budgie, a few hens and a hive of bees.

As the final symbol of change-over, we held the farm roup on Saturday, which turned out to be one of the most remarkable days in my fairly eventful life.

There I stood in the farm-close of Honeyneuk, looking down on the village which had given me a memorable childhood. Your thoughts at such times are too private for sharing.

Soon they were coming up the brae and along the farm road, by car, lorry and bicycle and even by horse and cart, till there were 500 vehicles in the grass park and nearly 1000 people clustering round the auctioneer's rostrum.

Honeyneuk had never seen so many people and I wondered what John Webster would have made of it all. That distant rumbling was thunder, I hoped, and not the sound of my father turning in his grave in the nearby kirkyard of Culsh.

For all his days he had jollied up those gatherings at farm roups, coaxing good prices with good humour. But now the tables were turned. It was the contents of Honeyneuk which were under the hammer of another auctioneer.

Old men of Buchan, ill-accustomed to speeches of gratitude, came up to say in plain sincerity what a grand chap my father had been. Younger ones wanted to tell me of his help and encouragement.

So they bought up his livestock and implements, his telescope, twine and tattie-riddles, sometimes no more than a souvenir of John Webster. As host for the day, I invited them to an out-house for mince-baps and beer and a floodtide of whisky which stirred fond memories and a warm fellowship.

The BBC came along to film it all for posterity and the result will be seen on the *Landward* programme, one Sunday in September. It could turn out to be a memorable documentary.

When the last of the drams went down and the handshakes were clasped, I took leave of old friends and neighbours, assuring them that I would always come back to Maud. For that was where I was born and grew up. And maybe, in a sense, I have never been away.

MENSA? JIMMY STEWART
HAD A BETTER IDEA

HAVING been consigned at conception to one of the more modest levels of intelligence, I have always been slightly wary of the so-called clever people and intrigued by what separates them from wise ones.

Wisdom, I suppose, has to do with the highest exercise of your faculties, inferring shrewd and honourable judgments on whatever basis of knowledge you possess. You can therefore be fairly simple-minded and wise.

But cleverness is another kind of cerebral story. It implies a facility of the deductive processes which puts you ahead of the mob, to the extent that you could take advantage of them if your scruples were not all they might be.

If clever people are not exactly ten-a-penny, at least they out-number the wise ones. Our jails are full of them. The chap who forged the Hitler diaries is an extremely clever fellow, as was that artist who faked the pictures. Even the late Professor Joad put his brilliant talent to the use of travelling on British Rail without paying his fare.

All of this came to mind the other morning as I was mulling over the muesli and reading some small item about the organisation known as Mensa. It reminded me of a rather enlightening experience I once had involving a member of that elitist body. But more of that later.

Mensa, as you may know, is a kind of international society of highly-intelligent people who pride themselves in an IQ of 148 or over—and have no intention of hiding the fact. The name comes from the Latin *mens*, for mind, and only about one in 50 of us would qualify for membership.

15

Whatever reservations one may have about such a convention of clever dicks, Mensa is a perfectly honourable organisation, not at all responsible for the excesses of any individual member.

Its ranks include that inventive genius Sir Clive Sinclair, and the creator of "The Saint", Leslie Charteris. Another who qualifies is Jim'll-Fix-It Savile.

Sir Clive (he of the pocket TV sets and funny little battery cars) has used the forum of Mensa to give the world a peep at his private crystal ball. After all, people of that mental calibre should be able to point the way into the future.

He looks ahead, for example, to the time when robots will keep human beings as pets and cars will drive themselves at more than 200 miles an hour.

A one-centimetre cube will contain the data from more books than mankind has yet produced. What's more, it could be implanted and linked into the human brain. And what's more than that, he is deadly serious about it all.

Sir Clive believes that the home meta-computer could become our doctor, a rather unnerving thought. But at least he leaves us with the one cheering forecast that science is on course to making lawyers redundant.

None of that, mind you, enabled Sir Clive to foretell that his business empire was about to run into financial problems, from which he was recently rescued by Robert Maxwell.

While we at the *Herald*, making no particular boast of our intelligence quotients, strive earnestly to produce a newspaper day by day by day, the Mensa people have recently produced one for an August day in the year 2020.

"The Mousetrap", you may be interested to know in advance, will just be closing after the longest run in British theatrical history. And Buckingham Palace will announce that a new royal clone has been activated.

Mensa was founded in 1946 by a Dr Lance Weare, to gather together people who shared similar views and understanding, always with that exclusive tag of an inflated IQ. There are about 14,500 members in Britain and four or five times that number around the world. I first encountered them many years ago, which takes me back to that memory which was revived over the muesli the other morning.

I had had a phone call from a Mensa member who was coming to Scotland and thought I should be updated on their activities. Would I join him for lunch?

I was duly hosted in the grand manner and given the a-la-carte while he consulted the wine list with all the flair of a connoisseur. That most expensive bottle of claret would do just fine.

When he had fully informed me of his Mensa movements and digested a splendid meal, a masterful snap of the fingers summoned the bill with all the assurance of a man who knows his Claridges.

What happened next will forever remain a bit of a blur. With the deceptive flourish of a mesmerist, he jumped to his feet, drew me to mine, clasped my hand and said "It has been nice meeting you, Mr Webster"—and vanished. Seconds later the waiter slapped the bill on the table!

Perhaps it was his idea of a joke, perhaps just thoughtlessness. But, whatever lessons I learned from that expensive experience, I have since felt more disposed to the stance of my Hollywood hero, James Stewart, who became chairman of a body called International Dull Folks Ltd., a club for poor slobs with sub-genius IQs.

With a potential membership of 4.5 billion, or nearly the entire population of the world, it attracts me by its safety in numbers. It may be more a case of Densa than Mensa but it has that invaluable virtue of not taking itself too seriously.

THEY STILL SETTLE FOR
LAUREL AND HARDY

IN the summer of '64 the world was still recovering from the shock of the Kennedy assassination.

More immediately, Nyasaland had become Malawi, the Beatles were attending the premiere of *A Hard Day's Night*, and the creator of James Bond, Ian Fleming, had just died, as had Edith Sitwell.

My diary tells me I was interviewing two of the best-known Americans of the century, Cassius Clay, later to be known as Mohammed Ali, who had just beaten the brutish Sonny Liston, and the man who revolutionised social behaviour by giving us Rock 'n' Roll, the late Bill Haley.

It was the year of four royal births, including Prince Edward, and a lesser-known one which landed me in a last-minute dilemma of finding a name for a newborn son before the registrar called in the prosecutor.

A plea for names in a newspaper column I was writing at the time produced more confusion than clarity, ranging from John, George, Paul, or Ringo, reflecting the flavour of the time, to the more prestigious Winston, indicating affection for the famous statesman who was within three months of his 90th birthday.

In the event we called him Keith, born on the anniversary of the Hiroshima bomb, August 6, from which a simple deduction will show that we had a 21st birthday celebration this week.

Those random thoughts of the sixties came together amid the cake and the candles, the gifts and the champagne, which set me wondering what goes through the mind of today's 21-year-old. Cautiously I pursued a gentle course of interview without intruding too much on the spirit of the occasion.

In that span from the mid-sixties to the mid-eighties, what has happened to impress itself on the young mind, seeking maturity at a bewildering point in human history?

The swaddling clothes of '64 have long since unwrapped a towering 6ft 2in, now favouring the stubble-crop head which fits more easily into the helmet of American football or takes him more tidily down the wicket to deliver a fast ball.

Mind you, that languid stage of laid-back contemplation is not the point of highest communication with the father of the species, but a surprising level of revelation was reached nevertheless.

The first event which impressed itself on the babe of the mid-sixties was evidently the landing on the Moon of the American astronauts in 1969.

Neil Armstrong's walkabout in slow motion, as watched on television with open-mouthed wonder, is as firmly destined for re-telling to the grandchildren of 2020 as my own grandmother's tales of the Tay Bridge Disaster.

Having perhaps just returned from their own mid-term moonshine break, they may well wonder what the fuss was all about.

If you have ever wondered what kind of effect all that blaring pop has had on the tenderness of your offspring, my 21-year-old son recollects a bewilderment about the screaming teeny-boppers, wetting themselves over the Bay City Rollers and the Osmonds, neither of whom he could stand.

Gary Glitter was the first pop star to make an impression, as a preliminary to greater maturity with The Police, David Bowie, Annie Lennox, and Bob Dylan.

He makes the point that teenage screams have tended to reach crescendo in the middle of each decade—for Elvis in the '50s, the Beatles in the '60s, the Osmonds in the '70s, and now Duran Duran and Wham in the '80s.

So he will drop into Glasgow gathering spots like the Rock Garden or Fixx, alternating with a game of snooker, enjoying a discussion but keeping a fair independence of mind in the face of youth's regimentation.

Considering the depressing prospects of work, there is a surprising level of acceptance among his age-group that life is going to be tough. How strange that young rebellion was at its height in the sixties, when jobs were plentiful and there seemed so much less to rebel about.

This week's 21-year-old was affected by the recent showing of *The War Game* and duly appalled by the nuclear consequences, though not at all tempted to join CND.

I sense in his age-bracket a growing distrust of pressure groups, while still discussing the issues with a seriousness that raises hopes of our world being inherited by thoroughly responsible people.

Inevitably there has to be an antidote of humour and for that particular safety-valve my son looks back to my own day. His favourite individual is Phil Silvers, as Sergeant Bilko, in whom he perceives a lasting universal appeal.

Laurel and Hardy top his double acts and, for a comedy team, he reveals his choice in regular re-runs of old Marx Brothers' films, claiming to find fresh nuances of humour at every showing.

So what about that name we gave him in 1964, when time was running out and the readers' choice extended from Lycidas, Laertes, and Lawrence to David, D'Arcy, and Dan?

I gather he is perfectly happy with Keith, which is a family name after all. There is just one other which might have pleased him more, he revealed with the mimicry for which he has a certain talent.

Screwing his face into the posture of a simpleton and scratching the crown of his head, as if to acknowledge that this was another fine mess he'd landed Olly in, he said: "I wouldn't have minded if you'd called me Stan!"

ON MEETING THE RICHEST MAN
IN THE WORLD

HAVING raised the subject of multi-millionaires in this column a few weeks ago, I make no apology for returning to it, in view of the discussions it evidently sparked off in assorted hostelries around the country.

Some correspondents have made the fairly predictable point that the folding stuff is no guarantee of happiness in this mortal marathon, though I should imagine there are a few men and women lingering outside the Jobcentre this morning who would be perfectly willing to give it a try.

But I take the point. Indeed, it was brought home to me very forcibly one day, about 10 years ago, when I went to visit the legendary Jean Paul Getty, the richest man in the world.

He was, of course, the American oil tycoon who was so fond of Britain that he settled here and bought the stately home called Sutton Place in Surrey, formerly owned by the Duke of Sutherland.

Getty was not exactly a rags-to-riches case, having been born into the family of a fairly wealthy oil man, but he developed a nose for the liquid gold which was nothing short of uncanny.

Shrewd men thought he had flipped, however, when he bought a stretch of the Arabian desert in 1949, in the belief that there was oil beneath them thar sandy wastes.

But shaking heads turned to gaping mouths when Getty's gusher revealed itself as one of the most productive oil holes in history. His wealth became even greater than that of another legend of the lucre, Howard Hughes, whose latter years were a pathetic story of paranoia, flitting from one hotel to another, enveloped in an anti-septic cocoon of refuge from germs.

Getty at least kept his sanity, to the point of having made a small side-bet of £100m on North Sea oil.

Not surprisingly in these days of kidnaps and hostages, such men are hard to reach. It took 18 months to elude the minders and finally speak to the man himself. (By mistake, a switchboard lady put me through to Mr Getty's private extension. God bless her!)

Somewhat alarmed by the extent of his own "protection", he invited me to Sutton Place the following week, and, if that seemed like a fairly straightforward operation, I can only say I found it easier to visit a certain well-known gentleman in the Special Unit at Barlinnie one night!

Mr Getty's prison was of a rather more upholstered order, of course, but there were striking similarities.

The formidable gates of Sutton Place were electronically operated and I had to be escorted through the grounds to the house itself, past a succession of guard dogs which were smacking their lips for a stranger.

In the vast acreage of the estate I calculated that Mr Getty's front lawn was 15 times the size of Hampden Park. Inside the mansion itself, built by Henry VIII for one of his knights, the minders were bouncing me from one to the other through long corridors, till finally I was shown into a small, plain room and left alone with the richest man in the world.

He was sitting on a chair with his foot on a stool, one shoe and sock removed and in mortal agony from an ailment of the big toe. Not all the millions in the world could ease the misery of a lonely old man who apologised for the indignity of his condition.

So there we were, discussing his North Sea investment, which he put into perspective by telling me that there was a single oil-well in the Middle East which had more reserves than all the Scottish waters put together.

From his window we could see the blossom of an English springtime, daffodils stretching by the yellow acre. From there he contemplated a life which had balanced the untold riches of the oilfields with a series of personal tragedies to match those of the Kennedy family.

One son, George, died of an overdose of drink and drugs. The child of Getty's fifth marriage, apple of his eye, took a brain tumour and died at 12. Then came the much publicised family squabbles, culminating in the kidnap of his grandson and the gory postal package which brought the boy's severed ear.

Getty looked sadly out to his daffodils and told me: "I am still an optimist. You have to be. There is no room for pessimism in the oil business."

When I finally left, he waved a frail hand and invited me back to his lonely den any time I wanted. For once he had been mercifully free of the company of tycoons and minders.

Today, the son who bears his name lives in his own particular form of seclusion, in Cheyne Walk, Chelsea, distributing his wealth with a generosity for which his father was not exactly noted. But he, too, is cut off from the world of reality, seldom seen outside the house and living like a recluse in the heart of London.

Real wealth, I suppose, has to do with matters other than money, which cannot even cure a big toe let alone provide immortality.

The fresh air we breathe, the friends we meet, the health we enjoy and the sun which used to shine . . . these are worth their weight in a currency which is the real kind of gold.

REMEMBERING MY OLD PAL NORMAN

IT was a phone call a few weeks ago which sparked off my new year resolution that I would try to keep better contact with old friends.

With the best will in the world we can still manage to neglect each other quite shamefully. Even people who have played a significant part at some distant stage of our lives can flit away like melting snowflakes, as if they had scarcely existed, to be replaced by new performers in an ever-changing scenario.

We may still exchange Christmas cards as an annual token of not having forgotten altogether, yet how often do we follow through those well-meaning postscripts about meeting before another Christmas comes around?

That phone call came from the closest friend I ever had, my boyhood pal from distant days in our native Scottish village. Though our paths had gone in different directions, Norman Rothney, by now living near Edinburgh, had just seen a television film I had written about the scene of our childhood and was spurred into phoning with the suggestion that we should not postpone our long-intended reunion any longer.

Let's meet soon. There would be so much to talk about. Of course, of course. It all came flooding back—carefree days in the remoteness of our rural haven, rambling over Aikey Brae, sledging down Banks Hill, dooking in the Ugie, camping with the Cubs and charging into the Den Wood with toy bayonets at the ready.

The war was at its height, and, in the fantasies of the moment, the tree trunk became a suitable substitute for the torso of a German.

Through that whole adventure of childhood, Norman and I forged a bond of friendship, deep and pure and abiding as children will do, unspoiled by words. We were barely conscious of our happiness and all the happier because of it.

When those wartime sirens first wailed out across the Scottish landscape, 200 children from Dowanhill and Hyndland Schools in Glasgow had come scampering north in the great evacuation intended to protect them from the bombing raids, labels round their necks, en route to village homes.

As they settled into an alien community, culture shocks vibrating in all directions, they spoke of their flicks and fairgrounds, polis and Partick Thistle, their shipyards and subways. We gaped in disbelief, as if their train might have come from Mars, surveying them in our slower, plodding country ways, unaccustomed as we were to running after tram-cars or eluding the pursuits of "ra polis".

Released from their bronchial back-streets and energised by the purity of our rural ozone, they ran riot in the new-found freedom, demolishing haystacks, tormenting bullocks and testing the elasticity of many a swinging udder, till the prospect of a cow jumping over the moon was in danger of being removed from the realms of fantasy.

If these were the comparatively harmless pranks of city kids, the situation darkened somewhat when they sought to superimpose upon our pastoral tranquility a version of the gangland they had left behind.

In scenes reminiscent of the O.K. Corral, they would approach in a solid swagger from time to time, thumbs in trouser-tops, eyes narrowed, challenging the Maud Loons to show their strength.

As rural innocents, we had little knowledge of such things, but the matter of pride was clearly at stake.

And that is where we return to my old pal, Norman Rothney. In the silence of quandary, all eyes turned to Norman for leadership. He was older than me. And bigger and braver. He was no aggressor but if these invaders wanted to cut up rough then here was surely the golden-haired hero to put them to justice.

With the rest of us making up numbers, Norman would grab them in twos or threes, flailing his powerful arms in all directions and inflicting enough damage to establish that the country cousins were not to be tampered with. (Little wonder he was later to become an Army champion boxer.)

In time we made it all up with the Glasgow boys, fell in love with their girls, and formed friendships which endure to this day. Of stuff like this are childhood memories made.

And these would be some of the recollections when Norman and I came together for that rendezvous in the early days of 1986. Let's confirm that date. Yes, yes.

Then the phone rang the other evening. It was one of his sons to say that Norman had died of a heart attack. We had left it too late.

It all seemed so unreal. In our previous meetings we had never acknowledged that an adult world existed. Our glorious days together had been boyhood days—and boys do not take heart attacks.

So the rendezvous in Edinburgh last week was very different from the one we had planned. Faces from our mutual past were there, and warm greetings exchanged.

There is no shame in shedding a tear for your best friend. But, oh, why do we procrastinate so?

THE LEGEND OF JIM RODGER

GIRTH apart, the portly gent who donned his hat and walked away from his typewriter last week would fit uneasily into any pigeon-hole of journalism that man has so far defined.

He belonged, in general terms, to that fraternity of sports writers who are usually trained journalists, like our own Jim Reynolds or Ian Paul, or former footballing stars, like Tommy Muirhead, Jack Harkness or Doug Baillie.

But the unmistakable figure of Jim Rodger was, to use the contemporary phrase, "one off", a legend of the Fourth Estate who carved for himself a position of power out of all keeping with his status as a journalist.

To allow such a man to retreat into early retirement without a few words of public tribute from his rivals would smack not a little of churlishness.

For here was no graduate of a university or school of journalism, not even the product of a local newspaper. Following a route of his own, Jim Rodger came out of the pits of Lanarkshire, a contemporary of other coal-miners like Jock Stein and Andrew Keir, the actor, determined to exchange the black alleyways for the light and fresh air and fellowship of sport.

To his new career of journalism he brought the miner's lamp which had shown the way forward at the coalface and would remain on his desk as a light to symbolise his past and guide him in the days ahead.

If writing talent was not the strength of Jim Rodger, he distinguished himself from every other journalist I have ever known by the incredible range of his contacts, the lifeblood of a successful newspaperman.

It all began with an early interest in schools football, where he

27

would carry a camera to snap at shiny-faced youngsters and present them with their first-ever team picture. Schoolboys like Bobby Clark from Sandyhills, destined to become Scotland's international goal-keeper, never forgot the jolly, kindly man who bothered to take that early interest.

Those who matured into professionals would later confide in him as a friend. In an atmosphere of total confidentiality, he became the mysterious middle-man of British football, a human crossroads for the hopes and aspirations of managers, players and club chairmen alike.

If an Ian Ure or a Jim Baxter were moving club, you could be sure that Jim Rodger would have a hand in it somewhere, perhaps conducting a cloak-and-dagger operation for which he would seek no reward except the story. Such was the essential secrecy of some transfer deals that sports editors would struggle to stifle their exasperated calls that a scoop was no good if it missed the edition.

In his own good time, with winks and nods and wry smiles, this portly patron saint of cream buns would produce the story.

He came to know absolutely everybody who mattered in football, far beyond the bounds of Scotland. But it didn't stop there. From his early days in Shotts, which remains his home to this day, he was well connected in politics. Margaret Herbison, the local girl who became a Cabinet Minister, was a close friend.

When Prime Minister Harold Wilson arrived at Glasgow Central Station, he was liable to walk past the welcoming party to greet his old friend, Jim Rodger.

The Jolly Jim had come of a rather remarkable working-class family. One of his cousins, whose father was a blacksmith at a Stirling colliery, was Bill Armstrong, a brilliant scholar who rose to become Sir William Armstrong, head of the Civil Service, and later Lord Armstrong, chairman of the Midland Bank. Another cousin became Sir David McNee, Britain's top policeman.

But Jim did not depend on such influential gentlemen to open doors which would be closed to most of us. He had an incomparable talent for doing that himself, turning keys not only for himself but for the benefit of the less fortunate. Visas would be charmed from reluctant Eastern European countries. No stone would be left unturned to help the sick, the needy, and the helpless, even if a degree of ruthlessness were necessary in the process.

On a memorable night in 1966, when England had been lucky enough to win a World Cup at Wembley, Jim and I landed where no journalist was ever allowed to land—inside the private banquet room, propelled there by the Prime Minister and Foreign Secretary of the day, Harold Wilson and George Brown no less!

Later that night, however, the considerable figure of Jim collapsed in my arms at the St Ermin's Hotel, in a fair imitation of death. I managed to revive him with an unaccustomed nip of brandy.

That golden heart was to falter alarmingly on several occasions thereafter, consigning him to the care of the Bon Secours nursing home, where his Protestantism proved no obstacle to a rare rapport with the nuns.

Visiting him one evening when he had suffered yet another attack, I found him talking riddles down a telephone. Jim tended to talk in riddles. Jock Stein was hovering in the background and the business which Jim was negotiating that evening, as I would later discover, was the transfer of Pat Stanton from Hibernian to Celtic!

There was no stopping him. But, in the cutbacks of Robert Maxwell at the *Daily Mirror*, the legend of Scottish sports-writing has taken his money and gone, a floating mass of jolly rotundity whose behind-the-scenes story of Scottish football and so much else would surely amount to a riveting revelation.

WHY I HAD TO REACH ABERDEEN
THAT NIGHT

LIFE is truly a paradoxical monkey-show, I thought to myself as I drove north in a snowstorm from Glasgow towards a rather special dinner in Aberdeen.

At least I was intending to drive north, but the whole adventure disintegrated into a nightmare when I slithered to a halt between Moodiesburn and Castlecary, amidst the biggest pile-up of icebound chaos I had ever seen.

With 50 accidents reported in a distance of 15 miles, I found myself at a standstill for a solid hour, unable to reach a telephone to alert my hosts at the other end.

So there was nothing for it but to fume in frustration and then resign myself to the inevitability of fate.

For reasons which will become apparent, my mind wandered back to a sad day in my life, in the summer of 1946. As a 14-year-old who had fallen far short of early promise, I was shown the vaulted gateway of Robert Gordon's College in Aberdeen and sent marching down the driveway with tears on my cheeks and the resounding ring of failure in my tender ears.

It was back to the village in my tackety boots to rethink the course of life in a world which had now returned to earth after the victory bells of 1945 and was facing the bleak austerity of the aftermath.

A serious illness compounded the disaster and, with the men and women flocking back from the war to four-page newspapers, the prospect of following my heart's desire to become a journalist could never have been so poor.

But nothing endures for ever. From the depths of my depression, the gods were to guide me towards what was probably the only vacancy for a cub reporter in Scotland at that time. Then, with the sacking of the boss, I became acting editor of the *Turriff Advertiser* at the age of 16, puffing at imaginary cigars and issuing orders to secretaries who were no less of a figment.

I had landed the job I wanted and would not have called the king my cousin. The career which followed has been more glamorous and satisfying than I had any right to expect. It has taken me to the ends of the earth and into the company of some fair-sized men and women, from Paul Getty and Sophia Loren to Maggie Thatcher and even into a bedroom interview with Christine Keeler!

The irony of it all was turning over in my mind as I sat there immobile, between Glasgow and Stirling, wondering if I would ever see that dinner in Aberdeen.

Normally my absence would not have mattered but, on this occasion, it would create a certain embarrassment. For that old school of mine, prompted by its former pupils, had decided to throw open that vaulted gateway through which it had despatched me with my tail between my legs in 1946, and to welcome me back as its guest of honour.

There would be a eulogy, to which I would respond in the manner of my predecessors (they included men like the British Ambassador to Vienna). Surely this must be a joke.

Suddenly, the traffic chaos was clearing and I made slow progress towards Aberdeen, sensing that I could still arrive at least in time to deliver my speech. Road conditions improved by the mile and I managed to sweep across the Dee, change into the dinner suit and make my breathless entrance before the meal had ended.

"Late again, Webster?" I could hear an old master mutter.

A large whisky cleared the cobwebs as I gathered myself for the most important speech of my life. Oratory was never a strength so I confined myself to a word-picture of those war years at school, the tram-cars clanking along, Richard Tauber singing at His Majesty's Theatre, a little girl making her debut at the Tivoli, by the name of Julie Andrews, and a German plane machine-gunning pedestrians in Union Street before crashing into the ice-rink at the Bridge of Dee.

There were air-raid warnings, as we dashed to the shelters, and the war news brilliantly encapsulated in the calls of news-vendor Patsy Gallagher. There was the smell of coffee as you passed the door of Collie's shop. And then the strange anti-climax of peace.

I had appreciation of the friendships formed, gratitude to Robert Gordon and his notion of free education for the poorest of children, and a hint of rebuke for a system which could send a boy out to a world which was bleak and inhospitable when he was no more than the tender age of 14.

They rose to applaud, familiar faces on all sides, and suddenly I knew that those gates had been well and truly thrown wide. I stepped inside, willingly back in the fold, with the new-found ring of approval somehow diminishing that earlier ring of failure which had dogged my footsteps on that nightmarish walk of 1946.

THE TRIUMPH AND TRAGEDY
OF CHRIS ANDERSON

SCOTLAND could ill afford to lose Chris Anderson, vice-chairman of Aberdeen Football Club and one of the game's ablest administrators, who has died, at the age of 60, from the same motor neurone disease which killed film star David Niven.

Chris Anderson was the fair face of sport, an intelligent and articulate spokesman and the brain behind so much of the change, not only at Pittodrie but throughout the game of football.

Destined to be the next chairman of the Dons, he told me, in a deeply-moving interview not long before he died, about his sadness at being robbed of the chance to lead the club towards the twenty-first century.

He was well aware of his fate and, with a courage which had characterised him as a player and a man, he told of his last visit to Hampden Park and how he looked around and knew he was seeing the great stadium for the last time.

The public knew less, perhaps, of his work as chief executive at one of Britain's leading polytechnics, Robert Gordon's Institute of Technology, where he took immense pride in the provision of higher education for talented youngsters in the North-east. Indeed, his OBE was in recognition of his service to sport and education. He had also been honoured with a fellowship from the institute.

But it was football which brought widest recognition, first as an Aberdeen player in the postwar era and then as the director who masterminded so much of his club's off-the-field success, like building an all-seated, all-covered stadium with executive boxes and so on.

He played just as big a part in laying the foundations of

33

Aberdeen's rise to dominance of Scottish football in the eighties, leading to the success as Cup Champions of Europe in 1983.

For the greater good of the game, he led the way to the creation of a Premier Division in 1975 and was advocating a British Cup and a Scottish National Soccer League (the change which nearly happened recently) when few could envisage the ideas. But a cruel twist of fate struck at Chris Anderson soon after he took early retirement from his college post at the age of 58.

While still able to communicate he talked to me very frankly about how it all happened. I leave it to the man himself to make his last public utterances:

"Now that I was taking early retirement, I looked forward to fulfilling my two remaining ambitions. I wanted to spend more time travelling the world with my wife Christine, who is a great tennis buff, and to take Aberdeen Football Club into the twenty-first century as its chairman.

I have always had strength. I had some money but I never had the time. Now I was making some time for myself.

Always superbly fit, I could be found in the gymnasium at Gordon's College twice a week, even after retirement, playing head tennis, or running along the beach at Barra, where I was in August 1984. I was always a fast mover, I suppose the fittest man for my age in the whole of Aberdeen, a teetotaller and non-smoker.

In September 1984, I had to go into hospital for a hernia operation but recovered from that. By the end of the year, however, I began to feel a stiffness in my right leg and right hand. There was a lack of thrust. I was also beginning to lose too many games of head tennis!

Christine and I went off to the Portuguese resort of Vale de Lobo last February and played tennis and golf. By then I knew something would have to be done about this leg so I went to see a specialist when I came home.

The trouble was diagnosed as motor neurone disease—and I was told there and then there was no known cure. Damage or disease of the central nervous system apparently affects the nerve fibres, which then fail to energise the muscles of the body. So the muscles waste.

Naturally, we were shattered by the news but decided not to tell anyone at that stage. We didn't want to upset people. So I soldiered on through last spring, getting stiffer and more restricted in my movement but still able to get about.

In July I went to Switzerland for the European Cup draw but things were getting more difficult and my condition was becoming apparent. So, in August, I told my family and friends that I had this disease and was heading towards being unable to move physically. There was total disbelief. They were so devastated that I found myself having to cheer them up.

I had also been trying to avoid creating any alarm at Pittodrie but, of course, I had to tell the chairman, Dick Donald, and our manager, Alex Ferguson, who were both shattered.

When I discovered there was nothing that could be done for me in Aberdeen I began to find out, systematically, what else might be done and that was how I came to visit Newcastle, which is a major centre for this kind of disease.

I learned about research going on in Boston—and that there are between 4000 and 5000 sufferers in the United Kingdom. I found a pattern is beginning to emerge showing that the victims are generally fit and athletic people and that the trouble often arises after an operation.

All along I felt some reaction to my hernia operation was triggered off in the body. The medical people say they might crack this disease in two or three years but time is not on my side.

Anyhow, I have faced up to my situation and, when people ask if I feel any bitterness that I have been afflicted in this way, I can only reply that I do not. If it hadn't been me it would have been someone else.

The prospect of a wheelchair was obviously a watershed and I set myself a target to stay on my feet till Christmas. I was

35

glad that I made it. I'm told that a less fit person would have been in the chair six months ago.

My mind is clear but I am now faced with the frustration of not being able to move and feeling I'm a burden on other people. I was always such an independent kind of North-east person."

He talked about the golden age of Aberdeen Football Club, starting with the managership of Ally MacLeod in 1975, continuing briefly with Billy McNeill and brought to fruition by Alex Ferguson.

"What we have done is succeeded in shifting the football base from Glasgow to the east coast. Having set such high standards, of course, we are now becoming the victims of our own success. Losing a few games, as we did this season, became a crisis but I knew it would all come right.

I have been deeply touched by the reaction of the younger players at Pittodrie. They have sent me cards of encouragement. When I went to Hampden for the League Cup Final in October and Willie Miller stepped up to receive the trophy, I found myself looking round the great stadium and knowing that it was the last time I would see it.

Afterwards, I went to congratulate the players and found I could face them all with one exception. Somehow I choked up when I came face to face with Eric Black. And so did he. It wasn't just that he had scored twice that day or that he set us on our way to victory in Gothenburg. I'm sure it was because he epitomised for me all that was good in football. He seemed to stand for all that Aberdeen had done in recent years."

In a close knit family unit, Chris and Christine Anderson have had the support of their journalist son Keith, and daughter Kay who moved recently from Aberdeen to Oman, where her husband is in the oil business. She was flying home for the funeral, at St Nicholas Church, Aberdeen, tomorrow at 1.45pm.

Though too ill to see Aberdeen in the Scottish Cup Final this month, he watched on television and tapped out his prediction of the result. It was: Aberdeen 3—Hearts 0.

In facing up to his greatest battle so courageously, Chris Anderson remained conscious till his very last day. But he was trapped inside an immobile body without means of communication, except for the flap of an eyelid.

The man who loved fitness and freedom was finally a prisoner. And, in the fading minutes of Tuesday night, he was mercifully given his release.

THE GOLDEN GRAVEL OF
ROBERT BOOTHBY

THERE is a weeping in the wind that whips up the Bullers o' Buchan and whistles round the lighthouse at Rattray Head, on that Northeast coast where they have special cause to mourn his lordship this week.

For Robert Boothby represented glamour on my childhood horizon, all flowing hair, bow-ties, disarming smiles, and voice of golden gravel, one of the finest orators and most rumbustious personalities this country has produced.

In a Buchan land of plain country folk, weaned on brose and bannocks, I had never seen that species before. Men admired him, women secretly adored him. Our country ways were in contrast to his own colourful life in the social salons of the wider world.

People of all political persuasions and none would flock to village halls, some unsure of the party he represented and believing only in a radical, common-sense phenomenon called Boothbyism.

Yes, Boothby was unique. Yet he might never have come our way but for the group of Tory farmers who went north to the Orkney sales in 1923. They went in search of bullocks and came back with Bob Boothby. As good livestock men, they checked his pedigree. Come of substantial Edinburgh stock, he may have failed in Orkney but would be just the chap the Tories needed to wrest their constituency from the Liberals.

He did just that in 1924, at the age of 24, and kept his huge majority for the next 34 years. During that period, the folk of Buchan were pleased to bask in the glory of their MP as he strode the international scene, picked out by Churchill to be his PPS while in his twenties.

He was close to people like the Duke of Windsor, Bernard Shaw, Somerset Maugham, and Compton Mackenzie. Society hostesses opened every door for him, pursued and pampered him.

Years later his explosive meeting with Hitler was related to me by the latter's press chief, Putzi Hanfstaengl. As he introduced the two, the Führer raised his arm and shouted "Hitler!" Not to be outdone, our Robert followed suit and shouted "Boothby!" Hitler was furious.

Boothby came back and told Chamberlain he was dealing with a madman. And every now and then he came back to Buchan and we would sit, open-mouthed, and listen to his personal anecdotes of people we could only read about.

Everyone knew Robert Boothby was the up-and-coming man. The tragedy was he failed to arrive. Perhaps he was too much of an individualist. Although a Conservative, he idolised Lloyd George as "the greatest man I have ever known" and was chosen to give his memorial address. Churchill was less than keen on the alliance.

From the plains of Buchan, his constituents followed it all with fascination.

Though divorce was not a word we knew much about in our rural setting, where men and women tended to thole each other through the worst of combat, he survived that personal crisis with ease.

His greater ordeal was a Commons investigation into his personal interest in paying out frozen assets to Czechoslovakians in this country, after Hitler's invasion, a matter which he failed to declare.

While all hell was breaking out around him, he turned for strength to the hard-headed folk of Buchan, without whose support he would not have survived. Nevertheless, it spelled the end of his route to the top, with Churchill taking a less than charitable view.

Buchan was, I suppose, a safe and comfortable base from which to conduct his colourful life, not that he ever neglected his people. No MP ever worked harder for the local economy, for the beef and oats of the land and the herring of the sea.

When he went to the Lords, we saw less of him but he took with him the title of Lord Boothby of Buchan and Rattray Head, representing the two sides of local life. What's more, he wanted to be buried there and, in 1962, wrote to the registrar in the parish of Crimond, thanking him for being "most helpful in the arrangements which have been made for me to be taken to Rattray Head when the end comes."

He added: "I don't think there is a more lovely resting place in the world. It almost reconciles me to my inevitable destiny!" He was talking about the old kirkyard at Rattray, between Peterhead and Fraserburgh.

By the time he wrote his last book in 1978, he seemed to have amended his plans when he wrote: "All I wish is that my ashes should be thrown over Buchan and the North Sea from the lighthouse at Rattray Head, which was built by Robert Louis Stevenson's father. Perhaps the Royal Philharmonic Orchestra might give a concert in my memory"—and he proceeds to give a suggested programme of Wagner, Debussy, and Delius, with Brahms and Tchaikovsky thrown in, but "no Beethoven, no Mozart, certainly no Bach." The common thread was melody.

I have no doubt at all that will happen in time. Meanwhile, I remember visiting Lord Boothby in his Eaton Square home and listening as he went on at length about his strange affinity with the North Sea. He would quote Harold Nicolson's *Tennyson*: "Let us recall only the low booming of the North Sea upon the dunes; the grey clouds lowering above the wold; the moan of the night wind on the fen, the far glimmer of marsh-pools through the reeds; the cold, the half-light, and the gloom."

In such a dramatic setting, the ashes of Robert John Graham Boothby would float freely from the bare lighthouse at Rattray Head, scattering themselves joyously upon the waves of the great North Sea and the furrows of the Buchan Land.

Where better for them to rest?

THE DAY THEY OPERATED ON
MY FAITHFUL FRIEND

AT least twice a day for the past 11 years my Boxer friend, Baron, has taken me for walks.

He has fertilised the bushes, promoted the growth of lamp-posts and put his master's arteries in better shape to cope with whatever bloodclots might lurk.

Occasionally of an evening we run into one of the foxes which roam freely in our suburban streets, leaping over garden walls and scraping at dustbins.

Baron is in good condition for his age, still capable of pursuing the offending cat or knocking you over in the enthusiasm of his friendly greeting. But there was this limp one evening, a persistent hirple in the back leg which prompted a call to the vet. Arthritis was the verdict. Age creeping up. Some pills would no doubt put it right.

However, there was something more sinister at work. In examining the limp, the practised eye of the vet had spotted a malignant tumour in a place no man could bear to contemplate.

Carefully, he explained all the possibilities. If left, the tumour would certainly continue to grow, though at what rate he could not foretell. In time it would lead to complications elsewhere, a spread of the tumour which may or may not have already begun. He explained very fairly the pros and cons of operating and left the decision entirely to the owner.

At the age of 11, Baron's natural lifespan might not be greatly affected by the progress of the tumour. On the other hand, his prospects of a longer than normal life would not be helped by the presence of a cancer. So the loving owner is faced with a decision. What would you have done?

It did not take long to decide that the tumour was better out of there. "Operate as soon as possible," was our request. To which the vet responded that, in view of Baron's natural exuberance, the deed had better be performed at home. Imagine the domestic drama as we prepared an operating table in the kitchen, kept an eye on the arrival of the vet's car and tried to behave as normal, though there was no fooling you-know-who.

There had been no food the night before and just an early morning visit to the garden. Something funny going on. He cocked his head and asked questions with those big brown eyes. Apprehensively, we anticipated trouble from such a big, strong animal when it came to administering the anaesthetic. It must have been the charm and expertise of the vet that worked wonders.

With our arms around him, poised between caress and firm control, Baron sat bolt upright and scarcely blinked as the needle went swiftly into his veins. The anaesthetic spread just as quickly to his brain.

Within seconds the body went limp and leaden. We eased him down on the lounge floor, allowed for the drift to complete unconsciousness, then the vet and I lifted him, like a sack of potatoes, and carried him to the operating theatre of the kitchen.

The time was 10.10am. Lunch would be a little late today. We left the vet to the privacy of the operation and withdrew to await the result. It was rather like waiting in the corridor of a hospital. There is nothing much to do; little to say. We waited for tell-tale signs from the kitchen.

An hour later it was all over. The tumour had been removed and Baron would now be left lying on the kitchen floor, to come out of the anaesthetic in his own good time. "Don't be surprised if he is still lying there at teatime," the vet had warned. "If he comes round earlier, he may try to get up and bump into things. Don't worry."

We kept a watchful eye on him hour after hour. Occasionally there was a stir before he lapsed back to unconsciousness. Lunchtime passed and the afternoon came and went without a further sign of life. The vet's warning about the time factor was appreciated when teatime arrived and our Boxer was still out for the count.

At 8.10pm, 10 hours after the anaesthetic had been applied, minor anxiety prompted an experiment. Knowing his partiality to pate— and having read those stories of people being talked out of comas by a familiar voice—we held a piece of his favourite bite in front of his nose.

The effect was instant. The Churchillian face came suddenly alive. Regaining some sense of where he was, his head went straight to the troublesome part where he licked the wound and then struggled to his feet.

Suitably reassured, he seemed to accept it had all been for the best. That night we went for a leisurely stroll to see that all the lamp-posts were in order.

Day by day he has regained his strength and the vet reports that the removal of the tumour seems to have been complete and that there may be no more trouble at all. We'll cross our fingers.

Thus relieved, we think even more of the old chap than we did before. He and I are back on the beat, morning and night, keeping each other in trim and following a routine without which our days would feel strangely hollow.

SO WHAT WAS THE POP MUSIC
OF MY DAY?

THE solitude of the den where words are put together is frequently invaded by bursts of teenage music, from which I could swear, despite a fairly practised ear, that one tuneless banality is quite indistinguishable from any other.

Noise, beat, pouting protest, sexual gesture. These seem to be the essential ingredients, whether it happens to be pop, rock, heavy metal or any of the other superfluous labels by which the pop industry seeks to subdivide its rhythmic ragbag.

In the interests of bridging the generation gap, I do try (honest) to understand the popular musical idiom of the day. After all, my own flesh and blood are to be counted among the hypnotised masses, presumably representing what I would have been if I were a teenager today.

Of course I can happily hum along with Abba, Manhattan Transfer, Air Supply, Carly Simon, Randy Crawford and a few others. But as for the rest . . .

All of which has set me wondering about the pop music of my own day, around the late 1940s and early 1950s.

For certain, there was no slavish adherence to fashion. When gramophone records became more freely available again after the war—and I discovered for the first time that not everything on wax was early Harry Lauder or Will Fyffe—I found myself buying a wide range of music.

Others of my age group might confirm or correct the impression. But was I alone in adoring the crooning tones of the late and forgotten Steve Conway ("My Foolish Heart"), the liquid ripples of that greatest of all saxophone players, Freddie Gardiner, or the strict tempos of Victor Sylvester?

Did you, too, rush out to buy the 10in. recordings of *Annie Get Your Gun*, *Oklahoma* and every other major show to hit Drury Lane?

Yet I was equally partial to the pre-war sounds of Lew Stone or Oscar Rabin, Carroll Gibbons or Billy Mayerl, or the more substantial works of composers like Albert Ketelbey, to whom I once wrote at his home on the Isle of Wight and suffered disappointment when there was no reply.

What distinguishes that period from today is that the teenage choice was liable to be the parents' choice as well.

Then there was Eric Coates, the king of light music, whose compositions had a particular appeal.

Coates had been leading violist with the Queens Hall Orchestra, under Henry Wood, but the success of his composing enabled him to exist by that alone after the First World War.

Some of the simple stories from that period help to evoke the mood of those inter-war years. In their flat in Baker Street, London, Mrs Coates was sitting sewing one evening in 1934 when the wireless burst forth with a new programme called *In Town Tonight*.

Finding the signature tune familiar, she called through to her husband: "Isn't that something of yours, dear?" Whereupon Eric wandered through, nodded his confirmation that it was something of his and went back to his desk.

Evidently, Eric Maschwitz at the BBC was about to launch a hastily-arranged programme when he realised it had no signature tune. An emergency call to the music library for anything with a London theme brought forth a new composition by Eric Coates. It was called the "Knightsbridge March".

Soon the tune was being played by every hotel and café orchestra, theatre organ and dance band, and whistled by every message-boy on his bike. When his "Knightsbridge March" was all the rage, Coates had occasion to visit the gents' toilet in a London hotel one evening when he found himself in the next stall to a bishop, who was murdering his tune with faulty whistling.

"No, no," said Coates, "you've got it wrong. This is how it goes," embarking on a demonstration.

Whereupon the indignant bishop said loftily: "And what do you know about it?"

"I composed it," he replied, continuing with the business in hand.

Happily, he composed many more of those theme tunes which somehow captured the mood of particular situations, from "The Sleepy Lagoon" (signature tune of *Desert Island Discs*) to "Calling All Workers" (*Music While You Work*) and the march for that epic film, *The Dambusters*.

I have been thinking a great deal about Coates in a week which marked the centenary of his birth. In fact, I was listening to some of his music when, suddenly, it was overridden by a loud volume from a teenage bedroom, not on this occasion the usual cacophony of pout and protest but the majestic swell of what was probably the Royal Philharmonic Orchestra, playing something from the classics.

What's more, the teenage son was singing along in total familiarity with every note. Disbelief! Ah well, perhaps he was shy about admitting disillusion with his world of rock and had been quietly educating himself in sounds more noble.

This called for some kind of congratulation, even celebration. When he finally emerged from his classical experience, I beamed in admiration and asked: "Was that the Royal Philharmonic you were playing?"

"Yes, that's right, Dad."

"Good, good. What was the piece they were playing?"

" 'The Queen Collection.' "

"The who?"

"No, not the Who, Dad. 'The Queen Collection.' "

"You mean that Freddie Mercury guy and . . . ?"

"Yes, their music has now been recorded by your Royal Philharmonic Orchestra. Not bad, is it?"

Picking the flea out of my ear, I had to admit—and it confirmed something I had always felt about the Beatles—that their music sounded much better when played by other people.

"Ah well, we're always learning," I muttered, diving back into "The Sleepy Lagoon" and rather wishing it would swallow me up.

WHEN WILL THE CENTURY REALLY BEGIN?

IT may not, I concede, be a matter of compelling urgency but it is worth some consideration nevertheless. I wouldn't even have raised the subject at this early stage had I not overheard a conversation about the approach of the twenty-first century.

"It will be some Hogmanay night in 1999," said one imbiber. "Not just a new year but a new century."

"Ay," said his pal. "What a blow-out that'll be."

I didn't dare intrude upon their anticipation of a rather special excuse for a booze-up but I could have tempered their enthusiasm by suggesting that the twenty-first century will come later than they think.

There are many intelligent people prepared to argue I have got it wrong. If the decade of the eighties, for example, began in 1980, they say, the new century will start at the beginning of the year 2000. Not so.

I have confirmed it with no less an authority than the Oxford English Dictionary, a custodian of such matters, that the century begins in Year One.

If you take the birth of Christ as the starting point, 1 BC was followed immediately by 1 AD so you must then complete 100 years to make up your century. It seems fairly obvious.

Admittedly the calendar systems have changed over the years but it is hard to see how you could measure it any other way.

The *Glasgow Herald* was in no doubt about the start of the present century, reporting, on January 1st 1901, a pretty wet, blustery and snowless day in which nobody appeared to be paying much attention to the arrival of a new century. Somehow I think it will be rather different in 2000.

With no desire to wish away the years, however, I'll content myself for tomorrow night with the ceremonial ushering out of 1986, which I can personally count among the better periods of my existence.

There is little doubt that our Scottish Hogmanay has been losing ground to Christmas as a cause for celebration, which is perhaps as it ought to be. It comes as a surprise to most people when I recall that, in my childhood of the 1930s, Santa Claus did not reach rural Aberdeenshire until Hogmanay night.

Out of our village classroom of 28 children, all but a handful saved their excitement for Hogmanay, rather pitying the few whose big night was over and done with a week earlier.

That heightening of New Year's Eve, pagan festival though it may be, no doubt explains why I still hold it in special affection as a milestone of my life.

In the fading light of tomorrow, you will find me strolling to some elevated point where I can view the horizon at the setting of the sun.

With the old year "dying in the night," as Tennyson said, I have come to regard it as a symbol of another chapter closed, a time to wander alone with private thoughts, to reflect on things past and to hear again the echoes of those whose laughter once brightened darker days and whose joyous spirits were a feature of many another Hogmanay.

If the stillness of the setting sun is a time to remember friends departed, I find it equally a time to take stock of those who are left, the ones who enrich the present and who would be just as sorely missed as those remembered.

In other words, it's a time to count our blessings, to resolve, without being too pompous about it, that we shall invest the daily round with at least the same proportion of effort as we would like to reap in eventual reward.

Maybe it is time for a few more simple courtesies, like speaking to people we normally ignore, and appreciating that most of us have a cross of some kind to bear and that a little kindness here and there will not go amiss.

As for that milestone of the year 2000, I'll let it take care of itself, knowing that, by the coincidence of my birth, it will lead me rather neatly to the limit of my earthly expectation, a climax at the personal level to be reached in tandem with the century.

Should I have the good fortune to arrive at that point, I might well throw caution to the wind and decide to welcome the new century in spectacular fashion, heralding the borrowed time and putting it in peril on the same night!

As for tomorrow, I shall exercise that caution so that I can face you next Tuesday without going on about the never-again miseries of a Hogmanay hangover.

When the bells ring—a happy new year!

HOW THE NEWSREELS
BRING IT ALL ALIVE

ARE you as much of a sucker for old newsreels as I am? Despite the pompous nature of some commentators, I still find these films more evocative than much of what I see on television today.

You may wince at the tones of a Ramsay Macdonald or a Neville Chamberlain and marvel at the unquestioning patriotism of men en route to the First World War.

The scenes themselves may have grown old-fashioned with time but how fascinating to study the faces and their reaction to events which, however much they may have dated now, were the latest issues of their time.

In sport, I can still watch those reels of Stanley Matthews streaking down the wing (even if he is tormenting Scottish full-backs) and feel that I am absorbing the exquisite skills of the man as well as the mood of the time in a way that has been quite unsurpassed by subsequent techniques.

I am reminded of all this by the BBC's *Attic Archives*, which ends tomorrow night. The fact that the last of the series, which I have just seen as a preview, takes us back to my own North-east corner has merely rounded off for me a nostalgic trip which was brimful of fascination.

In an earlier programme, I was scanning the parade of Winston Churchill's open car driving up Union Street, Aberdeen, in 1946 knowing that, somewhere in the footage, I was running alongside, as a 14-year-old boy, reaching out to touch the great man.

In tomorrow's showing, you see Aberdeen of the immediate post-war period, with the tram-cars clanking their way up Union Street and people going about their business.

The words of Laurie Lee and John R. Allan lend poetic depth to match the physical dimensions of Rubislaw Quarry, that massive hole within the city boundary from which the bulk of Aberdeen was hewn.

There are views of Aberdeen University, which was producing Britain's first doctors nearly 500 years ago, and artistic shots of the rural hinterland I knew so well, with horse-drawn plough and intruding "Fordie tractor".

A GPO film of a trawler heading for the wild North Sea had dialogue and touches of semi-professionalism yet I preferred some of the older films, like the wedding at Glasgow Cathedral in 1921, unearthed from the attic by a child of that marriage, who will now be approaching retirement age.

We have seen Will Fyffe, looking more like Harry Lauder and entertaining his audience to material which wears embarrassingly thin with time. There have been gems like the pensioners' picnic at Lochgelly and the queue for the opening of La Scala cinema in Hamilton in 1929, with its toothless grannies all dressed up in their finery. (Thank goodness for false teeth!)

A view of children in a cinema queue in Paisley in that same year raised a chilling reminder of the fire tragedy which engulfed so many of the town's youngsters in 1929.

Indeed the cinemas themselves have provided some of the best material, with promotional stunts like the rushing of film to Glasgow by Rapide plane for showing at the Vogue, an occasion of glory for Annie Macleod, a local lassie paraded on a lorry as Govan's answer to Jane Russell.

They made their own advertisements for the screen, promoting such local institutions as the *Alloa Advertiser*—"best for pithy pars." And who could resist the excitement of the mobs who greeted Laurel and Hardy when they came to visit Edinburgh in 1932?

So the series rolled on down memory lane, out to Colville's steelworks where they were shaping the girders to build the Tower for the Glasgow Empire Exhibition of 1938.

These old films not only took us doon the water but into John Brown's shipyard when they were building the *Queen Mary*, the greatest ship that ever sailed the seas.

Then there were the planes of 602 Squadron, City of Glasgow, looking like something out of Biggles in their build-up to the Second World War, and the famous flying circus of Sir Alan Cobham.

What wonderful impressions of those pre-war days when the old celluloid managed to show us people actually posting their letters straight into the mail-box on the train and buying their newspapers from the travelling vendor, who struck his head out through the window, station by station.

And what about those old turntables at the end of the line, where the big steam engines had to be pushed round by hand to face the other way? I must confess they got me going with this series, much of it salvaged from corners of neglect to assume an historic importance its owners didn't imagine.

Part of the fascination is in studying those faces and wondering what our forefathers are actually saying to each other and in what kind of language they are saying it. Were they really as vain as all the preening for camera attention suggests or was it just the novelty of the day?

Through all the hardships of the time, you are left with an impression of the innocence of the pre-consumer society, and the sense of the genuine and worthwhile nature of the people. The unseemly scramble of our competitive age may well have lost us something of that natural quality.

Thank goodness it is all retained in those amateur films which are emerging from many a loft around Scotland. Producer Dennis Dick has done well to draw it all together, along with presenter Jimmy Logan and Janet McBain of the Scottish Film Archives.

I hope their quest for more of this kind of material succeeds. It is not a matter of wallowing in nostalgia. It is a case of reminding ourselves about the way we used to live—and helping to get our present condition into better perspective.

WHERE DO THEY FIND
THOSE GORGEOUS NURSES?

FOR someone who has not lost a day's work through illness in more than 20 years, I can still sail fairly close to the hurricanes of hypochondria. Or so my wife says.

No minor twinge is allowed to pass without a frown of suspicion; no fleeting glow of well-being is accepted without a feeling that nature is lulling me into a false sense of security while all the time cooking up some sinister plot to cut short the mortal tenure.

There was a time when I had an annual visit to the surgery, usually at the first call of spring, with a form of overall aching which the doctor diagnosed as myalgia. I later discovered this was a bit of a medical ragbag, used by the quacks when they hadn't the foggiest idea what was wrong with you. But it sounded impressive and if it sent you away a happier hypochondriac then it didn't really matter if they called it myalgia, youralgia or anybody else's-algia. It served the purpose. (Come to think of it, I haven't suffered a bout for several years. Memo to self: Keep it in mind for a too-sunny day.)

In self-defence, I have to say that any anxiety about the state of play has nothing to do with "enjoying bad health"; it has everything to do with being passionately in love with the performance of life and appalled that the show can be cancelled at short notice.

The reason I tell you all this has to do with a recent virus infection which went the rounds, affecting the middle ear and sending people off balance.

I had a couple of nasty moments before going to the doctor. Now his diagnosis of a middle-ear infection would have satisfied any normal patient but not your Tuesday correspondent. Having

53

plumped for the worst possible scenario of a tumour, I was not to be diverted from a brain-scan which would hopefully prove, if nothing else, that there was at least a brain to scan, a fact about which some of my friends still need to be convinced.

So I duly turned up at the hospital and was met by a couple of crisp, efficient, good-looking nurses who laid me on a table and talked in such reassuring tones as to raise the highest suspicions of what lay ahead.

This brain-scan apparatus, which builds up a complete picture of the old grey matter in a process of multi-angled photographic "slices", belonged to the futuristic world of Star Trek (I have often wondered how the television people arrived at that particular form of weird electronic noise but that is exactly how the things work).

As I had been well warned, the table moved so that I was entering the scanning tunnel, the doctor and two nurses having escaped into Mission Control while maintaining that eerie contact through another of those space-age intercom gadgets.

The needle embedded in my arm had injected a fluid to facilitate the considerable task of finding my brain and showing what it might be up to.

I lay there for about half an hour, head stock still, till I nearly drifted off to sleep. In that halfway-house of consciousness, I emerged from the scanner, rather like a corpse at a crematorium, except that I was coming back and was, as far as I knew, still alive and kicking.

The nurse was bending over me, whispering more of those words of reassurance. Where do they find these gorgeous Nightingales? (Urgent thought: Could this brain-scanner possibly show up what I am thinking?!)

It is in such moments that one could almost welcome the kind of emergency which calls for the kiss of life; but it never happens that way.

Instead, I restored myself to sartorial decency and drove home to await the verdict on the state of the cranial sawdust. When the specialist finally phoned, it was to give me the news that "There is nothing there." Only later, when re-examining the form of words, did I realise that the poor man was probably trying to ease my mind when there was nothing there to ease.

After such a thorough investigation, however, I really had nothing to worry about. Except that nothing gives a hypochondriac so much to worry about as nothing to worry about. It is in the nature of the beast.

A moment or two of brooding and I was beginning to warm to the subject once more. What about all those X-rays which had been flashing through my brain like a ham-slicer? Don't they tell you that too much exposure to X-rays is a danger in itself?

And what about that needle they stuck in my arm? They are saying some peculiar things about needles these days. Could it . . . would it . . . ?

Now that should be enough to keep me going for a week or two. Yes, things are looking brighter already.

LOOKING BACK ON
THE PROFUMO SCANDAL

JOHN PROFUMO and I have at least one thing in common. We have both spent some time alone in a bedroom with Christine Keeler.

He was there for pleasure, of course. I was there in the cause of duty, conducting an interview for the enlightenment of the general readership on this notorious lady.

For some strange reason, that last statement usually sends the more vulgar of my acquaintances into paroxysms of disbelief, and produces even from the more sophisticated the ultimate proof that there is no limit to human cynicism.

Even as I try to explain that I was doing no more than pursuing the customary habit of arranging my journalistic encounters where the interviewee will feel most at home, I realise I am landing myself deeper and deeper in the mire of suspicion.

So I give up, leave them to their fantasies and try to convince myself that nearly 25 years now separate us from the biggest sex-and-security scandal of the century.

Whatever else the younger generation may not know about modern history, there must be few who have not heard of the Profumo Case which rocked the British Establishment in the early sixties and hastened the end of Harold Macmillan as Prime Minister.

The trouble was that John Profumo was his Minister for War, not the sort of post in which you should be exposing yourself to possible blackmail. Yet Profumo, bred from Italian aristocrats and married to film star Valerie Hobson, was going to bed with the beautiful young showgirl Christine Keeler who, in turn, was having some kind of liaison with Eugene Ivanov, a London-based officer of Soviet Military Intelligence no less.

His most faithful apologist would have to admit that, whatever the fleeting pleasures, that was not the most clever thing he ever did.

After Labour MP George Wigg raised a question in the Commons in March 1963, Profumo rose to tell the House there had been no impropriety in his association with Christine Keeler.

Harold Macmillan stood by him. Within weeks, however, Profumo was back on his feet admitting he had told a lie. He resigned in disgrace. The whole matter became a source of public entertainment soon afterwards when the key figure in the introduction of Keeler to the two men, Dr Stephen Ward, was charged with living on immoral earnings.

Ward was a famous London osteopath with such a flair for portraiture that he had sketched members of the royal family. Add to all that the fact that the high jinks involving the rich and famous were centred on a cottage at Lord Astor's estate of Cliveden and you have the ingredients of a pretty steamy, seamy story.

There have been books on the subject but nothing of an investigative nature until this past week. In the crazy way these things happen, after a lapse of nearly quarter of a century not one but two books are suddenly on the stands.

Best selling author Anthony Summers, who wrote Marilyn Monroe's biography, *Goddess*, told me this week how he had to speed up the process when he heard another book had been written.

Getting down to writing it as recently as Christmas, Summers has achieved a major feat in having his book out now. Called rather aptly *Honeytrap* (Intelligence parlance for a scheme to ensnare an espionage target through sexual compromise) it homes in on MI5 and MI6, who evidently spotted Stephen Ward as a man who could be useful to their need of supplying women.

The plan misfired and, as the famous ran for cover, Dr Ward seems to have become the scapegoat, deserted by his influential friends in the Establishment. Summers and co-author Stephen Dorril claim the Ward trial was a put-up job.

Having burrowed around in America they produce more evidence against the increasingly-discredited President Kennedy, who seems to have had carnal knowledge of at least one of Stephen Ward's young ladies, a certain Mariella Novotny, best remembered as the hostess in the infamous Man in the Mask party.

Among others now dead in the list of key characters are Lord Astor, Mariella Novotny, several more of Ward's girls (murder and suicide) and of course Dr Stephen Ward himself.

Just as the jury were about to bring in their verdicts (they found him guilty of living on the immoral earnings of Christine Keeler and Mandy Rice-Davies) Ward went home to his Chelsea flat, wrote a number of suicide notes and instigated the final act.

He lingered in an overdose coma for three days but finally went. Lord Goodman, legal adviser to Prime Minister Harold Wilson, had declared that Ward's girls were plainly not prostitutes, that the conduct of judge and prosecution left much to be desired, and that the case was "an historic injustice".

Mandy Rice-Davies proved to be the survivor above all, carving a career as actress and novelist. John Profumo, who went off to do social work in London's East End, is still immensely rich at 72. Summers grants him no more sympathy than he deserves.

Christine Keeler has been a loser, following a trail of broken marriages and dole queues. She is now 45, lives in a pretty depressing corner of Chelsea, and just the other week was arrested and fined for drunkenness and causing damage.

I remember studying her classical bone structure yet finding it difficult to reconcile her with the leading figures whose downfall she helped to precipitate. I suppose it only goes to prove that the High Life can be a pretty Low Life indeed—and that we really do live in a crazy, crazy world.

PEOPLE YOU MEET AT
A MALCOLM FORBES PARTY

THERE are weeks when not a lot happens between one Tuesday and the next; when the columnist's nightmare of a blank mind to match a blank page looms too close to reality. But the past seven days were different.

It all began with a phone call from the office of that American legend, New York publisher, art collector, balloonist and daredevil Malcolm Forbes, to say "Hey, come on over—we're holding a party Thursday night."

Now I'm not in the habit of dropping everything to rush off to a party, especially when it is more than 3000 miles away. But the parties Malcolm holds on his estate at Far Hills, New Jersey, are something different, even by the lavishly superlative standards of that remarkable country.

So come last Wednesday and I was heading across the Atlantic, wondering what kind of a bash this would be. The immediate occasion was the 70th anniversary of Forbes Magazine, the prestigious business journal founded in 1917 by Malcolm's father, Bertie, a poor little Scots lad who became known as the great humaniser of American business.

As a friend of the family, Bertie used to encourage my schoolboy enthusiasm for journalism. Since then I had been to the 50th birthday party of his magazine but had not expected another landmark event until the 75th.

Son Malcolm was taking no chances, however. Having narrowly escaped death at the Normandy landings of 1944, he was also one of the survivors when the King of Morocco's birthday party turned

59

into the massacre of an attempted coup in 1971, crawling away on his belly while 100 fellow-guests lay slain.

More recently he has cheated death in his famous hot-air balloons and on his motorbikes. One of the pithy sayings of Chairman Malcolm is "While you're alive—*live*," a dictum he follows assiduously. The fact that he is among the richest men in America merely heightens the sense of his own mortality.

Before changing into the dinner suit in my New York hotel, I encountered press speculation that, following his divorce last year, the 67-year-old Malcolm Forbes might announce his engagement to Elizabeth Taylor. Well, well. That added a new dimension to the evening ahead.

Off I went through the Manhattan teatime rush, across the Hudson River and out to the Forbes parkland estate. The fact that guests were already dropping in by helicopter should have alerted me that this would be no ordinary beanfeast.

Excitement stirred in the warm evening air as the family greeted guests on the tented lawn, surrounded by such a display of tartan and castellated splendour as to leave no doubt about the origins of the American family Forbes.

That effect was fortified when 140 pipers and drummers came skirling round the swimming pool declaring "Scotland the Brave" as the theme of the evening. And what an evening it turned out to be!

You really will have to pardon the name dropping, on the grounds that it is too good to resist. Amid people with monikers like Getty and Rockefeller, I also found myself chatting to people like Henry Kissinger, Sir James Goldsmith, and Rupert Murdoch.

Standing around us were Princess Lee Radziwill, Helen Gurley Brown, Mick Jagger's wife, Jerry Hall, General MacArthur's widow and Howard Baker, President Reagan's Chief of the White House Staff.

And did I forget to mention Elizabeth Taylor? Yes, she was there all right, as Malcolm's date for the evening and seated by his right hand at the dinner table.

There is a tale that the origins of one branch of the Forbes clan (pronounced with both vowel sounds in true Scots) came from a

Raleigh-like incident, where the gent threw down his cloak for the earlier Queen Elizabeth. She rewarded him with a title because he did it "for Bess".

Well, at Thursday night's party Malcolm did not exactly throw down his plaid for the modern-day Bess. Nor, for that matter, did he fulfil press speculation about an engagement. But he did something more useful. To Hollywood's Queen Elizabeth he presented a cheque for a million dollars to help her American foundation for Aids Research.

Once she had made her little speech of thanks and we had heard from two or three budding Presidents of the United States (Malcolm himself was once a red-hot tip for the White House) we adjourned to the lawns for the most spectacular display of fireworks America has ever seen. The pyrotechnics filled the sky to the thundering accompaniment of Gershwin and Beethoven.

Back in the marquee, Lester Lanin and his mellow saxophones danced us into the wee sma' 'oors of an event that left America breathless with admiration.

As Malcolm told the company: "If my Scottish father is looking down right now, he will be appalled at the expense but delighted that we can afford it!"

So the lights dimmed over Timberfield, the music lingered in the night air and the perfume of a heady whing-ding sent us floating back to Manhattan.

Come a new day and I would be heading back to the real home of the Forbeses, jet-lagged, hung-over and gloriously exhausted. And so to sleep.

If this space should remain blank next Tuesday, it may be less the sign of a blank mind than the onset of a miniature dose of the Rip Van Winkles.

REUNION TIME FOR LISBON LIONS

WHILE maintaining neutrality in matters affecting the rival sports establishments of Ibrox and Parkhead, I make no apology for placing the memorable Jimmy Johnstone of Celtic within the very top bracket of football entertainers it has been my privilege to watch.

That puts him in the company of some legendary names whose inclusion is demanded by their supremacy in different areas of the game. England's Frank Swift, for example, was without doubt the greatest goalkeeper I ever saw. (He was killed in the Manchester United plane disaster.)

Pele of Brazil had the best integration of skill and surging power; Franz Beckenbauer of West Germany was the most perfectly precise machine; Ireland's George Best and Holland's Johann Cruyff had the flair of the gladiator.

The maestro himself, Stanley Matthews, would stalk the right wing with a sleight-of-feet which would have been better performed with top hat and cloak.

But if you want my vote for the footballer who, by his own individual skill, could take on two or three opponents and beat them in a limited space, it would go without doubt to the wee red-head from Viewpark, Uddingston. And, if I needed reminding of that fact, it came in a recent television programme when Celtic's Lisbon Lions came together for a reunion on the twentieth anniversary of their European Cup triumph.

There they were, donning the togs of training and re-living a practice session at their customary haunt of Seamill, before gathering round a table for a celebration dinner.

Poignantly, the STV cameras moved from one face to the next, underlining with chilling effect the monstrously uneven hand of nature when imposing the rigours of age.

Fresh home from Australia, Willie Wallace looked ready to take the field as if time had stood still. For others the fates had been less than kind.

Around the table the banter was unchanged—the mischievous wit of Bertie Auld, the counter punches of Jimmy Johnstone and Tommy Gemmell, the moderating interventions of captain Billy McNeill. Wonderful stuff.

Behind it all the silent witness of Jock Stein was poised in portrait, the man who took a bunch of raw lads and moulded them into the finest club side Scotland has ever seen. Yes, the toast of the night was surely to an absent friend, the man to whom they owed so much.

Among the assorted thoughts and feelings which came to the surface as I watched that splendid programme was the question of how many of those Lisbon Lions would have taken their place in the all-time best XI of Scottish football.

Indirectly, it is a tribute to Stein's genius for blending a range of talents into a winning chemistry to say that, individually, perhaps not too many of the Lions could have claimed supremacy in their own positions.

But Jimmy Johnstone was certainly one. There is even an argument for saying that the world has probably never seen a player more gifted in the close control of a football.

I once had a rare opportunity to experience the exquisite skill at close quarters. When the euphoria of Lisbon was at its height, Celtic players were in demand with publishers who wanted to print their books.

Naturally, Johnstone was a prime target and I was engaged as ghostwriter for the Wee Man's story, which we entitled *Fire in My Boots*.

Calling at his home in Viewpark for one of our regular "ghosting" sessions, I found him out on a piece of waste ground, dribbling his way round dozens of local kids who worshipped him to the extent that they would follow on as if he were the Pied Piper of Parkhead.

Watching from the sidelines (and once having fancied myself as a footballer!) I called to him to bring the ball right up to me and demonstrate how he managed with such regularity to glide past opposing defenders as if they had never existed.

Secretly, I have to tell you, I thought I had the Wee Green Devil where I wanted him. I was going to nail him. This would be my moment of glory. Soon I was to learn what separates genius from mindless fantasy.

The Wee Barra brought the ball to within a foot of my clumsy feet.

"I've got him!" I said to myself as I lunged towards him with a potentially lethal tackle.

Suddenly, the ball was not where the ball had been. Wee James had not only jinked in one direction to commit my ungainly form to an undignified wild goose chase. He had also switched course to ride my tackle and disappear in the other direction with a single movement that mixed the skill of a conjurer with the sheer poetic beauty of a ballet dancer.

I really should have stuck to writing his book. As far as playing football was concerned, he left his ghost for dead.

THE REMARKABLE GARRYS—
ROBERT AND FLORA

THE Perthshire village of Comrie unfolded its arms in warm welcome as I rounded the final bend and knew that there was more than scenic beauty to be savoured within these hills of central Scotland.

I was heading for the garden gate of an extraordinary couple whose company I had enjoyed before and whose names I had known for as long as I could remember.

In contrasting careers, Robert Garry gained his first taste of fame at the very sunrise of his career as a doctor, while his charming wife, Flora, chose to wait for evening shadows before fully revealing the talent which has made her one of Scotland's outstanding dialect poets of the century.

At 87, they tend their garden behind a laich dyke, entertain you to a fine cup of tea and cast an intelligent eye down a century with which it has been their privilege to march, step by step, year by year.

Robert Garry, whose father was a teacher at Glasgow High, will take his own place in medical history because of what happened on a particular night of 1923, when he was a young resident doctor at the city's Western Infirmary.

From across the ocean, the fledgling Scots medic had been following events in Canada where, within the department of a distinguished Scots professor, J. J. MacLeod, a young surgeon called Frederick Banting had discovered a cure for diabetes. In 1923 it was still a killer disease. Now there was insulin.

Young Garry not only followed every move but managed to acquire a small phial of it and to learn how to measure the dangerous build-up of sugar in the blood. Then came that night, 64 years ago, when yet another patient was admitted to Ward 10 of Glasgow Western in a severe diabetic coma, from which there would be little likelihood of a return.

Young Garry could not act on his own but neither was this a chance to be missed. He phoned his chief, Dr Adam Patrick, at home and asked permission to use insulin. There was nothing to lose and he was given the go-ahead.

He still remembers dashing back to the ward: "The man's blood sugar was very high so I injected 20 units straight away," is his recollection. "We did not really know the amounts to use and this had little effect so I injected another 20 units. The sugar level began to come down. I gave him 60 altogether and by then he was practically down to normal."

Via the newly-qualified doctor, insulin had arrived in this country. In the morning there was rejoicing. The hospital superintendent was on his doorstep with the milk, eager to know all about it.

That was the first step in a distinguished career for the young Glaswegian who, in time, became Regius Professor of Physiology at Glasgow University.

At one stage in his career he moved to work at the famous Rowett Institute for Research near Aberdeen and there, by the happiest of coincidences, he was invited to become a part-time lecturer at Aberdeen University by none other than the Scot who had played his part in the discovery of insulin. Professor MacLeod had returned to become Regius Professor of Physiology at Aberdeen in 1928.

It was in that same corner of Scotland that Robert Garry found his future wife, Flora Campbell, the beautiful daughter of Robert Boothby's political agent, Archie Campbell, a well-known Tory farmer. Not even that political affiliation, however, could divert one of her ardent admirers, who happened to be the son of Ramsay MacDonald, Britain's first-ever Labour Prime Minister.

Herself a brilliant English scholar, Flora settled as the supportive wife of Professor Garry and only rarely revealed what she could do when she put pen to paper. In fact she was well into her seventies before her work reached publication stage and people began to take note of this talented writer. Where had she been all these years?

As we sat in their charming home in Comrie, I asked Flora Garry to read me the title piece from her poetry collection, *Bennygoak*, which catches the scents of the farmyard in rich dialect.

Too few Scots may now understand the language but here at least is a sample of the rendering I was given that day:

It wis jist a skelp o the muckle furth,
A sklyter o roch grun,
Fin granfadder's fadder bruke it in
Fae the hedder an the funn.
Granfadder sklatit barn an byre,
Brocht water tae the closs,
Pat fail-dykes ben the bare brae face
An a cairt road tull the moss.

Bit wir fadder sottert i the yard
An skeppit amo' bees
An keepit fancy dyeuks an doos
'At warna muckle eese.
He bocht aul wizzent horse an kye
An scrimpit muck an seed;
Syne, clocherin wi a craichly hoast
He dwine't awa, an deed.

So it went on. Flora Garry has no intention of dwinin' awa tae dee at this stage in her life. The sparkle of youth still glints from her eye. The crease of humour is ever ready at the corners of her mouth, as instance the remark which rounded off a perfect afternoon.

"When I do eventually go," she told me, "I know exactly what my epitaph is going to be: Here lies Flora Garry—much against her will!"

TO DUBROVNIK—
AND AN EVENING WITH MONTY

THE centenary tributes to Montgomery of Alamein must have been something of a revelation to a generation who perhaps knew him as a name and little more.

There he was, foxy little figure, the British General who turned the Second World War in our favour with his famous victory in North Africa, strutting about as a national hero with a kind of comic arrogance.

However rude he may have been to the Americans, Monty nevertheless inspired a fierce loyalty in his own soldiers of the Eighth Army, who would have followed him to the ends of the earth.

The reason for that loyalty was surely his outstanding success in mass communication. Yet how strange that a man who could strike a chord with tens of thousands was such a failure in his own personal relationships.

Such was his dislike of his own mother that he couldn't find time to attend her funeral. He was at odds with other members of the family. A proper enigma if ever there was one.

While the public portrait was being enacted on television and radio, I found myself musing over the occasion when, as a young journalist, I decided to seek an interview with the great man.

Having gone to sample Tito's Communism in Yugoslavia after the war, I made an early escape from Belgrade and took a lift on an old Dakota across the Dinaric Alps to Dubrovnik, long before that old walled city was opened up to foreign tourists.

Conditions were crude. The plane came bumping down on a field where farm animals were grazing. A fellow journalist and I found refuge with a local family.

It was during our stay in Dubrovnik, however, that we heard about Scheherazade, conjuring up those tales of the Arabian Nights, the telling of which in such mesmerising fashion was to save the good lady from the old Sultan's death squad.

President Tito had chosen the name of Scheherazade for the villa where he entertained his VIP guests. "Your own Princess Margaret has been here," whispered the locals. "And we hear your war hero . . . Montgomery? . . . is staying there at present."

We strolled up the hill to the sentry-box at Scheherazade, scribbled a note of request for an interview and handed it to a guard whose response was less than encouraging. There would be a reply if we returned at a given time.

Rating our prospects at little above zero, we nevertheless returned as promised. What happened next provided two young reporters with their first big break.

In the early dark of a September evening, the gates swung open to reveal the gloriously perfumed gardens of Scheherazade, ablaze with light, through which we were marched with a military guard, down the terraced slopes as they reached towards the waters of the Adriatic.

At a table in front of the villa sat the slight figure that was unmistakably Monty.

"What can I do for you, gentlemen?" he asked as we began to explain our innocent purpose. Chairs were pulled up and, in characteristic fashion, he more or less decided our drink would be vermouth, snapping his fingers at a gent in dark suit who appeared smartly, with silver tray.

We thought the waiter had now been dismissed. Instead, he returned to the scene, pulled up another chair and was introduced— as M. Popovic, the Yugoslav Foreign Secretary! Only the effrontery of Monty could have got away with that.

It reminded me of his moment of crowning glory at Luneberg Heath when he was taking the German surrender in 1945. Rubbing salt in the Nazi wound, he asked for the name of the German leader then snapped "Never heard of you."

When he told us of his recent visit to Churchill at Chequers, I was reminded of that other story about Winston telling King George VI: 'Montgomery is after my job, you know." To which the King, showing more wit than he was given credit for, replied: "Oh good. I thought he was after mine!"

In my first major interview, I thought I was doing pretty well till I realised I had been more the interviewee than the interviewer. Monty wanted to know about all we had seen. What about the people in their own homes? What had we seen of the agriculture?

At the end of a memorable evening, we were shown out in much the same way as we had been ushered in. But there was one parting shot. Having discovered we worked for Kemsley Newspapers, he said "You'll know C. D. Hamilton" (Kemsley's right-hand man in London). We explained that we hardly mixed in such elevated circles. "He was one of my best men at Alamein, you know. Good chap, good chap. Anyway, do tell my friend Lord Kemsley that I was passing on my regards."

Was it one of those courtesies which are not intended to be carried out? In our uncertainty, we decided to take no chances. With more than a hint of embarrassment, off went a note to his lordship.

A few days later there was another note on Kemsley's desk. It told of two enterprising young chaps who turned up at the Villa Scheherazade—and went on to give the kind of reference that job-hunters dream about.

It finished by saying: "I told them they were to send you personally my good wishes—and I hope they did so! . . . Montgomery of Alamein."

They tell great stories of his attention to detail in planning the Battle of Alamein. I can believe them. As my colleague and I wiped the sweat from our brows in relief that we had not ignored his request, we gained our first insight into the mechanisms which make great men tick.

We also began to understand why Rommel didn't stand a chance.

THOMAS THE RHYMER—
AND THE CURSE OF FYVIE

IAN GRIMBLE sent shivers down my spine the other evening when he took us on a television tour of Fyvie Castle and recalled a prediction of Thomas the Rhymer in relation to the occupants of that stately pile.

A thirteenth-century seer who also predicted the Battle of Bannockburn, Thomas the Rhymer gave warning of a time to come when no eldest son of Fyvie would succeed to the estate.

His words took time to become effective but, with the arrival of the Forbes-Leith family last century, they suddenly sprang into reality. In one generation after another, the assorted ravages of war and mishap began to claim the eldest sons of Fyvie Castle till the matter became a point of dreaded superstition.

That evil legend still hovered when I went thundering through the Howe of Auchterless, in my early days as a journalist, to pay a first visit to the Fyvie estate.

The purpose of the visit was to interview the head gardener about the floral abundance of that particular year and, as we wandered through the vast spread of walled enclosure, I cautiously mentioned this so-called curse which seemed to beset the Forbes-Leith family.

From what I could gather, it was not a topic of conversation to be encouraged but, before the gardener had time to respond to my scepticism, one way or the other, we were silenced by the appearance of a strapping young man who came striding down the garden towards us.

"Here's young John, the laird's son," said the gardener hurriedly. "The heir?"

71

"Ay. The elder of the two sons."

John Forbes-Leith had come to the end of his Army leave and was taking his farewell of estate workers before heading back to his battalion of the Guards in Malaya, which was then in turmoil.

As he continued down the garden and disappeared through the gate at the bottom, we watched with an uneasy sense of what fate can produce.

On the way back to Turriff by bus, however, I convinced myself it was all an old wives' tale, and turned my thoughts to the coverage of the latest excitements in local life (most likely a whist drive in the St Ninian's Church Hall!).

A few weeks later I was back on that bus to Fyvie. This time I was going to report on the funeral service of . . . yes, none other than John Forbes-Leith, the prospective Laird of Fyvie.

As he had disappeared from our gaze amidst the fragrance of a godly garden, he headed off to the guerrilla warfare of Malaya, deep in those sweaty jungles of Oriental scents and melodious birdsong.

In all the crossfire of bullets and grenades, there was writing on the wall for the heir-apparent of Fyvie Castle. Now they had brought his remains back for burial in the native corner better known to the outside world for its romantic song, "The Bonnie Lass o' Fyvie".

The aristocracy were joined by the folk of the farms and the village to pay their last respects to a fine young man, around whose head that legend lurked. Who could have believed this scene of mourning those few weeks ago when we met in the peace of a summer's day? I raised my head at prayer time, surveyed the congregation and wondered where reality lay.

Quoting from my notes of the time: "I slipped quietly away from the kirk to walk alone to the garden of Fyvie Castle, there to stand on the spot where I had stood before. It was as if time had lost its regularity and I was standing there as though never before, with the earlier visit but an imaginary figment rising now to torment and perplex.

"There was little knowing and even less understanding of the quirks of fate. But the blooms had faded in that bountiful garden and the wind that blew from a chill airt through the howe came echoing like the eerie call of a witch in the night."

The dead man's father, Sir Ian Forbes-Leith, was prominent in local government, becoming Lord-Lieutenant of Aberdeenshire, and there is one part of this story which came to me only recently, but on good authority.

While attending a council meeting in Aberdeen one day, Sir Ian suddenly rose and left to call his wife. Had there been any word of John? Evidently he had had a premonition. No, she had heard nothing. But news of his death arrived next day.

In a pattern now tragically established, young Andrew Forbes-Leith took on the mantle of future Laird of Fyvie from his late brother. In time he was married with a young family of his own. Then, as if the fates were starting to rumble again, his young wife just managed to survive a serious car accident.

They already had three children when she went to hospital for the arrival of their fourth. Nine days after the birth, she was dead.

The commercial considerations of running a big estate had no doubt been paramount when the magnificence of Fyvie Castle was passed into the hands of the National Trust for Scotland.

I wouldn't know what thoughts passed through the head of Andew Forbes-Leith about that relentless pattern of family curse. But, in the interests of his children and his children's children, would you have blamed him for wanting to be rid of the place?

THE VISIONARY THAT WAS
R. F. MACKENZIE

IDLY winding down before bedtime and thinking about nothing in particular, I turned on late-night TV and found myself engrossed in a programme in which southern pundits were assessing the remarkable Scottish educationist, Robert F. Mackenzie.

Suddenly, I was transported back in time to a day in the 1960s when I entered the Kingdom of Fife to seek out this rare individual about whom I had heard so much but knew so little.

Braehead School in Buckhaven was then gaining attention because of Mackenzie's presence as headmaster and, after negotiating long corridors, I settled to an interview with the visionary himself.

For those who may have missed out on the career of R. F. Mackenzie, it is hard to encapsulate him in a paragraph. Here was a man who wanted to revolutionise education.

He believed in the essential goodness of the young and blamed the system for turning them into the little monsters they sometimes became. That could have been a shade naïve.

He expounded to me his views in that slightly quivering voice of a passionately caring man, warm and humane, a prophet who would struggle for honour in his own country.

We struck up an immediate rapport, largely on the grounds of having attended the same Aberdeen school, albeit a generation apart. The gaping difference was that he ended up as dux of Robert Gordon's College.

For all it had given him, however, he was critical of that system. For a start, he regarded the belt as barbaric, especially when used on girls. But his philosophy went much deeper.

Striking right at the core of our education, he was appalled that we were failing to harness the creative energies of the young, asking them instead to sit at desks and memorise a vast amount of useless information.

We would ask them to measure the oxygen intake of the humming bird, write about the exports of Paraguay, or draw a map to show the millet-producing areas of Pakistan. (Does it ring a bell?)

Speaking to my colleague, Harry Reid, who made one of the most perceptive studies of Mackenzie, he once said: "I used to think we were different from the Russians but we push information into the kids in exactly the same way. We tell them the right things to say and they get marks for saying it. Our exam system is incredibly bad."

Instead, he wanted teachers to take children into the open spaces. "A week camping in the Highlands," he once said, "will teach children more about history, geology, botany, economics, and craft than a whole year in school."

Mackenzie was the son of a rural railwayman, a breed who so often produced clever offspring. I was fascinated by his early career. As a very young man, he set off with another Aberdeenshire lad, Hunter Diack, to cycle across the continent of Europe, then boiling up for Hitler's war.

Sending back despatches for the local daily paper, they met up with people like H. G. Wells before returning to publish a book about their adventures.

Mackenzie went back to teach in Germany and was living with a Jewish family in 1938 when the Nazis came smashing their way into the house. Back in Scotland, he teamed up with Hunter Diack, by then a teacher at Gordon's College, and two more of my old masters, John Foster and Johnny Mackintosh, to launch a weekly paper, which was intended to give some radical opposition to the local power of Lord Kemsley's empire.

But teaching, not journalism, became his vocation and Fife provided the base from which Mackenzie could begin to work out his theories. Predictably, there were critics and, in the midst of controversy, he moved back to his native North-east as headmaster of Aberdeen's Summerhill Academy in 1968.

Alas, it was there on his native heath, while trying to give shape to his ideals, that he finally came unstuck. His staff were split down the middle with complaints that, for all his progressive ideas, the net result was an increase in truancy, vandalism, bullying, smoking, even extortion.

They signed a protest, a document of school rules was drawn up and he was ordered to implement them. In fairness to the authorities, those rules were to do with such basics as turning up at school on time, with the necessary materials, entering by the appropriate door and doing homework when required.

But Mackenzie refused to follow the order and was suspended for ever in 1974. In a farmhouse near the River Dee he lived out his days writing and lecturing and still dreaming of a better future. (Ironically, Grampian region have just taken a decision to close Summerhill Academy altogether.)

He acknowledged, as a major flaw in his make-up, that he had not managed to carry his staff with him—and that must remain a failure of leadership.

R. F. Mackenzie died a few weeks ago and I am told that he quoted Gandhi to a friend who was paying him a last visit: "A thing I fear greatly is the hardness of heart of the educated."

There was no hardness in the heart of Mackenzie; only a touch of arrogance perhaps, but he was a kind and gentle and honest man. I am, however, haunted by the memory of that visit to Braehead more than 20 years ago.

Along those corridors, I passed room after room in which I could see little but bedlam behind glass doors. There was so much to commend R. F. Mackenzie and his theories, you felt. If only he would have acknowledged the need for some peace and order in which to implement them.

WE ALL HAVE A STORY . . .

THERE used to be a saying to the effect that inside every journalist there lies a book. To which the cynics might well have added that "inside every journalist" is exactly where it should stay!

It was, I suspect, a rather pretentious idea put about by the scribblers themselves. But if there happens to be any substance to the notion then it must surely apply to a much wider spectrum of the human race. Certainly, from the letters I receive from readers of this column, I am frequently given hint of a fascinating life-story which, in the normal course of things, will never be told.

The anonymity which covers the vast bulk of the population would include, for example, Miss Anderson, a dear old lady who lives on the South Side of Glasgow and bothers nobody. I doubt if her name has ever been in print before.

Yet her letter of recent weeks sparked off my curiosity and led to a most delightful evening in her company. Approaching her 98th birthday, she is probably my oldest reader, so far spared all the defects of sight and hearing, and conversing with the clarity of a much younger woman.

She does the *Herald* crossword every day and is an enthusiastic follower of snooker on television, to the point that her calculation of the various colours is well ahead of the game.

Indeed, a mathematical and business brain has been one of the strengths of Miss Anderson ever since her days in Fraserburgh, where she was born in 1890 and of whose local academy she was dux in the early years of this century.

To listen to her tales is to bridge the centuries. Her father, for example, was born in 1835, two years before Victoria came to the throne, and was serving on the old clippers when she was a child. Despite his long absences, Miss Anderson was the 11th of 12 children!

Her grandfather, Captain William Webster, used to sail his ship between Fraserburgh and Russia till he was lost at sea in the Great Gale of 1860.

As for Miss Anderson herself (she wouldn't suit a Christian name), there was a question of delicate complexion when she was young, giving rise to fears that she might contract the dreaded tuberculosis.

So in 1910 she set sail for South Africa, where two of her brothers had served in the Boer War. A third brother was engineer on board a converted cattle boat which was bought by Winston Churchill's mother to serve as a hospital ship in that same war.

With the onset of the First World War, and the men departing for battle, the young Miss Anderson from Scotland became a valued bank employee in Johannesburg, benefiting from a thorough grounding in the Three Rs and striking an early blow for her sex in a male-dominated profession.

She would be wined and dined in the fashionable Central Hotel, in a lifestyle which would have been maintained but for the calls from home. Back in Scotland at the end of the First World War, she gravitated to Glasgow in 1920 and found a job as book-keeper to the company which owned the famous Lauder's Bar at the corner of Sauchiehall Street and Renfield Street.

It was a new departure for the young lady from Fraserburgh but soon they found that her accounting capabilities were augmented by a particularly sensitive nose for the contents of a cask. In time they made her a director of the company.

Those were the days of people like Sammy Dow, who not only ran public houses but were exporters as well. During the Prohibition years of America in the 1920s, Miss Anderson found herself diverting North American supplies of the firm's whisky to Holland.

From there it was shipped to Canada and then (whisper it) across the border to the bootlegging speakeasies of a dry-throated United States. In time, Miss Anderson was sailing the Atlantic on the *Mauretania* to pursue her whisky business in a land which had, by then, returned to legal drinking.

Wherever she went, the little lady from Scotland would leave an impression. Nowadays she lives with these memories in the tenement flat into which she moved 54 years ago.

There we sat, raking over pages of history to which this wiry soul is a living witness. She turned out George Dey's delightful picture books of Old Fraserburgh and identified the people in street scenes of last century!

She even joined me in a wee refreshment, to use that quaint Glasgow phrase, and waved her beautifully expressive hands to emphasise a point. As she coasts towards a century of living, she claims that she would rather fade away quietly before that landmark arrives, despite the fact that she is so well blessed with faculties. I have a feeling nature may have other plans.

So I left this charming lady, with a promise to return; left her to the anonymity of her existence, where many a neighbour may have passed her by without an inkling of the story she has to tell.

To them, Miss Anderson has been no more than the little woman who always went to the bin with her hat on!

GOD BLESS IRVING BERLIN!

WHILE staying in New York in the 1960s, I tried repeatedly to fulfil one of my life's ambitions—to meet Irving Berlin, the greatest songwriter who ever lived. But luck deserted me.

He was either out of town or I had just missed him and his devoted secretary, Hilda Schneider, held out little hope of an interview. But she took my phone number and promised to let him know.

On the day I was packing my bags to catch the plane back to Britain, the phone rang in my Manhattan hotel room.

"Hello, Mr Webster? This is Irving Berlin. I'm back in town. D'you wanna come and see me?"

"Oh, Mr Berlin, my plane leaves in two hours. I'm just going to the airport," was my anguished cry.

Meanwhile, I stuck the tape-recorder to the telephone and picked up the husky voice of the man who had written some of the finest popular music of the century, without ever having learned to read it.

As a poor substitute, we conducted a high-speed telephone interview and he ended by inviting me to Claridges next time he was in London.

I still kick myself for not cancelling that plane trip out of New York and taking up the invitation because, for one reason or another, that Claridges meeting never did take place.

Personal regrets apart, let us rejoice that the inimitable Berlin has lived on to this day and, when he wakens up tomorrow morning, he will be celebrating one hundred years on earth.

For more than 80 years the melodies have tumbled like cascading waterfalls from his fertile imagination, yet usually so simple that we wonder why we couldn't have composed them ourselves.

From "Alexander's Ragtime Band" in 1910, he went through to

tunes like "Blue Skies", which Jolson sang in that very first talkie, *The Jazz Singer*, on to "Top Hat" for Fred Astaire and Ginger Rogers in 1935, and then to the postwar period of stage classics like *Annie Get Your Gun*.

The list of tunes which make our feet tap seems endless: "A Pretty Girl is Like a Melody", "How Deep is the Ocean?", "Always", "White Christmas", "They Say that Falling in Love is Wonderful", "You Can't Get a Man with a Gun" and, of course, "Easter Parade" and the national anthem of show business itself, "There's No Business Like . . ."

More seriously, he wrote what most Americans feel in their hearts to be their national anthem, "God Bless America." He told me that that pleases him most of all. For Irving Berlin has never stopped trying to repay the United States for the life and hope it provided for himself and his family and millions like them.

He was born in Russia on May 11, 1888, and was taken as a child through the filter of Ellis Island to the squalor of New York's East Side. His name was Israel Baline. Leaving school at eight, when his father died, he worked as a news-vendor and then as a singing waiter.

A rival café was drawing custom when its pianist wrote his own songs. Baline tried the same and turned out "Marie from Sunny Italy", which was good enough to be published. But the printer mistakenly called him "I. Berlin." He liked the mistake and kept the name

It was the beginning of a remarkable career. During the First World War, he was asked to put on a show on Broadway. It was packed out for weeks then, on the final night, there was a most extraordinary scene.

As the huge cast sang the closing song, "We're on Our Way to France", Irving Berlin led them off stage, down into the auditorium, up the centre aisle and out to the street. It took some time for a dumbfounded audience to realise that these boys really were on their way to France. Their transport was waiting by New York's waterfront.

After his first wife died tragically young, he came for his second honeymoon to Britain, was mobbed everywhere, and finally caught a train to Glasgow and sailed secretly for Quebec on the CP steamer *Montnairn*.

Irving Berlin is the last survivor of that incomparable crop of American composers who all knew each other and included Jerome Kern, George Gershwin, Cole Porter and Richard Rodgers.

It was Kern, such a supreme master of melody himself, who once said: "Irving Berlin has no place in American music. He IS American music."

But as well as being a songwriting genius, he has also been a most astute businessman, keeping tabs on his copyrights.

Bing Crosby once told me the story of making a Berlin musical in Hollywood. They realised there would have to be a single note inserted to effect a key-change but it wasn't as simple as it seemed. The director had to call in Berlin's lawyer for a deep discussion under furrowed brows.

Then a phone call was put through to Berlin in New York for permission to insert that note. After a long pause there came the reply: "Yeah. Yeah, I suppose that will be all right. But remember—it's MA note!"

"MA notes" have been dancing from keyboards throughout this century to lighten hearts in the darkest corners of the globe.

From Manhattan last night, Hilda Schneider was telling me that Mr Berlin is in pretty good shape and still draws a tune from those famous black notes (he has never had much time for the white ones).

They are holding a centenary birthday concert in the Carnegie Hall and once again a whole nation will be rising at the first rousing chords of "God Bless America."

I suspect that, come tomorrow night, the same nation will want to parody the song and say of that 5ft 4in giant of 20th century melody: "God Bless Irving Berlin too!"

SO WAS IT THE REAL HESS WHO
CAME TO SCOTLAND?

AN ATTEMPT to penetrate the fortress of Spandau Jail in Berlin and perhaps catch a glimpse of Hitler's deputy, Rudolf Hess, turned out to be one of my less successful journalistic exercises.

Despite the help of friends in high position, I found it easier to cross Checkpoint Charlie and cause some diversionary havoc to the annual VE-Day parade being staged by the Russians. The date was 8th May 1969.

Yet I am assured by Hugh Thomas that Spandau was not so impenetrable as I had imagined. Indeed, he believes it was just such an intruder who found his way inside last August—and brutally murdered the man called Hess.

Officially, the prisoner hanged himself. Officially, his name was Rudolf Hess. According to Hugh Thomas, both such notions are bunkum. The pilot who landed in a field at Eaglesham, on the outskirts of Glasgow, on a May night of 1941 was Hess's double and, for various political reasons, the pretence was maintained to his very last gasp.

Of course, the initial reaction is to tell Hugh Thomas to pull the other one. How could such a deception have been maintained through all those 47 years, from the moment he was arrested by farmer David McLean and taken to a Home Guard hut at Busby, right through the Nuremberg Trials and on to those lonesome years in Spandau?

It seems a thoroughly preposterous story. Yet, in the pursuit of truth—and in fairness to Thomas—we do need to take a second look at the facts. For a start, Hugh Thomas is no fly-by-night scribe in search of a sensational story. He happens to be a distinguished

83

surgeon who was a consultant at the British Military Hospital in Berlin to which the Spandau prisoner was admitted.

His examination of the man produced one astounding fact which sparked off his further investigation. The real Hess had been seriously wounded in the First World War, shot from a range of 30 yards with the bullet going through his lung from chest to shoulder blade, a wound which would never disappear completely.

The prisoner in Spandau had no trace of such wound—and there are X-rays to prove it. Working backwards from that startling piece of evidence, Thomas then satisfied himself that the plane in which the real Hess was supposed to have taken off from Germany was not the one which finally crash-landed at Eaglesham.

According to him, it all seems to have been part of a complicated plot by Himmler to get rid of Hitler's deputy, by shooting down the plane of the real Hess, sending on his double to negotiate some kind of peace with Britain—a settlement which would have been reached with Himmler, who would by then have disposed of Hitler! Ingenious stuff.

Certainly, the British Government turned down all offers of definite identification from people who had known the real Hess before the war. But why didn't the man himself confess the deception towards the end of the war to escape responsibility for Hess's crimes?

When I met Hugh Thomas in Glasgow the other day, he claimed to have more recent evidence that the man tried to do just that. Indeed, a gent called Colonel Pilcher of the Grenadier Guards, who tried to pass on the prisoner's confession to the highest authority, was allegedly put under house arrest in a Scottish castle and never seems to have been heard of again.

Can this be true? Is there anyone out there who can throw further light on this? As a surgeon-cum-sleuth who knows not a little of the workings of the SAS, Hugh Thomas is full of nods and winks about what can happen when few of us would really believe it.

Of course the ruse of planting doubles is by no means a fantasy. It was common practice during the war. The actor Clifton James was a perfect replica for Field-Marshal Montgomery, in voice and appearance.

Hugh Thomas believes that, committed to maintaining the deception, the man we regarded as Rudolf Hess tried to create as long a gap as possible before agreeing to see Frau Hess. When she was finally admitted to Spandau, the first thing she remarked upon was the depth of his voice, whereas it is a medical fact that the human voice invariably rises in pitch as we grow older.

Nevertheless she did believe, whether or not it was a matter of conditioning, that the man in Spandau was her husband, drastically changed though he undoubtedly seemed.

Thomas wrote a book about all this in 1979 but, when we met last week, he was just back from Munich, where he met the real Hess's son, who now firmly supports Thomas's theory that the man in Spandau, whoever he was, was murdered.

Thomas believes the Foreign Office know a lot more than they are saying. In fact he is highly suspicious of Britain's role in all this, though he doubts if Mrs Thatcher knows anything about it.

However ridiculous the story may seem in parts, the total absence of a wound is certainly a baffling piece of evidence. The surgeon is in no doubt at all that we are dealing with two different men.

So who killed the prisoner in Spandau last year? An ex-SAS man perhaps? I understand there are rumblings of activity in the Berlin prosecutor's office and I have a feeling we may not have heard the last of this story.

Meanwhile, as Hugh Thomas returns to his scalpel at the Prince Charles Hospital in South Wales, his updated book will do more than raise a few eyebrows.

PIPER ALPHA—THE PRICE WE PAY
FOR A MIRACLE

THEY will gather at the great kirk of St Nicholas in Aberdeen tomorrow to remember the 166 men who perished in the blazing horror of Piper Alpha.

For the Granite City and its immediate hinterland have borne the brunt of the biggest disaster in the entire history of mankind's attempts to coax oil and gas from the bowels of our spinning globe.

All over that Grampian corner there is hardly a living soul who doesn't know of somebody involved in the tragedy. The local joiner and undertaker at New Deer, Sandy Ritchie (himself no stranger to personal tragedy), abandoned his holiday last week to bury 24-year-old Michael Walker, the son of his close friend in the village. Everyone has a story to tell.

It was ever thus in the clustered communities which live by the sea and, all too often, have learned to die by the sea. More often their loss has come in the pursuit of that silver harvest which serves our table, the friendly waters which lap the doorstep of a summer evening turning suddenly to a raging cauldron of grief.

But now, with the coming of oil, their prayers for those in peril on the sea have found a new dimension. And, if there can be any consolation at all in a tragedy of this magnitude, it can be only in a greater public awareness of what is involved in the unimaginable task of finding oil in the depths of the great North Sea and bringing it ashore.

One day, much later perhaps, we may be able to measure the loss of so many human lives against the technological miracle which they were performing on our behalf.

I remember a day, just 13 years ago, when I stood by the beach at Cruden Bay, between Aberdeen and Peterhead, and marvelled at the fact that a pipe which came rising out of the sea like a dinosaur, then buried its head just as quickly beneath the farmers' fields, was carrying ashore the very first oil from the North Sea.

Here on this same beach, one of Scotland's finest, I had built sand-castles as a child and contemplated nothing more mysterious than the fact that a man called Bram Stoker used to stroll along this same stretch of sand when he was dreaming up his famous stories of Dracula. With the advance royalties, he had bought a house nearby.

Now it was oil, not blood, which was being sucked from this neck of the ocean and, as I hastened towards Aberdeen, it was with a keen sense of historical significance. A new industrial age was upon us.

At a carnival ceremony at Dyce, in the presence of Premier Harold Wilson and all her Ministers, the Queen pressed the button which symbolised the dawn.

Just a few years earlier, it had all seemed like an idle pipe-dream. Until that is, a man came knocking on the door of Aberdeen's Lord Provost of the day, John Smith (now Lord Kirkhill), and said he was from Shell and that they had opened a little office in an old city tram depot.

British Petroleum had crept in as well. It was not that they wanted the world to know—these companies play their cards close to the chest—but civic courtesies had to be observed.

I had ventured up by Cromarty towards Nigg and watched as they dug the world's largest hole in the ground, for the building of the first oil platform. Now they proliferate freely around the vast acres of the North Sea.

What we cannot actually observe, most of us find hard to visualise. But, in seeking oil from beneath the seabed, engineers have to drill towards hell to a depth which, if they were going upwards instead of downwards, would reach to the peak of Mont Blanc in the Alps.

Nor does the oil simply lie in pools awaiting the suction pumps. It secretes itself in sponge-like material from which it has to be extracted. Once that miracle has been achieved, it is then drawn to the surface of the oil platform and redirected by pipeline towards Cruden Bay, if it is oil, and to nearby St Fergus if it is gas.

Human beings have built great bridges and dug mighty tunnels but I doubt if any other feat of engineering begins to compare with the production of oil from the inhospitable depths of a stormy ocean.

The bigger the stake, the bigger the risk; alas, it is the familiar story which comes to torment us wherever the human race will take its gamble with nature.

In a thousand years of its history, Aberdeen has been enjoying, from the mid-1970s to the mid-1980s, its all-time peak of economic prosperity. As the oil capital of Europe, it has become a cosmopolitan city, accepting the good with the bad, the main beneficiary of 50,000 well-paid jobs and a popular centre with that international set of roughnecks and roustabouts whose quest for liquid gold is more often pursued in bleak and lonely corners of the earth.

The face of Aberdeen has smiled with the good times. Now, in the hour of tragedy, its granite façade is etched with grief. And tomorrow, as the great bells of St Nicholas peal out in celebration of human courage, the echoes will reverberate across a watery wilderness to a distant graveyard where, deep and silent now, so many lie asleep.

LUCKIEST DAY OF THE CENTURY

AT the risk of sounding like the Rev. I. M. Jolly, I am tempted nevertheless to ask the question: What sort of a day did you have yesterday? Or did you bother to ponder upon the coincidental nature of the date?

For your enlightenment, it was the 8th day of the 8th month of the 88th year, the sort of digital happening which comes round every 11 years or so. But, according to fung shui, the Chinese science of wind and water, yesterday's date is the one above them all which matters. In fact, I'm told they rate it the luckiest day of this century.

A friend of mine in Hong Kong, not unacquainted with Chinese culture, has been waiting for a major operation. Imagine the confidence with which he entered hospital at the weekend, having learned that his encounter with the surgeon's knife was due to start at 8am on 8/8/88. There could have been no better omen.

When the arithmetical sequence first struck this century, on New Year's Day of 1911 (1/1/11), the Glasgow store of Pettigrew and Stephens was also talking of good omens

Advertising its seasonal greetings in the *Glasgow Herald*, it said: "The signs of the times are pointing to a period of great and unexampled prosperity, with industrial and political peace reigning over the land, with the world expanding in every direction and means of intercommunication constantly growing." (Mind you, the First World War wasn't too far off.)

That same *Herald* recorded Glaswegians sobering up from another Hogmanay, "despite the growth of the observance of Christmas," which most of us would guess to have come at a much later date. A six-bedroomed house in Carlton Terrace, Kelvinside, was for sale at £800; the Anchor Line was advertising its Glasgow-New York sailings "with the Marconi system of wireless telegraphy installed." And, as if to prove the sanity of the age, Third Lanark were top of Scottish football's First Division.

By 2/2/22, they were flaunting the fact, on the front page of the *Herald*, that you could have your hair tinted at Giralt of 13 Newton Terrace, Glasgow. The Scottish Motor Show at the Kelvin Hall was offering a two-seater Bean car (with Dickey) for £385—and Sir Arthur Conan Doyle was due to lecture at the St Andrew's Halls on "Proof of Survival" and "Recent Psychic Revelations."

Sadly, the cruelty of inhuman beings doesn't seem to change. A man was appearing in court in Glasgow, charged with the attempted murder of a five-year-old boy, having grabbed hold of him on Stockwell Bridge and thrown him over the parapet into the Clyde. The wee lad put up a plucky fight to save his life.

On 3/3/33, the German people were on the eve of an election, with Hitler aiming to strengthen his hold on the country. There were reports that the Nazi Press had pilloried Einstein, Thomas Mann, and Remarque (author of *All Quiet on the Western Front*).

But a Glasgow coal exporter was telling the *Herald* of a conversation he had had with a German industrialist, who assured him that the Hitler regime was the best and most honest government they had had in years.

In lighter vein, Jack Payne and his Orchestra were entertaining at the Glasgow Empire—and this newspaper was reporting, in all solemnity, that the winding up of Bo'ness Football Club was "a regrettable and ominous phenomenon."

By 4/4/44, we were reaching vital moments in the Second World War. On this day, Anthony Eden gave up being Foreign Secretary to lead the House of Commons and enable Churchill to devote himself more completely to the war effort. (D-Day was just weeks away.)

By then, the Empire had lost 158,000 in battle, while 49,000 British civilians had also been killed.

Professor Sir John Fraser became Principal of Edinburgh University and, in that same issue, the *Herald* was showing the way with a feature article entitled: Feminism as Discussed in the Services.

On 5/5/55, Andrew Hood became Lord Provost of Glasgow, Karl

Rankl was conducting the Scottish National Orchestra at the St Andrew's Halls—and in court, Hughie Green was alleging a conspiracy to deprive him of a renewed contract for his popular show, *Opportunity Knocks*. His QC was Lord Hailsham. The *Herald* was still sporting advertisements on its front page.

On 6/6/66, there were, significantly, reports of finding gas reserves in the North Sea. Of more immediate interest, the US Air Force was reported to be planning a withdrawal from Prestwick Airport.

But the human story of the day belonged to 10-year-old Kenneth McDonald of Kelvinhaugh Street, Glasgow. Playing hide-and-seek, he was reported to have climbed into the back of a parked lorry where, for some unaccountable reason, he fell asleep.

By the time the driver opened up the back flap of his vehicle, little Kenneth was already in Nottinghamshire, 270 miles away! I'm left wondering if he was just after a joyride. At the age of 32, he should be around to tell us.

On 7/7/77, peace talks on Rhodesia were faltering and Britain was airlifting extra troops into Belize. There was cynicism in the East End of Glasgow about the £120 million plan to revitalise the area; and a former head of Scotland Yard's Flying Squad, Kenneth Drury, was jailed for corruption.

And thus to 8/8/88. Among the quirky happenings of yesterday, when the clock struck noon, the *Financial Times'* Stock Exchange index was UP—by 8.8 points!

On that rather special day of the century, I do hope the luck of the Chinese was with you.

And, of course, the Duchess of York gave birth to her daughter— at 8.18 on 8/8/88.

BAIRD AND WALLIS—
THE STRUGGLES OF GENIUS

AMONG the ploys of childhood, one of the more intriguing was the discovery that you could bore a hole in the bottom of two cocoa tins, connect them with the knotted ends of a long, taut piece of string—and play at primitive telephones by speaking and listening at the open end of the tins.

It all came back the other day as I watched the preview of tomorrow's television documentary on John Logie Baird, the Helensburgh boy who invented television.

At a similar age, it turns out, Baird was intrigued by the self-same game, except that for him it was a starting-point of development for the sheer inventive genius of the man.

He proceeded to advance the cocoa-tin theory to create a most realistic telephone service between the homes of his school friends, closest of whom was another Helensburgh boy destined for fame, that debonair legend of the theatre, Jack Buchanan.

By the time he was 12, in 1900, John Logie Baird had lit his parents' home with electricity and, within a short time, he was working on the possibility of "seeing by wireless", which was an early way of describing television.

I'll leave you to view the programme for yourselves, a compelling tale of unrecognised genius which proves that, if we Scots don't press the self-destruct button on ourselves, there is liable to be another Scot prepared to do it for us. (Baird's college classmate in Glasgow, John Reith, became the first boss of the BBC—two ministers' sons who detested each other—and the man who not only scorned Baird's invention but eventually adopted someone else's method for the BBC.)

Apart from cocoa tins and telephones, the Baird programme kept reminding me of another inventive genius it was once my pleasure to meet.

Just as Baird had raged at those who refused to implement his theories, popular legend had it that Barnes Wallis was a similarly frustrated being. Ages with the talented Scot, Barnes Wallis had invented the world's most beautiful airship, the *R80*, and the most successful, the *R100*. (It was someone else's *R101* which crashed and put airships out of fashion.)

He helped win the war by giving us both the Wellington and Wellesly bombers, the Tallboy and Grand Slam bombs and, of course, the famous bouncing bomb which produced the legendary Dambuster raids and knocked the heart out of the German war effort.

When he entered the supersonic age and invented the swing-wing aeroplane, it took the Americans to exploit his discovery, an ironic twist which Baird would have appreciated, considering the Americans thwarted his television discovery as part of their patriotic syndrome or NIH (Not Invented Here).

With all these thoughts in mind, I once drove up a leafy English lane and turned into White Hill House, at Effingham. There to greet me was the gentle figure of Barnes Wallis himself, white-haired and courteous.

We repaired to his attic den, where the inventing still continued, the walls festooned with a photographic testimony to this modest man's genius—the *R80* and *R100*, pictures of the Dambusters and the heroic Guy Gibson.

On his drawing board was an invention he was sorry he couldn't tell me about, though it seemed destined for the distant future. After his death I learned it was to do with an aeroplane which would fly out of the atmosphere like a rocket and bend itself to an appropriate angle for re-entry, so that passengers would reach Australia from London in about 90 minutes!

Like an absent-minded professor he pottered about the room, knocking down a tin of paint, apologising for this or that. His wife was away from home and he was feeling a little lost. We discussed our mutual migraine and the deteriorating standard of handwriting.

Then he came up with a model of his 10-ton bomb, proudly

reminding me that it had blasted the launching sites of the dreaded V1 and V2 rockets which bedevilled us during the war.

Finally I asked about the bureaucracy which was said to have thwarted his genius so often. He composed himself and said: "No, I'm not bitter at all. You see, there is a tendency in people to resist any kind of innovation. They don't like being pushed out of their conventional channel of life.

"The inventor is in a worse position because people cannot really gauge the effect of what he is on about. Besides, it is likely to be expensive. So there is opposition—but that's a good thing. It makes you go on to perfect your original idea and, if it is really worthwhile, the chap who opposes you has to give in at the end of the day."

Barnes Wallis was reckoning without the power of Lord Reith, that arch-enemy of John Logie Baird, who did not give in, even at the end of the day.

As I say, when I hear the Baird story, I cannot but be reminded of Barnes Wallis. The latter was at least honoured with a knighthood, though not until he was into his eighties. John Logie Baird died at 57, ironically just six days after Reith's BBC resumed its television service after the war.

Through all the frustrations, however, his son Malcolm, a professor in Canada, assures me that his father left him with no memory of bitterness. He simply funnelled his pent-up rage into a belated autobiography.

In this week of his 100th birthday the world is going some way towards repairing the damage. His widow, Margaret, is still here to appreciate it. So are his son and daughter.

What a pity we allowed the great man himself to go to his grave without the recognition he so richly deserved.

QUEEN ELIZABETH—
FROM CRADLE TO GRAVE

I SAILED down the Clyde the other morning under a bright November sun which merely helped to illuminate the derelict nature of those once-great riverbanks. No clatter of steel or sparks of industry, just the gloom of graffiti in a wilderness of silence. Yet the heart beat faster when we came in sight of the old John Brown shipyard at Clydebank, for it was here they built the greatest liners that ever sailed the seas.

I had made this same journey 50 years ago, in the final weeks of construction for the mighty *Queen Elizabeth*, when boatloads of visitors to the Empire Exhibition were ferried to Clydebank for a preview of the Cunarder which would take her place alongside the *Queen Mary*.

As a little boy, I gazed in wonder from beneath the hull, which rose with all the grace and beauty of a slender yacht.

Half a century later I had come to John Brown's for another launch; not a ship this time but a book about a ship—the *Queen Elizabeth* no less—written by Russell Galbraith of Scottish Television, who was pushing out the literary boat with a fine old splash of mellow blend.

He has called it *Destiny's Daughter* but gets to the heart of the matter with his sub-title, which is *The Tragedy of RMS Queen Elizabeth*.

For this great lady of the ocean was dogged by misfortune from the start, taking shape in the very months when Neville Chamberlain was being misled in Munich.

That war was upon us before she first caught sight of the open sea and, even then, she had been stripped of her regal finery as painters supplied an overcoat of grey so that she could sneak away in safety. Such were the requirements of security that even the men who arrived to sail her thought they were going to Southampton.

In fact they were heading for New York, from which she would embark on a wartime career as a troop carrier, taking up to 15,000 men at a time. When that war was over, the *Elizabeth* joined the *Mary* in those regular Atlantic crossings. But the glory was short-lived as the jet-plane overtook the maritime maidens in those post-war years.

Before that era passed away in the sixties, I sailed to New York in the *Queen Mary* and sampled the luxury which had so enchanted peers and princes, film stars and business moguls. This was a ship of the 'thirties, they said, all palm court and afternoon tea, gin-bars and foxtrots. It was all that—and it was wonderful!

Among the memories which will linger for ever is that hazy Sunday in mid-Atlantic when, out across the parish of wild water, the church bells summoned a congregation which gave thanks for those floating dowagers, for whom another bell was tolling.

A few weeks later, the two *Queens* passed each other in mid-Atlantic for the last time. Says Russell Galbraith: "The distance between them closing rapidly, heaven and sea their only witness, lights blazing defiantly, the sudden blast of their basso-profundo horns silences the wind.

"As Captain John Treasure Jones, aboard the *Queen Mary*, and Commodore Geoffrey Thrippleton Marr, on the *Queen Elizabeth*, doffed caps, both men knew they were saluting not just one another, and the two great ships under their command, but the end of an era in maritime history."

The *Queen Mary* was sold to the city of Long Beach, California, where she rests today as the glorious centrepiece of a conference and tourist complex. No such luck attended the *Queen Elizabeth*.

She seemed destined for Port Everglades in Florida but, amid local wrangles about her future, she was bought by a big ship-owner in Hong Kong, with ambitions to convert her to a sea-going university.

She reached Hong Kong all right but, on a ghastly day of 1972, was seen to be burning in no fewer than nine different places at one time. Sabotage? We'll never know the truth.

All I know is that, having seen the *Queen Elizabeth* at John Brown's yard in 1938, I followed her from the cradle to the grave and hired a little boat to take me out into Hong Kong Bay on a pilgrimage of farewell.

I was remembering some of the statistics. Cunard used to tell people that, if you stood the great ship on her end, she would measure 50 feet taller than the Eiffel Tower and nearly three times the height of St Paul's Cathedral. But when would we ever see her in such ludicrous postures?

Well, as I sailed around that wreckage in Hong Kong Bay, the position could not have been more ludicrous, or heartbreaking. There she lay on her side, as if hoisting herself on one elbow to utter a word of farewell from the deathbed.

I hastened back to Hong Kong and spoke to people who had wept as the great lady burned. They didn't have to tell me why.

A WEIRD EXPERIENCE AT THE
BRIDGE ON THE RIVER KWAI

PARDON my cynicism over the kind words being expressed about the Emperor Hirohito of Japan. How short can our memories be?

His reputation was in my mind as I drove westward from Bangkok the other week and came upon the Bridge on the River Kwai, made even more notorious by the Oscar-winning film.

And there the whole ghastly story came alive once more—of countless thousands of prisoners-of-war driven by the brutality of Hirohito's Japan to build a railway from Siam into Burma to further the enemy cause of reaching India.

In the tropical heat men of the Gordon Highlanders and the Argylls were among those who dropped dead where they worked, from disease, starvation or sheer exhaustion; at worst from the torture of their Japanese guards.

Some of the worst victims were taken back to the Death House at Chungkai, two miles from that Bridge on the River Kwai, where man's inhumanity to man went on the rampage and left us one of history's blackest episodes.

From a little tail-boat, I scrambled ashore and wandered through that former camp at Chungkai, now a beautiful cemetery, where the scent of camellias and wild orchid has long since won the battle with the stench of death.

Out of the shadows came a small, dark Thai who announced himself as Mister Lung. He had been a schoolboy here during the war, a close witness to the atrocities, and was later appointed a gardener at Chungkai. He was pleased and honoured to look after the graves. If this searing heat was an example of winter, what must it have been like on that Railroad of Death at the height of summer?

Across the River Kwai, in another cemetery with 6500 graves, I moved from one row of bronze plaques to the next, vaguely wondering if there was anyone from my own corner of Aberdeenshire.

For sure, there were Gordons but no addresses. I was moving towards the exit when, suddenly, I found one plaque with an address: Private R. W. Willox of the Gordon Highlanders: Died 7th June 1943, aged 25: Remembered by his father, mother and family at Sandford Lodge, Peterhead.

Sandford Lodge? That was a farm, not far from my own childhood home. How well I remembered the Gordons marching off to war that day of 1939. R. W. Willox? He would now have been 70. Would there still be relatives to whom I could bring back pictures of the grave?

For the moment, I found myself rooted to the graveside. Here was a Buchan loon, like myself, an innocent victim so far from the rolling fields of that native countryside we had both known and loved.

Perhaps not too many people from our Aberdeenshire corner had ever passed up this jungle route so I felt compelled to stay and keep him company in this place of peace at Kanchanaburi on the other side of the world. I took pictures and gave him a quiet word of farewell and knew that, whoever he was, there was one little corner of Thailand that would be forever Buchan.

Back home for Christmas, I wondered who might have known Pte. R. W. Willox. Then I remembered my old friend, Johnny Reid, a farm worker who, in later life, has become well-known for his writings about the rural scene under the pen-name of David Toulmin.

His wife Margaret answered the phone and handed me over to her husband, to whom I explained the story. There was a pause at the other end. Then Johnny spoke: "That'll be Rob Willox ye're speakin' aboot. Ay man, I kent him fine. In fact, he was my wife's brother!"

So Margaret came back on the phone and told me all about Rob, who worked at the farm of Pettymarcus of Clola. He was one of 10 children of James and Margaret Willox, a thoughtful lad who never forgot a kindness to his mother when he came home at weekends to Sandford Lodge, where his father was grieve.

Away he had gone that September day to train with the Gordon Highlanders at the Bridge of Don Barracks in Aberdeen.

He came home on his last visit at the back of hairst in 1940, before being posted abroad and landing in Singapore with the 2nd Gordons. The rest of the story is history. Singapore fell to the Japs in 1942 and our men were moved north to that infamous railway.

There had been a Christmas card and then a long silence before the Red Cross announced that Rob had died of the dreaded beriberi. Buchan folk mourn quietly but his mother broke her heart and died in the prime of life. Eight brothers and sisters are still alive.

Life has dealt me many coincidence but none that touched more deeply than that quiet grave in a faraway jungle—the last resting place of Rob Willox from Peterhead, whose death warrant bears the bloodied name of a man called Hirohito.

HOW THE FAMOUS MET THEIR DEATHS

MY FAVOURITE author, Lewis Grassic Gibbon, never tired of pointing out that nothing abides in this life, that nothing is true but change. In that frame of mind, he might also have added that the only certainty about life is death.

But this is not necessarily a cue for morbidity. It was merely the starting-point for a friend of mine in America who set out to investigate how the famous people of this earth met their demise.

His researches have turned up some fascinating facts. Did you know, for example, that Attila the Hun, a pretty despicable fellow who deserved whatever was coming to him, died on his wedding night—from a burst blood-vessel in his nose? It was said to be due to over-exertion!

The end of Aeschylus, the Athenian poet and dramatist, was no less peculiar. Apparently an eagle mistook his shiny, bald head for a rock and dropped a tortoise to crack the shell. Legend has it that the tortoise shell remained intact. Poor old thingummy was dead.

There was the even more bizarre case of the Bunker Siamese twins, Chang and Eng, who died in 1874. Nowadays they can separate Siamese twins but that unfortunate pair remained side by side for all of 63 years, still managing to sire 21 children between them (between them and others, I mean).

One night, Chang became ill and died while Eng slept. When Eng wakened up and realised his twin had died, he suffered a seizure and died an hour later. Come to think of it, I don't suppose he had much choice.

Aeroplane accidents claimed famous entertainers like Carole Lombard, Buddy Holly and Will Rogers, and car crashes took away James Dean and Princess Grace of Monaco.

Suicides included George Eastman (of Eastman Kodak) and

that great director of musical spectaculars, Busby Berkeley, while the modern craze for drugs has lost us popular singers like Billie Holliday, Janis Joplin, Elvis Presley, Sid Vicious, and Jimi Hendrix.

For me, one of the saddest losses of all was Karen Carpenter, that gorgeous lady whose singing tones said much about the inner beauty of the being. That was all to do with the slimming obsession which makes people anorexic.

Drink cost us Montgomery Clift, William Faulkner, W. C. Fields, Stephen Foster, Edgar Allen Poe and Dylan Thomas while the executioner brought final severance terms to Cicero, the orator of the Roman Forum, Mata Hari, the female spy of the First World War, and Sir Walter Raleigh, who may have given us tobacco and potatoes but had his head taken away in return.

Raleigh's wife, incidentally, kept his embalmed head in her red leather shopping-bag for the last 29 years of her life!

Assassinations have ranged from the Archduke Ferdinand whose shooting in Sarajevo sparked off the First World War, to the four American Presidents Abraham Lincoln, James Garfield, William McKinley, and John F. Kennedy.

As a newspaperman, I blush a little when recalling the insensitivity of one American scribe who interviewed Mrs Lincoln after her beloved Abe had been shot by an actor, during a performance at Ford's Theatre in Washington.

"Tell me Mrs Lincoln," said the journalist, "apart from that, what did you think of the show?"

In our own time, another man with thoughts of becoming President of the United States, Nelson D. Rockefeller, would probably rather have been assassinated than remembered for his own particular end. He was said to have been deeply engaged with a mistress at the moment of his going.

All of this, I suppose, reminds us that we should appreciate people when they are alive. How often do we suddenly find ourselves extolling the virtues of those to whom we haven't given a thought in years, just because they have died?

Can't you imagine what they will write in the obituaries of people like, say, Frank Sinatra and Ella Fitzgerald, no doubt to be claimed as the two greatest popular entertainers of all time? Well, they are still with us.

Just last year, an unconfirmed but convincing report reached this newspaper one day, to the effect that a recent legend of Scottish sport had been killed in a car crash. Suddenly, we were all elevating him to the peak of sporting glory and ready to say so in glowing tributes.

The news agencies were slow to confirm the event, however, and finally an intrepid reporter had the task of phoning the legend's wife to inquire, tactfully, if her husband had in fact been involved in an accident.

"No, no," she replied. "He's out in the back garden shovelling manure. Just wait till I get him."

Of course there was no need. We could all settle back to thinking of him as little as we had been doing for years. So isn't there a moral here somewhere?

OSCAR SLATER—
THE MYSTERY DEEPENS

NO case in Scottish criminal history has been more widely argued than that of Oscar Slater, a German-Jew who served 19 years for the murder of a well-heeled Glasgow spinster, Marion Gilchrist.

As every historian now knows, whatever kind of character Slater really was (gambler, pimp etc.), he had nothing to do with the murder of Miss Gilchrist.

However, this morning I bring you a new twist to the story, involving a famous Glasgow name, which will surely bring fresh impetus to the controversy.

But first to the facts. Slater was a wanderer who ran clubs in America but came to live in St George's Road, Glasgow, in 1908, with his French prostitute girlfriend. Miss Gilchrist lived round the corner, in West Princes Street. Just before Christmas, her maid, Nellie Lambie from Holytown, popped out for an evening paper and, when she returned, a neighbour was ready to accompany her into the flat, having heard alarming thuds.

As Nellie entered with the neighbour a man rushed past them from inside. Miss Gilchrist lay brutally murdered in her sitting-room. Whodunit? All Scotland was agog.

Suspicion settled on Oscar Slater, on the false evidence of a missing brooch which was pawned. A few days later, he sailed for America, which looked like a flight from justice, though he volunteered to return without extradition, to prove his innocence.

His dubious background was scandalously revealed during the case and even given weight by the judge in his address to the jury.

By a slender majority, Slater was found guilty and sentenced to death. The *Glasgow Herald* expressed immediate disquiet and, as doubts arose, the Scottish Secretary commuted the hanging to life imprisonment. Conan Doyle fought the case but Slater spent 19 years in Peterhead Prison before the appeal judges set aside the verdict and allowed him to go free.

Now Miss Gilchrist had been at loggerheads with her relatives and there were heated exchanges, thought to be over her will.

After the original trial, one courageous Glasgow detective, John Trench, was so convinced that his colleagues had framed Slater that he bypassed superiors, took the matter through a lawyer to the Scottish Secretary—and was sacked for his efforts.

What Trench had to say was that Nellie, the maid, kept referring to a man called AB, as if she knew him. AB was investigated but, mysteriously, his name disappeared off the police records. Why? And who was he? People have speculated for years, some concluding that AB was a relative of Miss Gilchrist, Dr Francis Charteris, son of a Glasgow professor who himself became a distinguished professor at St Andrews.

In a 1975 reprint of his book *Square Mile of Murder*, Jack House amended previous opinions to say there were two murderers. Dr Francis Charteris and a man called Austin Birrell. (Miss Gilchrist had relatives called Birrell.) Jack House said he had spoken to another relative who told him the family all knew it was "Uncle Austin" who did it.

Now for the new twist. A former Glasgow shop steward, Ted Ramsey from Springboig, began to study the case when made redundant several years ago. At his own expense, he is now publishing a book which gives a more plausible explanation of AB's identity—but proceeds to point the finger of suspicion at Nellie, the maid, and her boyfriend, Patrick Nugent.

Ted Ramsey may win no prizes for grammar or punctuation but all praise to him for his researches. Having studied the precognitions available after 75 years, he makes his own reconstruction.

When I told Jack House about it this weekend, he declared the accusation against Nellie to be "absolute nonsense", though he agreed that Slater himself pointed the finger in that direction. But then Jack made a very frank confession. He now tells me that, having been wrong in his original conclusions, he was quite wrong again about Austin Birrell—and that no such person ever existed. The man who told him about "Uncle Austin" had really said "Uncle Archie"—and that was Archie Charteris (brother of Francis), who became Professor of International Law at Sydney. So Jack House now believes the deed was done by two future professors, Francis and Archie Charteris.

Meanwhile, Ted Ramsey has more astonishing revelations. He has found an obvious person to fit the initials AB—Alexander Birrell, a nephew of Miss Gilchrist, who was investigated before vanishing from police records.

Ramsey has done some remarkable detective work to show the Birrells had changed their name from Burrell—and that Alexander was a cousin of Sir William Burrell of the Burrell Collection.

Worse still, Sir William had been an influential member of Glasgow Police Committee and is strongly suspected by Ramsey as the one responsible for the cover-up of the family name. Though Jack House still blames the Charteris brothers, Professor Francis Charteris died as recently as 1964 and, shortly before his death, gave what seems to me a fairly convincing explanation of how his name was drawn into the controversy.

My own conclusion? I may be no sleuth but I think Ted Ramsey's book, *Stranger in the Hall*, is worthy of some attention.

LADY WHO WROTE
"THE NORTHERN LIGHTS"

WITH "The Northern Lights of Old Aberdeen" rising quietly from an organ in the background, they bore away the remains of Mary Webb, the charming old lady who composed that popular song.

It was rather a pathetic finale to someone long forgotten and much neglected—just half a dozen people gathered at Oakley Wood Crematorium, near Leamington, to hear the vicar express a few sentiments about a name which would mean very little even in her own home area of Warwickshire.

Indeed, so tenuous were her family connections that she was taken to the mortuary of Charing Cross Hospital on Easter Monday and had to wait until the week's end, 24 days later, for a funeral.

In lingering with the past, we sometimes ignore the present; and Mary Webb stands as an example of such neglect. In years to come, she will be talked about, written about and elevated to some kind of legendary status as the English lady who wrote a popular Scottish classic, without having seen the city which was her subject.

For Mary had moved from her native Leamington to London where, through a short married life to Bill Webb and long after it, she remained the breadwinner, taking many a menial job to make ends meet.

It was while working in the kitchens of West London Hospital in 1951 that she met a girl from Aberdeen and invited her home to tea.

A former concert-party entertainer, Mary vowed she would write a song for her guest. She crossed to the piano, felt the melody swelling within her soul—and within a few minutes had fashioned a song that will last for ever.

107

As an Aberdonian, I'll be everlastingly grateful that I managed to meet her in those fading months. We spent a glorious evening together at her basic room-and-kitchen in a London back-street, ending up with the lady herself crossing to the piano upon which she had composed "The Northern Lights" and giving me a memorable performance of it.

No matter that a stroke had impaired her right hand; the fingers rippled with new-found ease as she gave a final flourish to the arpeggios and told me that her song, she believed, would live on long after she was dead.

Well, that day has sadly arrived and local historians will recall that she set eyes on Aberdeen only once in her life, well after she had written the song.

Incredibly, she gained the limelight only twice in all her days— at the Royal Albert Hall, London, in 1952, when Robert Wilson introduced her song and announced that the composer was in the audience, and again at the Tivoli Theatre in Aberdeen, where she was coaxed on stage to play her tune and take the plaudits of the people to whom it meant the most.

Thereafter, it was virtual oblivion, a baffling situation in an age of high profiles. Everyone seemed to think Mary Webb was bound to be dead. So, with the discovery of her actual death, there has been a sudden spurt of interest in her life.

When they heard that she had died lonely and penniless, the local authority in Aberdeen made an offer to take over the cost of the funeral and give her a suitable resting-place in the city. The few relatives decided, however, to go ahead with a cremation in her native town.

But I understand there is the possibility they will hand over the ashes, to be taken to Aberdeen.

One other point that niggled me since Mary died was the fate of her John Broadwood piano, on which she composed "The Northern Lights". It is a piece of musical history which deserves to be preserved.

I could envisage it disappearing into the anonymity of a London saleroom, never to be seen again. Time could be vital since she had been under pressure from her landlords to vacate her rented flat so they could sell it at the inflated prices of the south.

I took a gamble and made an offer for the contents of her little room, alerting the authorities in Aberdeen that I was doing so as a holding operation, until something could be worked out.

I did so together with John Mason of Troon, conductor of the Scottish Fiddle Orchestra, who was one of Mary's few visitors. We were given just two-and-a-half hours on Saturday morning to clear the room.

A lorry was dispatched from Scotland to secure the goods and bring them home for storage. There will now be an opportunity for the people of Aberdeen to lay out some kind of memorial to Mary Webb, perhaps a corner of an arts or music centre.

There the public will be able to see the lonely setting of Mary Webb's domestic life in London, complete with piano, and to hear again the echoes of an English lady who provided a Scots song that will never die—an anthem to Aberdonianism which leaps in many a heart and guarantees to stir the native blood.

SLAUGHTER AT KING'S BIRTHDAY PARTY

IT goes without saying that a day in the company of publisher Malcolm Forbes will call upon the last ounce of human energy.

As one approaching the limits of the allotted span, while still careering around the world by motorbike, balloon, or private Boeing—and keeping up with Elizabeth Taylor—he ranks as one of life's most persistent doers.

His motto of "While you're alive—*live*" sets the pace for a man who packs it all in as if tomorrow might be a non-starter.

It would have been enough for most people half his age to keep the Saturday date in Massachusetts, which was for the purpose of collecting his 59th honorary doctorate.

But he dashed back to New York in time for a viewing of the latest Batman film—before setting out on a day trip to Scotland! He was still fresh as the paint on Miss Taylor's face when I picked him up at Aberdeen airport at 7am for what would be a pretty hectic day.

By breakfast time we were wandering through the historic Pitsligo Castle at Rosehearty, near Fraserburgh, where he is spending a small fortune on stabilising and landscaping the ruins. The Scottish craftsmanship delighted him.

On we went to the magnificent Aden Country Park at Old Deer, where he marvelled at the efforts of Andrew Hill in recreating Scotland's agricultural past. By 11am we were joining in the worship at New Deer Parish Church, which his Scots father attended as a poor country boy a century ago—and witnessing a baptism at the font his father presented on his 70th birthday.

A pause by the family grave and on for lunch before being welcomed back to his father's native district of Whitehill, where he was piped into Hamish MacDonald's farm field to the applause of locals.

There were urns of tea and trays of pies and cakes, egg-and-spoon and sack races for all ages, a free-for-all tug-o'-war and a general air of warmth and good humour in a rural tradition that seems all but gone.

By late afternoon we were heading back to Aberdeen airport, where the luxurious' green-and-gold Boeing 727 emblazoned with "FORBES: Capitalist Tool", awaited its owner. Vanishing into the western sky, he would be back in New York within 24 hours of his departure.

Tomorrow would be just another day at the Manhattan desk which he reaches from home in New Jersey, 50 miles away, by 7.30am.

Malcolm Forbes will be 70 next month, and for the occasion he is chartering Concorde among the planes which will fly his guests for a birthday party at his palace in Morocco.

Mr Forbes's parties, incidentally, are like no other parties on earth, ending invariably with the breathtaking fireworks that remain a fascination for the boy within Mr Forbes.

Mention of Morocco recalls just one of the several occasions when this merry monarch of Wall Street came face to face with the fact that fate is no respecter of his £500m wealth.

He had already diced with death at the Normandy landings of 1944, when he was seriously wounded (and highly decorated). He had come close to his Maker in three hot-air balloon incidents, once when he struck a high-voltage cable and another when he plunged into Chesapeake Bay.

He was using up his nine lives at an alarming rate when he battled successfully with cancer. And then came Morocco.

As the owner of the Mendoub Palace in Tangiers, Mr Forbes had been invited to the birthday party of King Hassan in July 1971, a grand affair to be graced by the famous.

While the guests awaited the King to signal the start of lunch, a burst of firecracker noise suggested the fireworks display had come too soon. But this was no fun show.

A convoy of trucks came hurtling up the Casablanca road, swung into the palace gates, and 1200 armed military cadets began firing in all directions. By the time the attempted coup was over, more than 100 guests had been slaughtered in the palace courtyard.

The Belgian ambassador died in the arms of the French ambassador. The famous cardiologist, Jean Himbert, was crawling to the aid of the injured when he was callously machine-gunned to death.

Word reached Mr Forbes's own palace that he had been murdered. In fact the survival instinct had taken him on a leap over the palace wall and down on to the sands where he crawled away on his belly. Pursuing soldiers found him, however, and he was brought back and forced to lie face down among the dead and dying.

It seemed his moment had come when, miraculously, the revolt petered out, its leaders were executed and Malcolm Forbes had survived, along with the King himself.

I have no doubt the incident will cross his mind at the 70th birthday party in August. But it will not linger for long. He will be too busy getting on with the business of living—while he is still alive to do so.

JIMMY DELANEY—
GLADIATOR OF SOCCER

I WENT in search of a legend this week, by way of cleansing the palate of the bad taste that lingered from recent events in the game of football.

From all that publicity about the man now reviled by followers of Celtic Football Club, my thoughts were turning to the other end of that scale—to a man who gained immortality as one of the greatest footballers of all time, hailed from every side for being the kind of man he was.

I was thinking of Jimmy Delaney, a gladiator of the soccer arena for more than 20 years and darling of the Celtic Park supporters in particular.

What a contrast, I thought, between the pampered prima donnas of today, earning millions without being able to lace the boots of the dashing Delaney, who reached the peak of his income in the 1950s with a weekly wage of £14!

Like so many others of his day, including Jock Stein and Bill Shankly, the character of the lad was tested down the pits in his native village of Cleland, from which the only possible escape was a talent with a tanner-ba'.

Luckily, Jimmy Delaney possessed it to the point of genius, joining Celtic in 1934, at the age of 20, and playing until he was 42, rather in that Stanley Matthews mould of men who knew of nothing else.

His birthplace of Cleland always stuck in my mind as being important for nothing else but producing him; so it was to Cleland that I addressed my inquiries and it was there, in a quiet little street, that I found him.

Alas, the heroic figure was confined to bed, the man who fought

113

bravely in many a soccer skirmish now fighting the bravest battle of all.

The noble head lay tired upon the pillow, lips parched and the voice gone soft. But it took only the mention of great names and famous occasions to bring a spark to the eye; and maybe a tear as well.

I recalled a story which tells you not only about the greatness of Delaney but about the drastic change which has overtaken the behaviour of human beings. Having played 12 years for Celtic, he moved on to Manchester United and later to Aberdeen, by which time he was 36. When Aberdeen went to Glasgow to play Celtic on January 13th, 1951, they gave the former Celt the honour of captaining the team.

As Delaney ran out in the unfamiliar red jersey, the Celtic crowd rose to acclaim their new opponent. When one of their own players tackled him heavily, there were roars of disapproval. And when Delaney put Aberdeen on the road to victory with a splendid goal, there was a moment of silence before he was cheered once again!

Can you imagine that kind of decency being shown by football people today? Would there still be recognition of a memorable talent when an idol brings defeat to his former club?

My own outstanding memory of Delaney brought a wistful smile to the face of the great man. As a schoolboy I was paying my first ever visit to Hampden Park, for the Victory International of 1946, when a weakened Scottish team faced the might of England, the great Frank Swift and all.

I can still recall the mood of the terracings that day, with men just back from the war discovering one another in the crowd, giving rise to emotional reunions.

Down on the park, the Scots were more than holding their own as the game reached its very last minute. Husband of Partick Thistle took a free kick and flighted the ball to the head of Waddell of Rangers, who in turn headed it down to Delaney.

There seemed like a pause while the Scot told Swift that all his brilliance as a goalkeeper would do nothing to prevent what was about to happen. And it happened.

The final whistle blew, Delaney was hailed as the hero in a memorable victory over England—and the pent-up feelings of a nation after six years of war were finally released in a spree of celebration.

Which players linger in his memory? Typical of the man, the first two names belonged to Rangers: Willie Waddell and Bob McPhail. But they were soon bracketed with his former team-mates, Malcolm McDonald and Willie Buchan of Celtic, Stan Pearson of Manchester United and George Hamilton of Aberdeen.

"I had a great life in football," Jimmy Delaney whispered. "I loved the game so much that Saturdays couldn't come round soon enough."

In a previous interview, the man whose name was magic and whose talent brought him cup medals in Scotland, England and Ireland recalled the funeral of Tom Maley in 1935, when a Celtic jersey was placed on the coffin as it was lowered.

"I hope they do that for me." Delaney had said.

Let us hope and pray that time will be long delayed. But what human being would be more worthy of his wish?

BACK TO THE ABERDEEN OF
HARRY GORDON

AS you round that final corner on the northward journey, the grey-blue carpet of Aberdeen unfolds before your eyes, a sight to catch the throat of every returning exile.

I had come on a voyage around those childhood memories, recalling that the special treat of our school holidays in rural Aberdeenshire was a visit to the Granite City itself, which seemed like the gateway to a deliciously wicked world beyond.

For me, in the 1930s, it always happened on a Friday, when my father set out on his weekly mission to auction cattle at Kittybrewster mart. Aboard his little green Austin (RG 6502) we sped through Auchnagatt and Ellon towards the metropolis itself, each mile producing a fresh acceleration of excitement.

From Kittybrewster, my mother and I would join the Woodside tram-car as it hurtled down George Street towards the city centre.

There was morning coffee and a buttery at the old Empress Café, a rummage through Raggie Morrison's, a splendid lunch at Isaac Benzie's (with palm court accompaniment) and a visit to the Astoria Cinema, with its glittering organ played by Bobby Pagan, before my father emerged from the sharny sale-ring and we all went happily home to Buchan.

On this latest visit, I tried to re-enact that routine of 50 years ago, even to the point of acquiring a little green Austin from 1934, which I drove with much trepidation, since it had survived its 55 years without a single bump!

The re-enactment began to go wrong at Kittybrewster, where I just managed to catch the tail-end of my father's old headquarters before it moves out of town altogether.

Of course there was no longer a tram-car, which was just as well since it could not have reached its city-centre destination anyway. With their idea of wisdom, city planners have managed to block off George Street with two of those hideous-looking shopping centres.

From then onwards, however, this voyage around my childhood was little short of pure delight. Climbing atop the Salvation Army citadel at the Castlegate, I viewed the majesty of a Union Street enriched by the fortuitous appearance of the massed bands of the Scots Guards, resplendent in black and red.

Memories flooded back. Up that thoroughfare, in 1946, I had run alongside Winston Churchill's open car and reached out to touch the great man. Beyond Patsy Gallagher's news-stand, I could still recall the aroma of coffee which once wafted from Collie's shop.

Back at street level, I wandered into the Capitol Cinema and found, to my utter delight, that the old Compton organ still rises from the depths, the very last to function in a Scottish cinema. A local librarian, author and musician, Michael Thomson, plays it regularly and was on hand that day to transport me with sheer joy.

So I moved on past the Burns and Wallace memorials to glance again at the magnificence of His Majesty's Theatre, where a personal appearance of Richard Tauber around 1941 had introduced me to a magical new world.

A rare glimpse of the disused Rubislaw Quarry, in the city's west end, was a dramatic reminder of the hole from which most of Aberdeen was hewn. Down at the seafront I dropped in at a promenade café which occupies the old Beach Pavilion made famous by that memorable comedian, Harry Gordon.

At the back of the premises, you can still make out the proscenium arch of Harry's old stage. The ghosts came alive as I heard again his voice in that familiar refrain:

> There's Fittie folk, Kitty folk, country folk and city folk;
> Folk fae Constitution Street and folk fae Rubislaw Den;
> Wallfield, Nellfield, Mannofield and Cattofield,
> Lots o' lovely stories that you maybe dinna ken.

117

Round the corner from his beloved Pavilion lies that same Fittie (Footdee, in English) which the fisher folk regarded as their own village within a city. I had completely forgotten what a quaint and charming place it is.

On the nearby pier, two Frenchmen run an up-market fish restaurant from which you can view the lighted vessels sailing out to the dark North Sea.

Afternoon tea with two teachers was a special treat, since Miss Catto was the infant mistress who welcomed me to school in 1936 and Miss Morrison had recommended me for Robert Gordon's College. Then I went for a stroll round the quadrangle of that old school, in the company of a contemporary who has since made a name for himself—Buff Hardie of Scotland The What?

We ended up in a favourite haunt of 40 years ago, the lounge of the Caledonian Hotel, where once the fashionable of Aberdeen would go to see and be seen, soothed by more of those palm court strings which characterised the period.

All of this, I suppose, was really too much to keep to myself. So a BBC television crew came dogging my footsteps as I discovered a fresh glow in those dancing Northern Lights. All will be revealed no doubt—"in the autumn schedule", as they say.

A. T. MAYS—
THE MAN WHO DOESN'T EXIST

I WENT to a 70th birthday party last week. No, not that one, madam—my private jet was having its MOT that day. This was Troon, not Tangiers, and the profile was decidedly lower.

In fact, profiles don't come any lower than that of Jim Moffat, an Ayrshire man whose achievements in business are matched by his feat of wrapping himself in such anonymity that few in Scotland even know his name.

He has simply allowed his public persona to be represented by a figure called A. T. Mays who, just to confuse the issue, doesn't exist in human form.

In the course of a career, journalists interview many people and form friendships with few of them. But Jim Moffat is one of my exceptions. I took an instant liking to the man, who seemed like the fairest face of capitalism.

Yet his business success as one of Britain's big four travel agents is in sharp contrast to his early days in Saltcoats, where he reluctantly became a bank clerk at 17.

Things with wings had always fascinated him. Having inherited his father's interest in budgies, he bred the creatures and wanted to do a bit of flying himself.

Thus Jim Moffat became a wartime pilot, a taste of adventure which made his return to the bank all the more a misery. By now he had married Margie Robertson, a butcher's daughter from Ardrossan, who took his moanings until she could stand them no longer. "Either give up the bank or give up me," she said.

But Jim was approaching 36 and knew of nothing else, except . . . well, he knew about budgies. Maybe he could start a pet shop.

119

So he did, with a stock which amounted to one case of *Kit-e-Kat* and one of *Winalot*!

To eke out the living, Margie would open business in a hut across the street, selling rail tickets to Glasgow and boat tickets for emigrants. They would call themselves All Pets and All Travel.

The pet shop did well but travel did even better. When Jim and Margie bought the Kilmarnock branch of Mays (Shipping and Travel) they now had possession of a well-known name. Could they combine the two notions and call themselves All Travel Mays?

The registrar of companies refused but was quite happy if they used the initials and called it A. T. Mays. Thus that curious gent of non-existence became established as Scotland's biggest travel agent.

The rest of the story is business romance at its best. Step by step, the Moffats opened another branch and another, mostly financed from their own profits, until they had reached an incredible 250 or more.

They had come upon the travel scene at that most opportune of moments when the mass of society was forsaking places like Saltcoats and heading instead for Majorca. The package holiday had been the foundation of their prosperity.

Having taken his place alongside Thomas Cook, Lunn Poly and Pickford, Jim Moffat needed wider financing for the continued expansion. He could take his Saltcoats company to the stockmarket but that would inevitably mean being swallowed up by one of the other giants, with total loss of identity.

Instead, he accepted the wooings of the Royal Bank of Scotland, which sought diversity, laying down conditions that they would not change the name of A. T. Mays—and they would keep the headquarters in Saltcoats!

Isn't it wonderful, in this day of centralising all corporate cores in places like London, that a major national company stays loyal to the small town where it began?

But then that is the kind of man Jim Moffat is. Though financial control has passed to the Royal Bank in Edinburgh, the Moffats, including Margie and son Jamie, have been retained to run the business, just as before.

They take pride in driving home for lunch and viewing the hundreds of people wearing the company uniform, fully satisfied that they have brought jobs to a part of Ayrshire which badly needs them.

On his 70th birthday, Jim Moffat invited family and friends to lunch at the Marine Hotel, Troon, a splendidly civilised affair which included his very first A. T. Mays employee, Minnie Kerr, now Mrs Chalmers, wife of the farmer at Little Ittington, Ardrossan.

Among the guests was another legend of the Scottish travel trade, Lloyd Davies, the man who discovered Majorca in 1928, when it was only a winter resort, and pointed the way to its summer potential.

Another competitor, Roy Brabender, proposed a toast to round off an occasion of warmth and joy. Jim and Margie Moffat—Mr and Mrs A. T. Mays—responded with the modesty by which they have remained exactly the same kind of people as they used to be.

The disgruntled bank clerk may now be a millionaire 18 times over but you would never guess it. They indulge themselves in just one luxury—cruising. And that is why you would find them somewhere in the Mediterranean right now. I cannot think of a couple who deserve it more.

AS BARON APPROACHED
HIS CENTENARY

BY a recent calculation, I discovered that my faithful friend Baron and I had walked the equivalent of New York and back during our years of mutual exercise. His sense of relief had promoted the growth of trees in the neighbourhood and my arteries had been kept in better shape than would otherwise have been the case.

He had come into my life so many years ago, a bouncing little Boxer who could mistake a chair leg for a lamp-post but was soon showing the character of his Crufts-champion grandfather, with a Churchillian face and determination that was prepared to fight other dogs on the beaches, in the streets or wherever they happened to meet.

He ruled the roost and nobody minded, for we all knew he was a big softy at heart. He and I established a routine of walking and talking in which I could pour out the woes of the day and be sure that I would receive not only a sympathetic hearing but a definite nod of approval.

From time to time he would seek to sniff around and stick his flattened nose into this column but succeeded only once—when I was deeply anxious about his health and felt I had to confide in someone.

My faith in the essential goodness of the human heart was restored by public reaction to the news that poor old Baron, then aged 11, was undergoing an operation to remove a malignant tumour from a place which no man dare to contemplate.

The vet performed the operation in the kitchen and it was an anxious 10 hours later before the old man blinked his way back to consciousness.

122

We appreciated him even more thereafter and he and I were soon back on the beat.

Despite the many inquiries about his health, I did not burden you with the further news that what happened to his left side had later to be repeated on his right.

Old age was creeping up and soon we would have to face the inevitable, since Boxers are lucky if they reach 11 or 12. But his outline was still in perfect shape, his brown coat as sleek as ever, and we crossed our fingers that he would live on for some time yet.

Just before his thirteenth birthday, however, he suffered a serious heart attack, the vet was summoned and it seemed as if our man had breathed his last. There would be one final attempt at revival. Could he possibly live after this?

Well, old Baron bounced back, large as life, showing his Churchillian determination to stay with us and settling down to a daily dose of pills which gave him a surprisingly good quality of life. A magnificent vet in Mount Florida showed the kind of skill and caring concern which many people complain they don't find in their doctors.

We had a fourteenth birthday party in July and calculated, according to the doggy years of seven-to-one, that he would reach his centenary on October 31. The Queen might not acknowledge the event but surely there would be a telegram from the Corgis.

Last week, however, things began to go wrong. The steroid injections which had lent new strength to his back legs were no longer having their effect. Though the old warrior was still keen to walk and pick up his scents and supervise his lamp-posts, he was beginning to stagger and fall.

The eyesight was failing and the hearing too. There came that night when he could no longer raise his legs for the final visit and we all knew, in our silence, that there must be no selfishness in love.

A sign of distress in the night brought the 7am phone-call to the vet, who was on the doorstep within 20 minutes. We gathered round and accepted his guidance without question.

The limp figure lay in all his animal beauty as the vet prepared the injection.

"How long will it take?" I asked.

"About three or four seconds," he replied.

Gently, he slipped the needle into a foreleg and, without a twitch or a murmur, old Baron was gone to wherever dogs go. (If the rest of us could go with that amount of ease, we would surely lose all fear of dying.)

We wrapped him in his favourite rug, with a final pat, carried him out to the van and watched it disappear round the corner. Baron had measured out our family life, from the time the children were at school, through their adolescence to adulthood, and given us a focal point of affection and endearment to which he responded in abundance. I suppose it explains why people keep pets.

You lose a bit of yourself when you lose your dog. One more phase is over. Then you walk with your thoughts, alone in the night—and feel there is more dew in the air than you had imagined.

MANHATTAN REQUIEM
FOR A MEMORABLE SCOT

EVEN in the crisp cold of a late-winter evening, New York remains an exciting city, one of my favourite places on earth. A concrete jungle without a soul, you've heard them say?

What kind of soulless creature, I wondered, could fail to pick up the rhythms of such a vibrant community, as I sauntered up Fifth Avenue and turned right by East 50th Street, to the most stunning of all Manhattan's thoroughfares, the glass towers of Park Avenue?

Quarter of a century on, the sight of it by night never fails to thrill me, that vista which leads to the Helmsley Building, rising to its golden crown with a rare majesty.

Invariably, my Park Avenue promenade ends in the cocktail lounge of the Waldorf-Astoria, where the cocktail is less important than the sound of Cole Porter's own piano, bequeathed by the man himself to the folks downstairs, from the apartments next door where he spent his latter years.

It was all a particular novelty for my companion of last week, the Rev. Russel Moffat from New Deer, Aberdeenshire, who was paying his first visit to the United States.

It was an enviable sight for a minister that evening to see the Manhattan crowds queuing up to enter their churches. For it was Ash Wednesday, first day of Lent, when the clergy was marking the sign of the cross on the foreheads of its congregations, with the accompanying words: "Remember thou art but dust and ashes, and to dust thou shalt return."

It was a timely preparation for the following day, when we would attend the funeral service of Malcolm Forbes, the Scots-American publisher, on that same Park Avenue.

125

How appropriate that the minister from the Scottish parish of Malcolm Forbes's father should take his officiating place in the vast church of St Bartholomew. When invited, he didn't even have a passport, and it took an early morning battle through an Aberdeenshire snowstorm to reach the issuing office in Glasgow.

Any further pain in getting there was totally removed when the Forbes family sent its luxurious Boeing 727 to pick us up at Aberdeen Airport. As we curved in an Arctic direction, Greenland's Icy Mountains became more than a name in a hymn book, sparkling in the midday sun like an elaborate wedding cake.

And now, in the high-domed church of St Bartholomew, the mighty organ was leading an angelic choir in a swell of sound which tingled the blood.

As the minister spoke I was reminded more than ever of John Donne's memorable words: "And therefore never send to know for whom the bell tolls; it tolls for thee." Because we are all involved in mankind, as Donne said, and "any man's death diminishes me".

Somehow it was driven home, more than usual, that the sound of that bell is not for the immediate deceased alone but an echo for all who have gone before, our loved and remembered ones, and even for ourselves in time to come.

I couldn't help thinking of the human race, with all its foibles and frailties, parading before us even now in that Manhattan church. There was old Richard Nixon, come to say farewell to his Republican colleague, now doddering down the aisle with a kindly smile for his fellow mourners, benign as a bishop. From across the aisle I studied him discreetly and tried hard to fit the scandal of Watergate upon his quite distinguished head. It sat with difficulty.

Soon he was joined by Elizabeth Taylor and, once again, it was hard to fit the legend to the reality, Elizabeth of the many films and many husbands, one half of that Burton-Taylor partnership which intrigued a generation.

Now there was little more than a pair of recognisably sparkling eyes to distinguish a dumpy little woman. I thought it was perhaps the bulk of the fur coat which was deceiving me but, even as I talked to her at the reception back in the Forbes Gallery, the uncoated Miss Taylor still had more girth than was good for her.

The gossip columns had had their fling in recent years, linking Miss Taylor with the fabulously rich Forbes, who had been her close companion since his divorce at the age of 66.

They found joy in each other's company, of course, but the value of the publicity to Forbes's publications was not lost on the canniness of his Scottish nature.

Liz Taylor was in the front pew of the memorial service to hear one of his sons tell the congregation: "My father had no difficulty with women—he simply married the best."

Well, he didn't marry Miss Taylor, for whom the party was now over. But he did marry the charming Roberta Laidlaw, with whom he lived for 39 years.

And when the service was over, it was Roberta who walked with dignity from that magnificent church. She may have had the worn look of sadness, no doubt wishing that matters had turned out differently. But, in the end, she had the triumph as well.

DANNY GORDON—BAILIE O' BENACHIE

THE Mither Tap o' Benachie juts proudly as a landmark for shipping down that Aberdeenshire coast, declaring itself the eastern
extremity of the Grampians.

Like many another mountain, Benachie holds a fascination even
for those who will never touch it, standing as silent witness to the
passing of centuries, a privilege denied mere mortals of the human
race.

The Gadie runs at the back of it, as the song tells us, and the
Don flows quietly by, on its way to Aberdeen. But Benachie just
broods there.

I've known it all my life but not so intimately as Danny Gordon,
who grew up under its shadow and whose life has revolved around
it for close on 90 years.

From his childhood home at Tayloch Farm, in the parish of Clatt,
he could gaze in wonder at its massive presence, silhouetted against
the moonlit sky and all the more dominant in a land better known
for the gentle contours of its rolling farmland.

The magnetic pull of Benachie has never loosened its grip on
Danny Gordon, who still lives by the banks of the Don, at Inverurie,
with an elevated view of the river and his mountain calling from the
west.

For it is very much Danny's mountain, to the extent that, in 1973,
he summoned all like-minded people and suggested that, for the
production of a pound, they could call themselves the Bailies of
Benachie, custodians of its breadth and beauty, protectors of its
flora and fauna.

They would preserve its rights of way, study its geology, defend
it from vandals. They would celebrate its presence at an annual picnic, and so they do, at a good old-fashioned gathering every August.

128

I had known of Danny Gordon for 50 years but had never met him until I drove up to his picturesque farmhouse of Coldwells.

In the shadows of Benachie, where he was born just a few days before the death of Queen Victoria, he was one of the five children of Robert Gordon, lay preacher and story-teller, who farmed a bare scrat of a place and made wills for his neighbours.

Missing the First World War by two months, Danny paid his way through Aberdeen University by working at hay, hoe, and harvest and milking the kye at five o'clock in the morning (not a student loan to protest about).

He struck that university year of the returning ex-servicemen, people like Eric Linklater, boys grown to men in the horrors of the Somme, glad to be alive and determined to savour life. There has never been a student period like it; in that one class, for instance, there were a dozen Military Crosses.

In that well-rounded tradition of learning, Danny Gordon graduated in both arts and medicine and became a doctor at Insch, close to Benachie, before heading off to work in the east end of London. They were primitive days before antibiotics and he shudders at the memory.

His earliest brush with doctors had been unforgettable. At 11, his tonsils were sliced out by Dr Grant of Rhynic, using some new-fangled instrument—and without anaesthetic.

"Jist open yer mou, loon," the good doctor had said. "That's fine. Noo, we'll hae a slash at the ither side!" And of course they grew again.

He became family doctor at Ellon in 1928. Soon after his first wife died in childbirth, he was off to the Second World War, serving with the RAMC at the debacle of Dunkirk, returning to Ellon in 1945 and marrying a local teacher.

Danny Gordon's education was guided by his uncle, that legendary Scottish dominie, Benjamin Skinner of Strichen, who ruled by fear. But, by jove, if you were taught by Skinner, you stayed taught! As a measure of the standards, he was qualified to teach, at the Higher level, not only English, French and German, but Latin, Greek and Maths.

He retired in 1930, at the age of 60, and took over Coldwells farm at Inverurie, which he then passed on to his nephew, Danny. He, in turn, retired at 60 and is still at the farm, happily accepting his 90th year but giving me the opinion that the ideal lifespan is 80 years.

"I have studied people all my life," he says. "They are fine until about 80. Then they just begin to wear awa."

Danny hasn't "worn awa" very far. He credits his good habits of health and fitness to the Boy Scout movement. He ends his ablutions, incidentally, with a cold shower.

He plants acres of trees for the well-being of future generations, looks after his 92-year-old wife, Betty, watches the Don flow sweetly by to the North Sea—and turns again towards Benachie.

When he raised the public profile of his beloved mountain, one matter-of-fact old lady said: "Fit's a' this fuss aboot Benachie? It's aye been there!"

It's aye been there, indeed; symbol of a world that keeps on rolling through the millennia while we, the inhabitants, drop by for a fleeting visit.

NOTALOTTI PAVAROTTI

WELL, that will teach me to keep my waving hand to myself. There I was at a charity lunch the other week when the chairman announced a pair of Pavarotti tickets for auction.

As the son of an auctioneer, I should have known better. But, considering the black market value of those £50 tickets, the bidding struck me as sluggish. So I gave the man a bid at £150 and set the carnival atmosphere a-rolling.

I was still wheeling at £450, with a counter-bidder who seemed set upon his night out at the Scottish Exhibition Centre. "I'll give him one last turn," I was saying to myself when, suddenly, the crafty fellow pulled out and gave me a turn instead!

Yes, no need to spell it out. At £500, I was the owner of two tickets for the Pavarotti concert in Glasgow last week. Deciding to initiate economies immediately, I chose to walk back to the office from that Holiday Inn lunch, a first act of penance for my folly.

Well-heeled colleagues waved cheerfully from taxis and a song kept buzzing through my head as I consoled myself with two thoughts: The money had gone to charity; and, if the black market was all they said it was, I could always recover my money, maybe even double it, and further assist the charity from my new-found profits. That song which kept annoying me, by the way, was Anthony Newley's "What Kind of Fool Am I?"

As the day drew near, thoughts of profit-taking began to recede and I was set upon a course of giving my wife what would surely be one of the nights of a lifetime.

Any hint of misgivings was firmly put out of sight as we joined the great traffic jam towards the Clydeside venue and prepared for our memorable evening with Mr Pavarotti.

Now, it would be unworthy of my better instincts to make facetious comparisons with a night of the toothache; but you get the drift.

Opinions have varied widely, mainly based on the level of expectation which the individual carried into that vast barn of a place which masquerades as a concert hall.

With a fairly keen sense of music in my soul, I thrilled to the sight of the Scottish Opera Orchestra, with its choral accompaniment; with that kind of background to one of the finest tenor voices in history, surely we were set for a night which would linger in our memories forever.

Mr Pavarotti had exhorted us, nay warned us, to be there 15 minutes early if we did not wish to be locked out for the first half. Little did I expect to view that, in retrospect, as more of a promise than a threat.

For a series of bad blinks might have prevented any knowledge that he had appeared in the first half at all. (Having all turned up, as instructed, those 15 minutes early, hadn't we the right to demand a time-keeping courtesy for ourselves, instead of enduring a further and disgraceful delay of 15 minutes?).

The second half wasn't much better than the first and we had to thunder some applause in anticipation of an encore before the Big Man deigned to give his musically-mixed audience anything resembling what they had come to hear.

Of course the biggest bungle of all was to imagine that that steel-girdered monstrosity could ever pretend to be a concert hall. I kept waiting for the bombers to return from a raid over Germany; or to hear the buses coming in for the night. As colleague Michael Tumelty said, in a very perceptive review, the Exhibition Centre rules triumphant over live music—and kills it stone dead.

This was the night when a combination of wonderful musical talents should have engulfed us all in a great cauldron of sound, vibrations each unto the other, till we would walk from the place in a quiet ecstasy of spent emotion.

Instead, no sweat was broken. In an event so sadly lacking in theatrical presentation, the rich musical tapestry was confined to a distant tableau, better seen by those in the closed-circuit television hall nearby.

132

Luciano himself kept disappearing to what was presumably his backstage couch, before re-appearing in a fresh entrance which raised hope of better things to come. But the hope was in vain. Notalotti Pavarotti, as my Fish-and-chip man might have said.

With his right hand poised for the majestic walk through the orchestra, his left hand carried what was presumably a towel (super-fluous in the event) but which looked more like a clootie-dumpling from which the dumpling had escaped.

Maybe the dumplings were all in the audience, paying more than £500,000 on a night which for such a variety of reasons fell far short of expectation.

In an idle moment, I toyed with thoughts of a prize for the biggest plum-duff in the hall. Then, remembering that distant dinner, I realised it might seem as if I had fixed it!

TROUBLE OF CHOOSING A NAME

IN my regular column of 26 years ago. I was preoccupied in this particular week with a dilemma, for which I sought the help of readers.

I had just met a crinkle-faced stranger with a Churchillian scowl who seemed to have inherited a great deal of character and intelligence. His other distinctive feature was that he had no name.

Of course, the situation should never have arisen. There was a boy in the family already and this was to have been a girl. My wife, who had been blessed with the name of Eden, had searched the garden and come up with Avon, which seemed to flow with all the ease of that beautiful river. (It was pure coincidence that Sir Anthony Eden had become Lord Avon.)

But what were we to call a second boy? With a certain absence of imagination, our family had been Johns for generations (seven of my preceding John Websters are buried in one kirkyard!) and I was modified to Jack in the hope of avoiding "Old John and Young John".

Choosing a name, which will bless or blight a child for the rest of its life, entails a fine balancing act between a mellifluous, rhythmic sound of good metre and something which will not be contracted into playground ridicule.

Fashions of the day were followed long before the appearance of a Jason or a Kylie. When I saw the sizeable mouth of my second son, I thought of Cassius (does it need to be explained to a new generation that Mohammed Ali was known as Cassius Clay in 1964).

The suggestion of noise and fisticuffs led me to young Geoffrey. What would he like his new brother to he called?

"Well," he began, "he could be John . . . or George . . ." (A traditional boy, I thought) ". . . or Paul . . . or Ringo . . ." Then I knew we were back among the insects.

Readers came rushing to my assistance, with no lack of imagination. They ranged from Stephen, Lawrence, Brian and Vincent to Conrad, Derek, Winston and Stuart.

A man called Dan thought he shouldn't suffer alone, while a Mr Stuart Paul, from Arundel Drive, Glasgow, went overboard about Shakespeare. He suggested Laertes, Claudius or Hamlet and, if all that failed, he was reasonable enough to settle for the classical name for a boy—Lycidas, from Greek mythology.

In a year when the poets were scrabbling in obscurity at the Edinburgh Festival, the versifiers were rushing to my rescue. One lady wrote:

> Hullo, little lonely stranger
> Are you looking for a name?
> What about D'Arcy Dagenham,
> If you want to rise to fame?
> You could still be useful and happy
> —and it wouldn't matter a damn—
> If your name were Billy or Bobby
> Or Jeremiah or Tam.

The most popular readers' choice in 1964 was David (meek and mild and beloved) but someone touched on Keith and that set us thinking about the obvious. My wife's maiden name was Keith, from her distant relative, the Earl Marischal, so how would that match up with Webster?

Wondering if the boy might, by chance, turn into a scribbler in need of a byline, I concluded that Keith Webster had a fine enough ring about it.

Mixing some family names, we inserted Barron Raeburn in the middle, which rather clumsified the overall effect—and I dashed round to the registrar's office just minutes before I became liable for prosecution. I concluded my column that week by saying: "The boy will probably think we are nuts."

Well, the world goes round and round and the innocent babe of 1964 celebrated his 26th birthday yesterday. He had indeed grown up to be a journalist, landing in Fleet Street and, only last week,

135

had his father drooling over a two-page tabloid spread, written "by Keith Webster".

"That's my boy!" I was muttering to myself as I phoned up to wish him a happy birthday. And by the way . . . what had he thought of his name? Had we really been nuts, as I feared?

Well, the middle parts had been for concealing at school, he revealed for the first time. When questioned by other children about the initials B.R., he had passed them off as British Rail! The rest was fine, however.

In any case, he now fully sympathised with the dilemma. In the way that life keeps repeating itself, he and his wife are preparing for their own first child and he could have been tempted to write the same kind of article I wrote for him in 1964.

The thinking in the next generation, however, has been a little more positive. In good time, they have decided that a boy is likely to be called Fraser and a girl could be Sinead.

That, I thought, might be after a well-known actress but I'm told it is also the name of a pop star who did well in the charts. It is pronounced Shin-ade—and I'll sure have it before Kylie!

REMEMBRANCE FOR WALTER

THE November damp of an Armistice Day never fails to stir a mood of reflection in those of us who remember the major conflicts. It must, of course, be hard for the young to share any sense of a Second World War which is now as distant for them as the Boer War was to my generation.

Yet it is not enough for a protesting young man to set fire to himself, as happened in London, or for others to pontificate about the futility of a conflict like the one with Hitler, in tones suggesting that aspirations of peace have been the preserve of a later and more enlightened generation.

There would not have been a later or more enlightened generation if their forefathers had not stopped the Madman of Munich in his tracks.

That is why the parade at the Cenotaph is for all of us, with the 11th hour of the 11th day of the 11th month falling, appropriately this year, on a Sunday.

My own memories date back to those Armistice Days of the 1930s, when we stood in the school hall, bowed our heads and tried to imagine the glaur of a foreign field, in a war which was already 20 years away.

Little did we know that an even wider holocaust was just around the corner: one which would add to that granite slab by the village kirk some names from within those ranks of children who now bowed their heads in some vague search for a meaning to it all.

So they came down Whitehall on Sunday, old soldiers squaring up in a brave reconstruction of more energetic days, the story of a thousand agonies etched on their weather-beaten faces.

It was the men of the RAF who brought a special lump to my throat. For I was wearing a very special poppy for my good friend

137

Walter, who served that force with distinction in the Second World War.

We had been together on Friday night, in an atmosphere of warm fellowship. He was the usual gloriously cheerful Walter, known to a large circle of friends as well as to generations of students at Springburn College, where he had been head of English and general studies.

He was back in our house, large as life, on Saturday. But hours before that Armistice Day broke, he was slumped dead in his chair. I was there within minutes. No pleading for a word, for a sign of life, could reach him now.

We just stood dumbfounded. Where does a human spirit go in the briefness of a few seconds? It was a deeper question which could wait. For now, it was a case of coming to terms with the fragile nature of our existence.

That moment of sudden death, and the bizarre silence of the aftermath, seem totally unworthy of the life that has gone before.

I looked at him and read again, in the repose of his features, the story of Walter Macphail's life. He was the typical Glasgow boy, fresh from his Highers, who was off to war in the days beyond the Battle of Britain, training as a pilot and already dicing with death on bombing raids over Germany before he had reached the age of 20.

Boys became men in the flash of a searchlight. And when it was all over, he came back to Glasgow University to study English and become a teacher, adding to his profession that dimension of the world-travelled ex-serviceman, which served him well in further education.

In recent years there was the squadron reunion delighting him in the friendships renewed yet saddening him in the havoc which time had wreaked on some of his older comrades.

The ravages of war had finally caught up with many a dashing young pilot for whom the uncertainty of another day had lent a special quality to the rest of their lives.

Walter was the "baby" of the squadron, well remembered by older pilots for the courage and maturity with which he conducted himself in the hell of a bombing raid.

138

He carried those qualities into his later life, a manly man, a truly good man, a straight, honest, decent human being who toiled and sought no reward, who served and was pleased and proud to do so.

With the baser side of our natures so much glorified in a perplexing world, it is not so fashionable these days to be a good man. But I cannot help feeling the world would not be any the worse for a few more Walter Macphails.

Maybe that war was catching up with him too. Who knows the strains and stresses which build up within the human frame and precipitate a premature exit?

He left us quietly at the weekend, only the echo of a familiar laugh ringing in our ears. They could be a disappearing breed, those men who march with their memories on an Armistice Day.

At least that is how it seemed to me on this poignant Cenotaph day when the morning was dull and damp—and appropriately so.

THE LORD'S MY SHEPHERD

JUST when you are ready to concede that this crazy old world of ours has slithered beyond redemption towards a pit of vanity, greed and downright evil, driven by individual performance which puts a question-mark against our claim to be *human* beings, what a joy it is to discover that matters are not at all as bad as you had imagined.

In the saddest of times, I have been overwhelmed by the flood of human kindness, flowing even from people I may never meet but who felt it in their hearts to offer a word of support. It does wonders for your faith in human nature.

Through 35 years of marriage and my gallivanting journalism, Eden had stayed very much in the background, the quietly intelligent lady exerting a fine influence on three sons and proving once again what an anchor to family life the mother really is.

In all the millions of words I have spilled down the decades, I can recall only one phrase which was worthy of its place in an American collection of quotable quotes.

That was when I wrote that "whoever created the cliché about no-one being indispensable must surely have forgotten about mothers".

The boys came with me to the little parish church of Crimond in Aberdeenshire, where the Keith family had originated. And there they heard her former Guide mistress recall their mother as a little girl in nearby Fraserburgh.

She had stood in the guard of honour at the Guide mistress's wedding in 1948 and, while still at school, had flashed an engagement ring as she announced that she would not be coming back to the classroom.

Some passing journalist, who could surely be up to no good, was sweeping her away in marriage.

There were many more memories as we stood in that little church at Crimond and raised the rafters with fine rural vigour, singing "The Lord's My Shepherd" to the tune which took its name from that same little church and was made famous when the Queen chose it for her wedding in 1947.

Indeed, back in the 1880s, Eden's crofting grandfather, Alex Keith, had sung in the choir of this very church, alongside Jessie Seymour Irvine, whose father preached from the pulpit above.

Jessie had written it for a competition and was later to suffer the frustration of seeing her musical creation being credited to David Grant, a more worldly-wise Aberdeen organist, who helped her to harmonise it.

Genteel ladies of the manse were not supposed to raise a voice in those far-off days; in any case, Jessie died young and it was eventually left to her sister to protest about injustice.

Down the years, and even today, there have been academics who have sought to stir controversy over the claims of Grant. Plain, honest folk from Crimond, still alive a generation ago, needed no documentary evidence to remember the time when Jessie composed the Psalm tune. They *knew*.

If her authorship had not been genuine, they asked, how would such an unassuming lady ever have been associated with the melody called after Crimond, where her father was minister? It seemed a good point.

These thoughts filtered through my mind as we reached the closing verse of "The Lord's My Shepherd". It was here that Eden's father had sung as a youth, a typical lad o' pairts who cycled the daily nine miles to Fraserburgh Academy, where he was dux, before graduating at Aberdeen and returning to his old school as principal maths teacher.

The war had spirited him off to the Gordon Highlanders, to be captured in Rommel's presence at St Valery and to spend five years as a prisoner in Germany.

As a student, he would rise at 3am on summer mornings to hoe his father's turnips before cycling across Aberdeenshire to wherever there were Highland games, using his athletic prowess to earn a few pounds and save his parents the cost of his lodgings.

141

So we laid flowers on the family grave and repaired to the local inn, consoled by happy memories and the warm fellowship of kindly Buchan folk. There was also a consoling sense of relief that the agonies of her particular cancer were over.

At 54, she had just held her first grandchild and was looking forward to a second. This time it would surely be a girl, to help balance up a family bias of males. Would the child arrive in time for her to be told?

Alas, it was not to be. In the shelter of her own home, Eden's remarkable fight to stay alive finally gave out. Just a few hours later, the first cries of a new-born babe were heard, 300 miles away in an Oxford hospital.

As one life ended, another began. A girl indeed. In the hour of grief, when the world became a lonelier place, it was time to give thanks that life goes on, come what may.

There is really no other way for it.

THE DILEMMA OF
A SON'S PHONE-CALL

I SUPPOSE I have always taken it as some kind of compliment that all three of my sons decided to follow in the old man's footsteps and become journalists.

Throughout their childhood, they had seen my various wanderings around the world and the occasional encounter with the famous as a glamorous way of life which had far more appeal than other means of making a living.

Even the occasional adventure in Northern Ireland, when I was caught up in some hair-raising nights of bombs and bullets, merely added an element of danger which did nothing to dissuade them from a career in newspapers.

But the phone call which came at the weekend was different. It threw me into one of the biggest dilemmas of my life.

The call was from my youngest son, in the south of England, agog that he had been offered a journalistic assignment which would almost certainly be the biggest one of his lifetime. It could also be his last.

In all the scramble to report the events which could break upon us from today onwards, his newspaper group had come first out of the hat among the few who can put a correspondent right up there in the front line of whatever holocaust erupts in the Gulf.

They fly out tomorrow and will be taken by armoured vehicle right to the Kuwaiti border, from which point they will be on their own.

If only because of recent family bereavement, the boy was sensitive enough to phone his father to see how I would feel about the risk he was taking. Would I approve of him going?

A number of his colleagues in the newspaper group had already turned it down and now it was decision time for young Martin. I looked across the editorial floor of the *Herald* and remembered it was not so long ago that he was the junior copy-boy here, full of enthusiasm for the prospect of becoming a reporter.

Off he had gone to his college course at Lancashire Polytechnic, graduating from there with good reports before joining an English newspaper and, within two years, collecting awards as both weekly and young journalist of the year.

He moved south in the name of progress and now he was being given the chance of a grandstand view of what could turn out to be one of the nastiest of all wars.

With an instant decision awaited, I tried to run it all through in my own mind. Having been all my life an enthusiast for journalistic adventure, I knew that my son was being offered the chance of a lifetime. Did I have a right to deprive him of it?

As far as his career was concerned, he would never look back. Then again, he might never look forward either.

For if the scenario of a Gulf war is enacted as we predict, then Saddam Hussein will unleash such horrific weapons as to make the consequences unthinkable.

I cannot even claim to belong to the lobby which thinks the Iraqi dictator does not have to be countered. By all appearances, there may be no alternative. And if my son had made a career of the armed forces, I could only accept that he had laid himself open to the possibility of a nasty war.

All wars are nasty but some of them have to be fought if we are not to fall under the heel of demons like Hitler or Hussein. Volunteering to fight in a professional army is one thing; was volunteering to report it quite another?

All these thoughts were buzzing through my head as my son waited on the other end of the line for his father's response.

What would you have done? Would you have told him to go ahead and make a name for himself as one of the front-line reporters, possibly coming home at the end of it all with a commendation for bravery and the chance of some glory and quick promotion in his profession?

Or would you have hesitated over such advice on the thought that you might well, within a matter of days, be putting your son in the line of a chemical attack and possible death?

We talked it through, he and I, and I found myself wondering what his mother would have said. By now I knew I had to ask myself one more question: What would I be saying this day next week if I advised him to go to the Gulf War and he became a front-line victim of whatever horrors the Iraqi dictator decided to throw at us?

I would have been putting his career before his life—and I couldn't have lived with that. Having lost the anchor of our family in recent weeks, I was in no frame of mind to risk another heartbreak. So, rightly or wrongly, I asked him not to go. And he didn't.

FACE TO FACE WITH CHURCHILL

IN London last week, I thought I would drop into the House of Commons to catch the tail end of the big debate on the Gulf War. It was, after all, a fairly poignant occasion.

Having just seen policemen at Glasgow and London Airports parading openly with rifles at the ready, I should have found it no surprise at all that security was so tight.

I just hadn't bargained for the fact that a break-out from Barlinnie might be a simpler proposition than an entry to the Palace of Westminster.

Security men all but turned me upside down and inside out before placing me on a set of footprints, where I stood for a full minute before the red light of a highly sophisticated detector was persuaded to change to green, presumably signifying that I had definitely left the gelignite at home and could be passed on to the next stage without too much risk to the Mother of Parliaments.

Guy Fawkes wouldn't have stood a chance. Finally, I had to fill in an identity form, promising to behave myself in the public gallery. Misdemeanours were never further from my mind.

Much of that performance took place by the steps of Central Hall, Westminster, within a few yards of the spot where, just quarter of a century ago, I had filed past the coffin of Winston Churchill. What a different world we live in, I thought, even from Churchill's day. What a different type of war we face.

In those days, the full potential of individual and small-group terrorism had not yet dawned on its likely perpetrators. What a pity it ever did.

Finally cleared of all suspicion, I mounted the narrow stairway to the public gallery, comparing the effects of modern terrorism with the mood and atmosphere of 40 years ago, when first I set foot in these historic premises.

I remember meandering without let or hindrance, through a wood-panelled corridor, rather losing my way and intending to ask the only other person in sight.

He was coming towards me from the far end—and it didn't take long to recognise the familiar outline of Winston Churchill. He nodded and smiled as we passed and I turned, open-mouthed, to gaze in admiration at the man who, in my childhood, had seemed to be all that stood between me and the worst horrors of Hitler's regime.

How, I was asking myself, do you reduce the great figures of history to the wholly recognisable form of a flesh-and-blood human being in a dark pinstripe suit?

In that same year, on Armistice Day, I had crossed from Horse Guards Parade, through Downing Street on my way to the Cenotaph and passed Mrs Churchill, out walking alone with her little dog. They can't do things like that any more. Even Downing Street itself is blocked off.

By now, I was seated in the gallery of a crowded house, trying to concentrate on the final speech by Defence Secretary Tom King but distracted by sensitive microphones which pick up very clearly the bad-mannered babble of some members who evidently regard their own tittle-tattle as of more importance than the business of the House.

I tried to control a certain nostalgia for men and women of stature. Those 40 years ago, there were personalities like Churchill, Eden, Macmillan, Boothby, Bevin, Morrison, Foot, Barbara Castle, Aneurin Bevan and his wife, Jenny Lee. Only two are still alive and Michael Foot alone survives in the Commons.

He was there that night, white hair flowing as he moved around in the style of elder statesman, looking as if he might dodder on for ever.

If that breed has not died out, it certainly doesn't give its life to politics in the latter stages of the twentieth century. We are into a new mould of men and women, no less articulate or driven by integrity, I'm sure, but somewhat lacking in colour and originality.

The lights and cameras of television have added their own dimension but nothing has changed a certain eeriness in the House of Commons as Big Ben reaches for 10 o'clock and the sound of division bells.

Something else which doesn't change is the sense that they all belong to an exclusive club down there, divided into cliques perhaps but incestuous nevertheless. Some members suddenly appear in the spectators' gallery, like participants in the school play who have come flushed to the bosom of proud relatives and friends in the audience.

As the lights begin to dim over Westminster, you wonder what happens to those actors on our political stage as they drift outwards to the dangerous moonlight of a troubled world, presumably back to the loneliness of their bed-sits in Pimlico.

A stiff whisky, perhaps, to help them unwind from a day and a life which, for all our cynicism about MPs, I would not envy them.

As Big Ben struck eleven, I pulled my collar to the wind, nodded an acknowledgement to the bronze of Churchill and headed briskly for my hotel.

PAVAROTTI OF PITTODRIE

AT first sight, you would struggle to find a connection between Luciano Pavarotti of Italy and Willie Miller of Aberdeen, yet for me they came together in a curious way the other evening.

I suppose you could say that, for 20 years now, Willie has been the Pavarotti of Pittodrie, singing with his feet to such fine tune that already he can be hailed as the biggest name in the entire history of Aberdeen Football Club.

But nothing lasts for ever and Willie's career has sadly come to an end after an injury sustained, characteristically, when he was giving his all for Scotland at Hampden.

Now, at 35, he must look elsewhere for a living and, as part of his farewell to the playing of football, his home town of Glasgow turned out in magnificent numbers to honour him at a splendid dinner in the Normandy Hotel.

Those who ply their trade in Glasgow and follow the local teams had, you would think, very little for which to thank Willie Miller. After all, he was the Bridgeton boy who reached world-class rating without playing for any local team other than Eastercraigs.

As a schoolboy of independent mind, he had resisted the pull of his friends to follow-follow on the routes to Ibrox or Celtic Park and had gone instead to the Granite City, where he became the most famous of adopted sons.

Of course he was by no means the first boy from the Strathclyde area to beat a path to Pittodrie. It has been happening for nearly 90 years, all the way from Donald Colman, Alec Jackson of the Wembley Wizards, Willie Mills and George Hamilton to Charlie Cooke, Jimmy Smith, Joe Harper and Alec McLeish.

In some ways it has symbolised a long-standing connection between the West and the North-east, dating back to those days when

149

the Fair folk of Glasgow headed for Aberdeen perhaps more than for any other single destination.

You will find even today, when holidays abroad have eroded the link, that older Glaswegians still exchange Christmas cards with the children of their old landladies in Wallfield, Nellfield, Mannofield or Cattofield. The golden sands were nearby and so was the Beach Pavilion, home of the great Harry Gordon, who became as big a favourite with Glaswegians as any of their own home-based comedians.

That tradition of Aberdonian humour is now safely in the hands of the highly-talented revue group, Scotland The What?, but it is an interesting sign of the changing times that they are not yet so well known to Glaswegians as Harry Gordon, despite their biannual visits to the King's Theatre and occasional exposure on television.

That could be set to change when they return to the King's in September. For they came south to entertain the company at that Willie Miller dinner—and proved a sensational hit with their audience, some of whom had heard of them but had no idea just how cleverly funny they could be.

They came to his own home town to honour the Bridgeton boy who had brought unprecedented football honour to Aberdeen, all the way to European glory at Gothenburg in 1983.

And they were joined by people as diverse as Scotland's manager Andy Roxburgh, the voice of authority on the BBC's *World At One*, James Naughtie, and our own Jack McLean, who rounded off his gravel-voiced performance by producing his mouth-organ and leading the company in "The Northern Lights of Old Aberdeen"!

But where did Pavarotti come in? Oh yes. Readers of this column may recall my experience of last year when I turned up at a Press Fund charity lunch and found myself bidding at an auction of two precious tickets for Luciano's big concert in Glasgow.

Without pausing to consider my particular brand of insanity, I paid £500 for the pair!

It all came back to me on the Willie Miller night, when we were auctioning one of his special Scottish jerseys, to raise funds for his own chosen charity of cancer and leukaemia research.

The most persistent bidder was the editor of the *Glasgow Herald*, Arnold Kemp, who finished up paying £400 for the jersey. It was only then that the significance of events came clear to me. Mr Kemp had been chairman at the press lunch and now, with me being chairman at the Willie Miller dinner, he was returning the compliment for another charity.

Being himself a Hibernian supporter, he promptly presented the jersey to his deputy, Harry Reid, who is strongly rumoured to be an Aberdeen supporter. Mr Reid, in turn, has handed it back to be auctioned at yet another function, raising more money for cancer and leukaemia research.

So those old routes between Aberdeen and the West of Scotland are still wide open, flowing not only with football rivalry but a sense of generosity as well. Who knows? With cutbacks in foreign travel, we might even see a restoration of those traditional holiday links at the Fair this summer.

LIFE ON THE FIDDLE—
WITH MAX JAFFA

THAT pre-war London scene, where you could enjoy the music of Carroll Gibbons at the Savoy or Ambrose at the Mayfair, has always fascinated me. It was part of a distant, untouchable, magical world created for us by the wonders of radio.

Names of big-band leaders became legendary, from Roy Fox and Henry Hall to Harry Roy, Geraldo, and Maurice Winnick. Imagine walking into the Piccadilly Hotel and finding Rachmaninov sitting there—or the great Fritz Kreisler or Artur Rubinstein.

It was all within the daily orbit of another memorable musician, who knew every one of those people and many more. So what a pleasure to spend some time last week with Max Jaffa, for whom life on the fiddle has been such a rewarding adventure.

Max was back in Glasgow, where he first arrived 60 years ago to become leader of the Scottish Orchestra. That had been a chilling experience.

With a seasoned player like David McCallum standing by, they had passed him over for this Jewish kid from London, barely 20. McCallum didn't speak to him for four days, until finally the youngster turned in desperation and said: "Is there something the matter? Do I smell?"

"I'm finding out whether you can play the fiddle or not," McCallum growled. Then, after a pause, ". . . You can play."

So they relaxed and became friends and, when Max Jaffa returned to London, he told his bosses there was no need to search the country for a new leader.

"They had their man in David, who was first-class," Max Jaffa told me. "He modelled himself on the great Fritz Kreisler and,

152

indeed, there were times when he sounded more like Kreisler than the man himself."

It was the great Austrian violinist who gave Max one of his best lessons. While playing at the London Piccadilly, he noticed the maestro sitting at a table nearby.

Kreisler sent for him and said, "Whenever you play, you must always give a performance. If it happens to be a piece of music you don't like, you must give it an even better performance. Then the music will always be enhanced and your playing will never suffer."

Max Jaffa has been living up to that standard ever since. Yet he can let you into a secret known to many top musicians of that day— the great Fritz Kreisler could sometimes play out of tune!

"But even Kreisler's out-of-tune notes were far more beautiful than other people's true ones!" says Max.

His own favourite fiddler was not Kreisler, however. Quite the most exquisite player of this century, he tells you, was Russia's Jascha Heifetz, a name which, curiously, didn't establish itself in the public mind.

Considering Max will not be 80 till December, what a span of musical experience he has known. Playing in London cinemas and Lyon's Corner Houses in the 1920s, this son of a Jewish tailor was performing on a luxury liner and stopping off at Rio to appear as a guest-star at the famous Copa Cabana Hotel on the way to Buenos Aires—all by the time he was 17.

As a top student at the Guildhall School of Music, he was unaware that others studying in the building at the same time included Noel Coward and Fred Astaire.

He can tell you about playing at Buckingham Palace for King George V, a Viennese enthusiast, who danced past with Queen Mary and kept calling: "Let's have 'The Blue Danube'." Max played little else for hours!

It is fascinating to hear what top musicians think of their con- temporaries. One gathers that big names don't always live up to reputations. Maurice Winnick was a better band leader than a musician, so much so that pianist Jack Byfield reckoned he had studied at the Gas, Light and Coke Company—and failed!

Max can vouch for the fact that the famous echo-sound of Mantovani's strings had nothing to do with Mantovani. It was all the work of arranger Ronald Binge, who cleverly invented the sound—and fell out with the boss when he failed to get the credit. Max was leader of the orchestra when it recorded that classic example, "Charmaine".

He spent 27 summer seasons leading his orchestra at the Spa in Scarborough—many of his players came from Scotland—but is best remembered, surely, for his association with Jack Byfield and cellist Reginald Kilbey. Splendid musicians all and, in 35 years, they never had a cross word.

Jack died in 1977 and Reg two years later, and Max carried on till a few months ago. Then, after a lifetime of delighting his vast audience with a very special talent, he put the fiddle in its case and tucked it away for good.

Now, at his home in St John's Wood, he just listens to music, occasionally taking out the fiddle to look at it. But no more. The neat and nimble fingers which once danced on strings were turned instead to writing his life story. *A Life on the Fiddle*, from Hodder and Stoughton, is a fitting farewell.

SOUND OF THE SIXTIES

THE sound of the sixties has a harshness about it, in sharp contrast to the mellow outlook that tends to accompany old age. Old age? Is that what I reached last week with the entry to a new decade?

As the old conveyor belt carries you inexorably on the long and winding road, I suppose there are facts to be faced, preferably with humour.

Making light of the new milestone, I phoned the bus company to see if I qualified for a bus pass. Not unless you are a woman, said the voice at the other end of the line (I didn't think my trousers were that tight).

Because of this shameful discrimination of sex, by which the bus pass must wait for the 65th birthday, a man is expected to work five years longer, even though his average expectation of life is five years less than a woman's.

Ah well, if there ain't no justice, what about a Saga holiday, I thought. Surely I qualify for that. "Oh certainly, sir," said the lady. "In fact you qualified when you were 55."

Well, nobody told me that. Nobody had even told me the truth of what Saga stood for. Originally I thought it was Send All Grannies Away. But visions of blue rinse and bulging midriff were revised when someone let me into the secret that it really stood for Sex And Games for the Aged.

No wonder they were overbooked and had emergency plans for the unexpected heart attack.

For the record, the real meaning of those initials, which signify holidays for the retired, is Social Amenity and Golden Age. Not a lot of people seem to know that.

Forsaking the possible excitements of Saga, I took to reflecting on how I had entered those earlier decades.

155

If the arrival day of July, 1931, escapes me altogether, the accumulation of memory by the 10th birthday is quite staggering. By 1941 I had clear impressions of the mid-thirties, King George V's silver jubilee, followed by his death and the rumpus over Edward VIII.

There was the Empire Exhibition in Glasgow and Chamberlain in Munich, leading into the Second World War. There were warm summers on Fraserburgh beach and bombing devastation of that same small town, where they made munitions for the war effort and Maconochie's food for the nation.

Within the limited consciousness of those first years I had sensed the possible excitements of living; learned to dread the tuberculosis and diphtheria that stalked our classrooms; wrestled with the bewildering emotion that stirred at the touch of a pristine innocence in her dark-brown ringlets.

Even in our small village there were gas masks and air-raid sirens, children evacuated from the greater dangers of Glasgow, convoys of soldiers coming and going, postmen delivering the dreaded telegram that gave notice of "missing" or "killed in action".

With the young men off to war I was paid 10 shillings on a Saturday night to play the drums in my uncle's dance band, in which the accordionist was a local farm servant called Arthur Glennie, later to be the father of Evelyn Glennie, world-famous musician. So much living crammed into the formative years.

By the time I entered my twenties, in 1951, the Second World War was six years behind us; I had been in journalism for three years and was now a daily newspaper reporter in Aberdeen. I bought my first car, a 1947 Ford Anglia, and managed to ruin two big ends before someone told me about putting oil in the engine.

The highlight of that year was attending the Festival of Britain at Battersea Park, London, which seemed much less of an event than the Empire Exhibition at Bellahouston Park in 1938. Elvis Presley was still an unknown schoolboy.

By 1961, when I entered my thirties, I had been married for five years, had a toddler son, moved to Glasgow journalism and put behind me an unsettling decade that was perhaps the least

156

attractive of them all. Kennedy had become President of the United States. Nobody had heard of the Beatles.

The decade when life allegedly begins was a welcome extension of the previous one, just as the Swinging Sixties spilled over into the 1970s. Three children were now at school.

On the 50th birthday in 1981, I paid a sentimental visit to my birthplace in Maud and opened a bottle of champagne in the room where my mother had lain. Now that decade has gone and the next milestone will round off the allotted span, if I should happen to get that far.

If not, I will have enjoyed at least 60 years which were, on balance, more glorious than I had any right to expect. Youth gives way to maturity, then maturity gives way to youth.

Now the toddler son of 1961 has a toddler son of 1991; and the conveyor belt rolls on inexorably. It's the way of the world.

THE REMARKABLE LIFE OF
OTTO BUCHER

THE grim obsession with putting a little white ball in a hole, not once but 18 times—and repeating the monotonous process day after day—is a charm which has so far eluded me.

Given that public attention was riveted to a blanket coverage of the Open at the weekend, however, I concede the deficiency must be mine.

Saturation golf did at least remind me of one of the most delightful encounters of my life and raised the question: Whatever became of Otto Bucher?

You won't find his name among the great golfers of the world, though he has met most of them over the years and can claim a special niche of his own.

I first set eyes on this remarkable character in 1984, while strolling in the Spanish golfing resort of La Manga. He looked like a man in his seventies, swinging down the fairway with an easy gait and refusing the transport of a motorised buggy.

My interest deepened when someone claimed to know that this same smart figure was already into his 100th year. I couldn't believe it; but there was one way to find out.

Over a glass of his favourite Scotch, Mr Bucher not only confirmed that he had been a teenager in the reign of Queen Victoria —and was now the oldest active golfer in the world—but revealed a personal story which I found truly fascinating.

As a Swiss-American based in Geneva, he had been born into the family which owned the world's first chain of hotels, stretching across Europe to Cairo. Young Otto was sent to learn the business at London's Savoy, came to know the legendary Mr Ritz and was running Cairo's best hotel by 1907.

Settling in America in 1912, he made money in textiles and lost it again but finally married the daughter of a wealthy Cuban, from the Havana cigar business.

Even in his 100th year, he was still involved with hotels, his son Robert running the popular L'Angleterre in Geneva and daughter Carmen owning the very exclusive Hassler Hotel in Rome.

Having learned his golf in America, Otto told me about winning the Swiss Seniors tournament four times, most recently in 1983 at the age of 98, and how he was prevented from defending his title by a silly fall down a stair!

We were joined by Brian Barnes, another of golf's great characters, who had also been watching the old man on the fairway and said he had never seen a man anywhere near that age producing golf of such quality.

After our memorable meeting in La Manga, he invited me to visit him in Geneva, an engagement I fulfilled in 1986, accompanied by a friend, Bill Brown, who happened to be captain of Caldwell Golf Club, near Glasgow, that year.

Now approaching 101, Otto had just written himself into the *Guinness Book of Records* by scoring a hole-in-one, the oldest man ever to do so. Was there no stopping this centenarian?

Bill Brown was so intrigued by the story that he invited Mr Bucher to become an honorary member of the Caldwell club, a gesture from the land of golf which he accepted with pleasure.

Having previously played at Turnberry, he could recall visiting Scotland as far back as 1916, when he happened to be nearby at the death of the great Lord Kitchener, a tragedy caused by the mining of HMS *Hampshire* off Orkney.

Yes, he was honoured to be recognised by a Scottish golf club and would hope to pay a visit one day. Without putting too fine a point on it, soon perhaps?

There was really no hurry. Otto had just been out to buy a brand-new Burberry coat—"one that will last me a while," he said optimistically.

159

But a strange silence fell over Geneva. There was no more word of Otto Bucher. Clearly he had passed on to that great fairway in the sky, where eternal sunshine would render the Burberry superfluous.

It only remained for his connection with Caldwell to be written into the story of the club, now being prepared by one of its members, Bob Cowan, a well-known publishing executive.

"Could someone find out when Mr Bucher actually passed away?" said Bob Cowan the other day. It would be a delicate phone call but surely they would understand.

"My father?" said Robert Bucher, at the other end of the line to Switzerland. "He is very well, thank you. Just celebrated his 106th birthday. Now the oldest man in Geneva. He's just back from the South of France and is off again to a hotel near Basle. There's no stopping him really.

"No, he doesn't drive the car any more—gave it up at 103—but, yes, he is still very clear in the mind, has all his faculties; tires a little but that's all."

"Well that's splendid news," I said. "Do pass on the regards of his Scottish friends."

Good old Otto, I chuckled to myself. He's certainly getting the use of his Burberry.

IN SEARCH OF "NO MEAN CITY"

AS a preparation for moving to Glasgow more than 30 years ago, I read the obligatory book, *No Mean City*, written by Alexander McArthur, a well-known character in the Gorbals, and a London professional, H. Kingsley Long.

If it stiffened my apprehension about coming here, it also had about it the ring of truth.

Once I had settled in, there was nothing for it but to walk the streets of the Gorbals, talk to residents and, where possible, visit their homes. Thus I gained an even closer acquaintance with the territory of Johnnie Stark in *No Mean City*—Rutherglen Road, Thistle Street, Hospital Street, Crown Street (where Stark lived), and Waddell Street (where McArthur lived).

I came to know the smell of a close, the restrictions of a single-end, and what a jawbox looked like. Did they really pee in the sink in the middle of the night?

Yes, oh yes. McArthur got it right, the older folk assured me. The swagger of the Razor King, the gang fights on Glasgow Green, the pride and the poverty, the class structure of the tenements.

It was all there in *No Mean City* and, even in the late 1950s, you could sense its authenticity in a Gorbals which had not yet been physically destroyed.

The book helped me get to grips with Glasgow, its history and traditions, down to such details as the origins of a "wee hairy" and the fact that Thursday was always courting night in the city.

But times change and attitudes change with them. In recent weeks, the suggestion that Glasgow might consider some recognition of Alexander McArthur has brought strong reaction from people like Labour leader Patrick Lally, who calls *No Mean City* "a distorted

161

work of fiction" and fumes about the image which he and his like have striven to remove.

Mr Lally himself grew up in the Gorbals, albeit after the days of Johnnie Stark, and must know that McArthur came very close to the truth of life on the south bank in the 1920s.

He should also know that, however swiftly you may remove a mural from a concert hall, you cannot as easily cut away a city's social history just because the warts annoy you.

In Councillor Lally's position, I would feel proud of the civic effort which has so transformed the image of Glasgow in recent years that the parish of my origins can now be seen in broader perspective.

The controversy over *No Mean City* inspired me to reread the book, which became a million-seller and continues to flow from the presses 56 years after its first appearance.

I have to say, it is by no means a classic piece of writing, showing an uneasy alliance between a raw Gorbals talent and a smooth professional from another culture. There are phoney phonetics, like "canny" for "cannot", and an infuriating habit of putting quotation marks round "hoose" wherever it crops up. But the authenticity of the whole work is strong as ever.

Repeating my earlier ritual, I followed the rereading of the book with a wander through the Gorbals the other evening. Not much of it remains. The brown-brick tenements have been replaced by those architectural monstrosities of the 1960s, for which Sir Basil Spence received an award. A police summons would have been more appropriate.

I crossed the Clyde to Glasgow Green, where Johnnie Stark had his "fair fight" with big McLatchie from Townhead, and walked among the ghosts of the 1920s. Well-spoken boatmen now practised their rowing in full view of winos and junkies on the riverbank.

It was along these same banks, one day in 1947, that they found the body of Alexander McArthur. At 46, he brought his bachelor life to an end by drinking disinfectant. He had lived with his mother, worked as a baker, and tried hard to be a writer.

His share of the royalties for *No Mean City* went first to a brother and then to a half-brother, Johnny Milligan, who lived in Duke Street, Dennistoun. When Johnny's wife died, her neighbour, Margaret Wood, saw to it that Johnny got a square meal.

In turn, he left the McArthur share of the *No Mean City* royalties to Mrs Wood, who now lives near Chelmsford in Essex. The rest goes to Kingsley Long's family and the original publishing company.

The whole sad story came back to me that evening last week as I wandered through what is left of the Gorbals.

Each generation will no doubt produce its academics who will make cool pronouncements on the worth or worthlessness of *No Mean City*. Over the years, I have learned to pay most attention to witnesses of the period. And they were in no doubt that, whatever the deficiencies of the book, McArthur's powers of observation were nothing short of brilliant. I'm sure they were right.

Whether or not Pat Lally wants to deny him a plaque is a matter of little consequence. His memorial will be found on the shelves of libraries and bookshops in Glasgow and elsewhere for as long as people will seek out their social history—and want to enjoy an interesting story.

LIFE IS A MONKEY SHOW

I HAVE just made the first jottings for a book I must write one day. It will be dedicated to my offspring—them and theirs—in the hope that they can benefit from the experience of a forefather and in the belief that, in the ridiculous brevity of the human lifespan, there simply isn't enough time to learn only from your own mistakes.

The idea for a volume of *Webster's Condensed Wisdom* flashed into my mind during a visit from the grandchildren, little innocents absorbing their first impressions of a world gone crazy enough already, with whatever to follow only the mysterious gods may know.

As they grow to assess the full spectrum, from wonder to woe, what are they going to make of it? I was asking myself.

Seeking to avoid the pompous cautions of a grumpy grampa, which are so readily put down to doddering dotage, I'll simply put it all into print and leave the young ones to decide, in the fullness of time, how much of a sage or a sucker the old codger really was.

So what, if anything, have I learned on this long and winding road which is worth passing on to the descendants?

First things first. You will hear much discussion on the value of first impressions and may well find yourself revising them. But don't be surprised if you return time and again to find that your initial instincts were uncannily correct.

Then, as your great-great-granny used to say, be careful of beginnings. The first step on any path, particularly a downward one, is always the most difficult. From the second step onwards, I have observed, the will weakens, the conscience dims—and it's downhill all the way.

Try to measure your life in decades and don't be downhearted if the second one, teenage, is a bit of a let-down. It can be a difficult

164

period in your life. The twenties may not be much better. You probably start work, find your life's partner, marry, buy a house and have a family. Too much, too soon.

Make the most of your thirties. Whatever you intend to do, creatively, in this world should have started by now. The mantle of maturity begins to settle. From my amateur researches, I have found that, for some strange reason, the first great pangs of nostalgia hit the human being around the age of 33.

There's nothing wrong with nostalgia but keep it in perspective. Try to remember, for example, that the present is the past of the future and therefore deserves the same respect and attention as the past.

Expect very little of the human race and you won't be disappointed. There is an essential goodness in people but, take it from your cynical old grandfather, there is an essential badness too.

Whoever said that no-one is indispensable in this world must surely have forgotten about mothers. They are the backbone of all family life. Appreciate yours.

The two "puncts"—punctuality and punctuation—have one virtue in common: good manners. Punctuation helps to clarify your meaning and saves the reader's time. Good manners.

Make your own judgment of people who boast of bad spelling, inferring that the genius survives despite it!

A few random thoughts and suggestions:

• Do all things in moderation.

• Appreciate a truly impartial opinion. However much they seek to disguise it, people tend to say exactly what suits them.

• In your entire existence, you will encounter no bias which comes near to matching that of a football fanatic.

• Talk to people as if it might be your last meeting. It sometimes is.

• As you grow older, take a vigorous walk every day.

• Good health will outstrip all your other assets.

• Flee laich, flee lang.

165

Shakespeare got it right when he spoke of all the world being a stage. You may well come to believe that all human behaviour is a performance.

A wise old German friend of mine put it more crudely when he told me: "Life is a monkey show, a cruel joke, a nothing."

It is certainly a monkey show. There will be times when you see his point about a cruel joke. But a nothing?

That will be for you to decide. It will lead you into discussions about the existence of God and far be it from the old grandfather to influence you in that direction.

There is one thought worth considering, however. If the Deity doesn't exist, believers will be none the worse at the end of the day. If He does, atheists are, literally, going to be in for one hell of a shock!

Ah well, on the basis that there are plenty more homespun clichés where these came from, this could just be the start of that book I was talking about. And just a final word of warning on superstition: never cut your nails on a Friday. . . .

SEEKING JUSTICE FOR JESSIE

A MINISTER called Bell set off a few alarms recently when he told his television audience, quite categorically, that the famous Scottish psalm tune, "Crimond", had really been misnamed.

Contrary to what some people thought, he said, that great tune which brings haunting depth to "The Lord's My Shepherd" was written by an Aberdeen tobacconist, David Grant, and not by Jessie Seymour Irvine, daughter of the parish minister at Crimond, between Peterhead and Fraserburgh.

Of course the Rev. John Bell, of the Iona Community, was not the first to make the claim. It is a controversy which has surfaced throughout the century.

Having had some acquaintance with the story, I wondered if Mr Bell could tell us why the tune had been called Crimond in the first place. Who misnamed it? How did a genteel lady of the manse come to be credited with the composition if she had nothing to do with it? Worthy of some investigation, surely.

Having grown up within 12 miles of Crimond, I can only give the version of the story as I have understood it.

Jessie Seymour Irvine was indeed the daughter of the Rev. Dr Alexander Irvine, minister at Crimond in the second part of the last century. She sang in his choir and composed her tune as an exercise, set for the organists' class she was attending at Banff.

When she met David Grant, a well-known figure in the music scene of Aberdeen, she confided she wasn't satisfied with the harmonising of her melody and he agreed to help.

Grant's great friend, William Carnie, well-known Aberdeen journalist and musical figure, was then compiling the *Northern Psalter* of 1872.

167

Jessie's tune was included for the first time in print—with the composer given as David Grant!

"Crimond" didn't become famous until much later, when it was requested by the Queen for her wedding in 1947 and recorded by Sir Hugh Roberton and the Glasgow Orpheus Choir.

If there is no record of Jessie's protest at the time, she probably thought her simple little melody hardly justified a rumpus. At least Grant had got it into print.

Only when it became the best-known psalm tune in the world was there a fresh interest in who composed it.

As a young man, I had several witnesses to the story as I understood it. First, I came to know the Rev. Robert Monteith, who had been minister at Crimond in 1909 and had conducted his own investigation. He could produce a letter from Jessie's sister Anna confirming the story of how Jessie composed it and Grant harmonised it. (Jessie herself died in middle-age.)

Then I married Eden Keith, whose father was a crofter's son from Crimond. It turned out that her grandfather, Alex Keith, had actually sung in the choir, as a young lad, alongside Miss Irvine.

In the earlier part of this century, he was only one of countless witnesses to that self-same story.

Finally, it seemed, justice was coming to Jessie. Her name began to appear in psalm books.

Several books on church music continued, however, to credit Grant—in much the same way, I suspect, as newspapers sometimes perpetuate falsehoods because the journalist accepted as gospel the evidence of previous cuttings, without re-checking.

Some take their cue from an Aberdeen architect and historian, Fenton Wyness, who upheld the claim of David Grant in a book in 1958. I remember Fenton Wyness well.

A florid man with a little bristle of a moustache, he used to visit my Aberdeen newspaper office in the 1950s and, much as I appreciated his lively mind, I detected within his flamboyance a touch of mischief. (He also tried to convince us that Shakespeare appeared on stage in Aberdeen in 1601.)

So church historians, feeding on each other I suspect, once more gave Grant the credit, some suggesting that the other version was mere second-hand gossip—a rather insulting view of solid country folk.

Jessie suffers from lack of the documentary evidence which so impresses academics. They find it easier to support Grant, whose name is there in black and white. But, in my lifetime as a journalist, I have learned to pay attention to what locals say.

Would the people of Crimond, a breed I know well, really have invented the story?

So back to Mr Bell and his TV programme. My inquiries at the BBC had an interesting sequel. The producer, Dr Ian Bradley, author of the *Penguin Book of Hymns* and a respected voice on church music was quick to take responsibility for John Bell's words.

He was, however, prepared to hear the other side of the story, with which he was less familiar. As a result of our exchanges, I can now report that Dr Bradley has revised his opinion.

He told me: "I am now inclined to change my mind. I think I have been hoodwinked by the musical establishment. The more I reflect on it, the more I think the story you have told me is the correct one.

"I can now see how it all happened and I would take the first opportunity to put the record straight."

I think Jessie Seymour Irvine deserves no less.

ROUNDING OFF A YEAR WITH
ALISTAIR MACLEAN

THERE was spring in my step but all else had the scent of autumn as I wandered up from Hyde Park Corner towards Marble Arch one day last week.

Great gatherings of brown leaves, crisp and crackling in the breeze, came hurrying across Hyde Park as I launched myself into a rhythmic walk, breathed in the cool air and marvelled that you could be in the very heart of London with scarce a soul in sight.

This would be the constitutional to clear the lungs before a rather special day in the personal calendar—publication day for my biography of Scotland's famous storyteller, Alistair MacLean, when I would be expected to reverse the normal role of interviewer.

Crossing at Marble Arch, I continued along Oxford Street, past Selfridge's till I came to Regent Street, turning left towards a building which has always fascinated me. Put it down to a wartime childhood but Broadcasting House, along with Winston Churchill and Big Ben, symbolised for me the solid authority of Great Britain which seemed to be all that stood between us and the invading designs of Adolf Hitler.

And there she was last week, her distinctive shape like the prow of a mighty ship, riding the airwaves on what looked like her majestic progress down Portland Place.

In reality, she stands at anchor, her mast a beacon of intelligence which speaks unto nations by the kind of invisible beam which kept the beleaguered Mr Gorbachev well informed on the recent coup within his own land. (He duly expressed his gratitude and admiration.)

To this day, there is about that building something of the stern authority of its first captain, the redoubtable John Reith, the

Scottish engineer who laid down standards which made the British Broadcasting Corporation such a respected organisation.

I had been here only rarely since that first visit of 40 years ago, when I joined the audience of *Grand Hotel*, in the days when the Palm Court Orchestra was led by that fine fiddler, Tom Jenkins.

This time was different. My appointment was with a Scotsman who is at least as tall as John Reith, that genial giant of a man, John Dunn, who runs one of my favourite radio programmes during the teatime hours.

When it comes to interviewing, big John, along with Jimmy Young, leaves the Wogans of this world at the starting-post.

I am usually listening to the John Dunn show on my homeward drive from work. That night, however, I would be *on* it.

Approaching the main door of Broadcasting House, you wonder how they can conduct the world's greatest service from the location of a noisy traffic island. Since my earlier visits, they seem to have turned Portland Place into a major London thoroughfare. Nevertheless, if they ever decide to leave that site, they will have taken the soul out of the BBC.

Once inside, however, you witness a miraculous transformation of sound-proofing in those warrens where the Derek Jamesons, Jimmy Youngs, and Ken Bruces perform their routines.

I was taken up in a lift, along a corridor and down a stair before being delivered to the John Dunn studio, a typical padded cell of a place where I would face the Big Man across the console.

He could have fooled me but some of those smoothly relaxed interviews are actually pre-recorded and slotted into his live broadcast with such technical skill that you wouldn't notice the join.

The illusion extends to those chats with authors, where John Dunn seems so well versed that you could swear he had read all the books himself. Clearly that is an impossibility.

Instead you are rung up on the previous day by a researcher who chats about your book just long enough to formulate a list of questions. The presenter's own intelligence, allied to his easy manner, does the rest.

While interviewing has been an important technique in my own career I have seldom relished the role in reverse. In fact, after the recording, I left Broadcasting House feeling less than happy with my responses.

There must surely have been some skilful editing before it reached the 2.5 million listeners. I didn't hear it for myself but, from what friends tell me, it obviously sounded better than it really was.

Anyway, I wandered into the late afternoon, passing a wee woman who turned out to be Gloria Hunniford and recognising the distinctive voice of the night-time man, Chris Stuart.

It was time to treat myself at the Inn-on-the-Park and to round off the day with drinks on the rooftop of the Park Lane Hilton, acquiring a glow to match that spectacular view of London by night.

After spending a year with the ghost of Alistair MacLean, it was the perfect end to a rather special day.

THE MAGIC OF BEVERLY HILLS

A DAYTIME flight across the United States drives home the vastness of that remarkable country, as well as the totally unpredictable contrast of its weather patterns.

Heading for the West Coast, I witnessed the devastation of a dust-storm that caused a pile-up of vehicles and killed 17 people, cutting into a blizzard stretching all the way from Montana in the north to the Grand Canyon country of Arizona where, incredibly, they were clearing 10ft drifts.

Yet when the 747 glided gently upon Los Angeles that favoured pocket of Southern California was warm and welcoming in the December sun.

Further to confuse the wearied traveller, the glittering entrance to the Beverly Hills Hotel twinkled with seasonal lights as Bing Crosby relayed his annual dream of a White Christmas.

It was here, by the poolside of this very hotel, that Irving Berlin wrote that record-breaking song; and here that I would soothe away life's troubles for the next 10 days, absorbing the heat, walking the silent, palm-lined avenues of Beverly Hills and dining quietly in the famous Polo Lounge, where the motion-picture moguls still thrash out their deals.

I never come this way without paying homage at the former home of George Gershwin in North Roxbury Drive, now occupied by Rosemary Clooney. Eleven years ago I had been admitted to the house next door, where George's brother Ira still lived.

But now so many of the legends are gone. There was a time when Jimmy Durante would suspend his gardening to give you a cheery wave, never objecting to the public attention.

Nowadays they mostly cower behind heavy security, threatening dire consequences if you dare approach their distinctive palaces.

I have seen Jimmy Stewart draw into the drive with his Rolls-Royce and observed, through the casements of his Rodeo Drive home, the unmistakable figure of Gene Kelly hosting a dinner party.

But the best chance of encountering celebrities is still the Beverly Hills Hotel, a fact underlined once more on my first evening. Coming down to the foyer I found myself weaving through a gathering of local residents, come to honour a backroom boy of filmland.

Carol Channing was holding court as Brooke Shields drew admiring glances. Ann Miller did a neat step-and-shuffle to let me past but big Cesar Romero still blocked the way.

I brushed past a handsome figure whose velvet tones prompted a double take. Yes, it was Gregory Peck, as rich and resonant on inconsequential chit-chat as in his more weighty scripts.

I carried the echoes of his screen performance in *The Guns Of Navarone* into the Polo Lounge, where I was about to renew acquaintance with a man he knew well, the director of that epic film, J. Lee Thompson. The pianist played Gershwin.

At 77 Mr Thompson, from a Scottish family related to the great Jack Buchanan, is the oldest active film director in Hollywood. His 50-odd credits range from *Northwest Frontier* and *Tiger Bay* to *Ice Cold In Alex* and *MacKenna's Gold*. Indeed, come 1992 and he will be remaking the Hayley Mills classic of *Tiger Bay*, but in an American setting which seems the route to box-office success these days.

For once in California I joined the tourists, visiting Universal Studios, where they create all those celluloid illusions—then shatter them by revealing how it is all a fake. I'm not sure this is sensible.

Back at the Beverly Hills, the staff had just heard that the famous old hotel was to close down in 1992, for a refurbishment that is likely to take at least two years.

Built in 1912 (the hotel gave its name to the city that grew up around it), the building has been overtaken by the more modern ones. The plumbing and kitchens belong to the original days; bedrooms and bathrooms are on the small side.

So the 262 rooms will be reduced by about 40, but Kerman Beriker, the general manager, assures me they will not tamper with the Polo Lounge, which somehow remains the heart and soul not only of the hotel but of the film world itself.

For all the Californian vulgarity, I must confess to being a sucker for Beverly Hills. But the grandeur belies the problems now affecting its residents. A real-estate man was telling me the repossession rate of those magnificent homes is every bit as high as we are currently facing in Britain.

Back in my room I switched on the television set and tried to figure out local news values. On a day of rejoicing about hostage release—and watching the live transmission of William Kennedy Smith's trial—the top item of that evening's bulletin was a warning that overnight temperatures would get down to the 40s. In preparation for this catastrophe, the lorries would be out on the streets to bring in the homeless.

I put a phone-call through the hotel operator, who restored my sense of balance with a refreshing flow of Clydeside. From Bellahouston to Beverly Hills has been the route of the highly efficient Jeanette Shand.

Suddenly I knew that true sanity was less than 7000 miles away.

HOW WE FILMED "WEBSTER'S ROUP"

IT was just an idea which crossed my mind several years ago. Should I? Well . . . why not? So I lifted the phone and called the BBC to say, rather sheepishly, that I had a suggestion for a television programme.

Oh yes. They had heard this kind of thing before. So what was my bright idea? Well, eight years after his death, I had just sold my father's farm in Aberdeenshire and it occurred to me that on that last day, when the auctioneers would sell the implements and livestock and I would break my family ties with the land, they could make an interesting documentary.

Hmm. They would call me back. It didn't take them long. Yes, that was a rather good idea. It would suit the farming programme on Sunday lunchtime. But as a journalist, would I write the script myself?

Knowing nothing about the mechanics of television, I could only try. So I discussed advance details with director Dick Colthurst, who duly arrived with his camera crew for that rather poignant day in my life.

They shot a few scenes around my native village of Maud, including the cattle mart where my father had spent his entire working life as the ebullient auctioneer.

So to the farm of Honeyneuk, sloping on a picturesque setting towards the edge of the village. As a crofter's boy without capital, my father had dreamed of buying his own few acres one day and nothing would please him more than to buy Honeyneuk.

When it was being sold off by the Brucklay estate 40 years ago, he borrowed every penny of the purchase price—and realised the dream of a lifetime.

We moved from our council house in the village into the

176

comparative grandeur of Honeyneuk, though my mother missed her neighbours and their fly-cups and their gossip.

In time, my father paid off the loan but, alas, there's always a catch. As the only child, expected to follow the tradition of the land, I had not inherited his passion for farming. I was already on my way to the *Turriff Advertiser* with a comparable passion for journalism, which my down-to-earth father dismissed as "a tippence-ha'penny bugger o' a job!"

When his lifetime drew to a close that May evening of 1977, I walked across his beloved braes, now gaunt and silent, and resolved that I would keep it all going in his memory.

That is what I did for another eight years, but farming needs more than long-distance attention and lukewarm interest. So, in 1985, I took the difficult decision to sell.

And now the folk were coming up the farm road, a thousand of them in all, to buy John Webster's cattle and implements. And, as they did, a crack of thunder resounded from the heavens and I could have sworn it came from the direction of the kirkyard at Culsh.

The young men he had trained as auctioneers at Maud down the years were now applying those skills to the break-up of his beloved Honeyneuk. It was a mixture of a day, of torn emotion and warm recollection.

Crofters came up to say what a shrewd judge and good friend my father had been. His guidance and advice were always free to the small man, whose cause he championed.

We had tea and mince baps and a dram and the folk drained away and we saw the last of the light up at the kirkyard, where I made my peace with the old man. As the credits rolled, we played one of my mother's favourite pieces of music, Dvorak's "New World Symphony".

The film was completed within 24 hours, I wrote the script in one evening and the cost was a mere £1000. When it was seen on the farming programme, viewer reaction was such that the BBC decided to give it a wider airing.

It picked up a television award that year and the BBC, knowing a bargain when they saw it, encouraged me to keep going. So, in

1987, I wrote a full-length drama-documentary about growing up in that same corner of Scotland and followed it two years later with another film about the North-east.

Two years on again and I have turned my attention to Glasgow, with a film which has yet to be seen. It is called, appropriately, *Webster Goes West*.

It will save a thousand stamps if I tell those who have been asking about that first venture into television that the roup-day at Honeyneuk is due to be shown again next Monday night. It will act as an introduction to the other three films, which are being presented as a trilogy.

John Brown. In 1926 he started designing the *Queen Mary*

The great *Queen Mary* leaves Clydebank in 1936

Paul Getty: I meet the richest man in the world

Harry Benson: world-class photographer from Glasgow

Rudolf Hess: the mystery of Hitler's deputy

Robert Boothby: the golden voice of a great orator

Malcolm Forbes: "Come on over—we're having a party"

George & Ira Gershwin: Fascinating Rhythm

Irving Berlin: a giant of 20th century melody

left:
Matt Busby as a player,
with goalkeeper
Frank Swift to the right

below:
Jock Stein—created
the Lisbon Lions

above:
Gothenburg—
Aberdeen's night
of football ecstasy

right:
Chris Anderson:
the fair face of
Scottish football

right:
Harry Gordon,
at home in the
Beach Pavilion,
Aberdeen

below left:
Luciano Pavarotti:
he cost me £500 . . .

below right:
Bob Hope in
Scotland—with a
goodbye wave

above:
Scotland The What?
An emotional
farewell

right:
Alexander
Mackendrick:
a Scottish legend
of the cinema

above: The *QE2*—what a reception in Scotland!

left:
Tait's Tower: symbol of the 1938 Empire Exhibition at Bellahouston Park, Glasgow

ROYAL DAY FOR MAUD

IN a new book about his life as a soldier, Frank Coutts tells of the preparations for D-Day and the seven months of training he spent with his battalion of the King's Own Scottish Borderers in a small northern village.

He remembers the day they left that village for good, marching the 28 miles to Aberdeen, and how a schoolboy who had become fascinated by the bustle of military activity in his rural backwater marched alongside his heroes, unwilling to let them go.

At the first halt, miles from the village, they had to persuade the boy to go home. It was a minor incident which nevertheless stuck in the mind of Frank Coutts for nearly 50 years.

"I've never seen a sadder laddie," he writes in *One Blue Bonnet*, the autobiography of a distinguished soldier who reached the rank of Brigadier and became Colonel of the Regiment, as well as heading up the British Legion and the Earl Haig Fund.

I can vouch for the accuracy of his observation for I knew the laddie well. It was me.

I obeyed the military order, delivered in the kindliest of terms, and stood waving through a blur of tears as the Borderers marched away for the grim reality of the Second Front.

I knew some would never return from that battlefield, but Frank Coutts now puts me better in the picture as to who they were and how they met their deaths.

The fleeting contact with our village of Maud was a mere tenth part of their war, taking its modest place in the greater drama. But for us it was the most memorable period in the entire history of our community, where nothing much has been known to happen, before or since.

A sleepy village of 500 people was suddenly brought to life, its

179

population trebled in a day, as dashing soldiers spilled out of their vehicles and took up residence in halls, hotel and nearby castle. They would remain with us for seven months.

With pipes and drums and silver band, they brought music and colour and a new excitement to our village square, not least when their Colonel-in-Chief, the Duchess of Gloucester, made a royal visit to a place which, otherwise, could never have contemplated such a spectacle.

The Borderers were country folk like ourselves and still, I believe, the friendliest people in Scotland. I exchange Christmas cards with KOSBs to this day—one of my heroes, Eddie Edwards, died in Edinburgh last week—and have a standing invitation to their annual reunion in Hawick. (There, I am remembered as "the wee loon fae Maud"!)

As for Frank Coutts, now in his seventies, I remember him as a popular officer in his mid-twenties, a son of the manse, able piper and the man who introduced us to that funny-shaped ball beloved of Borderers.

As they staged seven-a-sides on Winnie Tait's rough grazing, little did I realise that I was looking at Scottish rugby internationalists like the great full-back, Tommy Gray, and Frank Coutts himself.

I knew vaguely that Frank had gone south to be a London bobby before the war but not that his central beat saw him on duty for the Coronation of 1937, or that he was standing nearby as Chamberlain came back from his historic meeting with Hitler, waving that pathetic piece of paper, or that he drew his truncheon on Oswald Mosley's troublesome stormtroopers.

Among other revelations which came later, Frank Coutts's sojourn in the North-east was a return to the land of his maternal roots. His mother, Granny Rose, a wonderful character who lived to be 101 in 1987, was the daughter of Sir John Fleming, Lord Provost of Aberdeen and Liberal MP for West Aberdeenshire.

In his earlier days, John Fleming was working in Dundee when he wandered out for a walk one night and saw sparks flying from a railway engine at a peculiar angle as it crossed the river. Only later did he realise he had witnessed the tragedy of the Tay Bridge Disaster of 1879.

Frank's grandfather, his mother and brother Ben, the well-known Scottish farmer, are just three of the family who have written books about their lives. Now Frank has addressed this one to his grandchildren, taking them through the glaur of war but setting it in the context of a warm-hearted human story, from the pen of a brave soldier who is also one of the most civilised and peace-loving gentlemen you could ever meet.

As well as remembering the sad little boy in Maud, he recalls a delightful story from our village scene, concerning a frail wee woman called Maggie Smith, who fed the farmers on market days and extended her hospitality to the soldiers with no thought of profit.

As so often with saintly souls, Ma Smith was saddled with a lazy, useless, malingering creature of a husband, old Jimmy, who was advised by an impatient doctor to go dig the garden and get a good reek of the soil. "Dig and sniff" was the instruction.

When Ma encouraged him to the task, providing a spade for the purpose, Jimmy paused and growled: "You dig, Maggie—and I'll sniff!"

One Blue Bonnet is published by B&W Publishing, Edinburgh, at £7.95.

THE MAN WHO GUARDED
RUDOLF HESS

THE Government files on Rudolf Hess, Hitler's deputy who came on a mysterious mission to Scotland in 1941, have now been opened up to create another mystery: why they needed to be wrapped in secrecy for half a century.

The fact that they tell us practically nothing we didn't know before has been well established. The theorists will merely continue to have their long-running field day, from his reasons for coming here in the first place to the fact that he may not have been Rudolf Hess at all.

Having met some of those with notions of conspiracy, I suspect an infinite capacity for fertile imagination.

What we know for sure is that the man who crash-landed in a field at Eaglesham, south of Glasgow, on the Saturday night of May 10th, 1941, was eventually produced at the Nuremberg trials of 1946 alongside the other Nazi criminals, who seemed to recognise him as the real Rudolf Hess.

Unlike most others from Hitler's hierarchy, he was spared the gallows and spent the rest of his life in Spandau jail, Berlin, where he died five years ago, aged 93, apparently by suicide. Or was it murder?

Back in 1969, I went to Berlin with the secret ambition of observing him in Spandau. With friends in influential places, I got closer than the law permitted. Beyond that, however, the mission came unstuck.

It all came back at the weekend when I ran into Bob Shaw from Blanefield, a former professor at Strathclyde University, now retired with the precious memory of an extraordinary night in his young life.

182

Bob Shaw had grown up in the Springburn district of Glasgow and by 1941 was a young subaltern, stationed at Maryhill Barracks. Sunday night was dancing night and Bob was all dressed up in his tartan trews and white spats, about to leave for the Plaza, when he was called to the orderly room.

Apologies, but he was needed for special duty at the Buchanan Castle military hospital near Drymen. Get over there now. A German prisoner had been taken to hospital with an ankle injury and Shaw's duty was to guard him.

He could treat himself to dinner at the Buchanan Arms Hotel, but first he would check on his man, who was to be found in a small side-room. Shaw made the acquaintance.

"His name was given as Captain Alfred Horn but his face and large, penetrating eyes reminded me of someone I had seen before," he told me. "After dinner I heard the nine o'clock news. Rudolf Hess was rumoured to be a prisoner somewhere in Britain. Now I knew my man."

Bob Shaw couldn't wait to resume guard on his prisoner. "You are Rudolf Hess, aren't you?" said the eager young officer as he settled down to spend the next few hours alone with Hitler's deputy. The figure in the bed just shrugged.

Interrogation would come later that night with the arrival of the Duke of Hamilton, the man Hess wanted to contact, and Ivone Kirkpatrick, a former official at the British Embassy in Berlin.

His watch and personal belongings were on the window ledge. Since he was not allowed to leave the room, a chamber-pot was provided. In such circumstances the ice soon breaks, and it was not long before Hess was exercising his considerable command of English on the young guard.

Bob Shaw was not slow with his questions. Why had he come? How did he get here? He said he was on a reconnaissance flight, with a plane provided by his friend, Willi Messerschmitt. He knew the Duke of Hamilton, he said. Had met him at the Berlin Olympics in 1936.

In time, the two men struck a level of almost light-hearted exchange.

"We're going to beat you," said Hess.

"Never. We'll knock hell out of you in time," replied young Shaw, who took the liberty of asking about the Jews and the labour camps. Hess told him that the position had been greatly overstated.

So they rambled on in a free-ranging discussion about Poland and Russia and the Hitler Youth, leaving the young soldier from Springburn trying hard to absorb the fact that he was at the centre of a significant event in the history of the Second World War.

At a late hour, Ivone Kirkpatrick and the Duke of Hamilton arrived and Shaw discreetly left the room.

"But I was so curious about the historic events going on inside that I used a shaving mirror above the door to see what was going on," he now confesses.

When the two distinguished figures emerged, Kirkpatrick confirmed that Shaw was aware of his prisoner's identity.

"Don't let him out of your sight. And don't allow yourself to be interviewed," were his instructions.

Bob Shaw was relieved in time for an early morning plate of scrambled eggs, amid all the buzz of speculations, heightened by a call from the telephone operator to say Mr Churchill was coming on the line.

The next he saw of Hess was on newsreels of the Nuremberg trials, when he reckoned his vastly different demeanour was an act to escape the gallows.

By coincidence, Bob Shaw became captain of Buchanan Castle Golf Club and still plays there to this day—glancing over from time to time to that building in which he crystallised his own precious memory of the strange tale of Rudolf Hess.

THE SPIRIT OF THE SEA

IT'S a special breed of men who go down to the sea in little ships, prepared to risk their lives for the safety of others. And they come no more special than the fishermen of Fraserburgh, a town which has been marking the 400th anniversary of its royal charter with a visit from the Queen.

Amid the celebrations, Her Majesty also met 20 widows of local men who lost their lives at sea, among them the crews who perished in three lifeboat tragedies within living memory.

It all came flooding back to me at the weekend when I re-visited this town they call the Broch, to help raise funds for the lifeboat service.

For I grew up within 15 miles of that Kinnaird Head lighthouse which divides the waters of the Moray Firth from the great North Sea, anticipating with unbearable excitement those sunlit days of the 1930s when we went by train to Fraserburgh's golden beach for school picnics.

Then came the clouds of war with the disproportionate threat to a small community which happened to have a Consolidated Tool-works making munitions and a Maconochie's food factory turning out rations.

I can still remember the terror of Guy Fawkes Night, 1941, as the German planes came droning over our village on their way to Fraserburgh. Within minutes we heard the thud of their bombs, a direct hit killing 35 people in the Central Bar, where my father had joined some farmers for a drink that very afternoon.

The devastation of bombed-out buildings and the lorry-loads of coffins had a profound effect on the child mind. In the heaviness of my young heart, I had gained first hint of the calibre and quiet courage of the Brochers.

But I came to know even more about it on a February day of 1953, by which time I was the resident reporter of the local daily paper. The Great Gale of January 31st, nature's wildest demonstration in that part of the country, had blown itself out and a spring-like calm descended upon that North-east shoulder.

But under those blue skies and sparkling sun the lingering turbulence of an angry sea still swelled towards the shore. Fraserburgh's after-lunch nap was shattered with a cry "The lifeboat's over!"

The whole town ran to the foreshore to confirm its worst fears. The *John and Charles Kennedy* had gone to escort back to port some yawls that were caught in a dangerous swell. Returning to harbour, it was caught by a freak wave and turned on its face.

We were there in time to see Coxswain Andrew Ritchie, a powerful swimmer, thrashing his way to safety, when up came a piece of wood and struck him on the head. He was one of five men to perish that day. Only Charlie Tait survived, his father having gone under.

That night I had the melancholy task of visiting the widows to collect details and photographs of the dead men. Old Mrs Tait, a widow by a few hours, sat by her fireside and was able to rationalise on the good fortune that at least her son had survived, him with his wife and young children.

I marvelled at her spirit. And I marvelled again the following week when they called for volunteers to replace a lost crew and the first man on the doorstep was her son Charlie. With him was his younger brother, come to replace their father.

Close behind them came Joe Ritchie, offering himself as coxswain in place of his brother Andrew.

At moments like that you choke up and wonder how deep is the reservoir of courage and character which lies hidden in the souls of so-called ordinary men and women.

Fraserburgh had lost a lifeboat before, in 1919, and it would lose another in 1970. By then I had gone off to the south, but the news of yet another Fraserburgh lifeboat disaster sent me scurrying back north.

I was there that night, appalled by the whole sense of *déjà vu*. In 1954 I had seen HRH the Duches of Kent christening the new boat which took her name and now, 16 years later—exactly the lifetime of the previous vessel—it too had perished at sea. Five more men were gone, with one survivor.

So I went back to Fraserburgh on Saturday and there I met Albert Sutherland, coxswain of the present craft, the *City of Edinburgh*. Now 46, Albert remembers being taken by his father to witness the wreckage of the 1953 lifeboat.

By the 1970 disaster, he was himself a lifeboatman but escaped death by the chance that he was fishing at Scrabster that day.

None of that dissuaded him from what fishermen see as their duty to the fraternity. And you can see it in his honest face that he is hewn from the same rock as his predecessors.

And when you ask if the family traditions of lifeboat service still survive, he silently points to his No. 2 coxswain—his brother James. Then to his No. 3 coxswain—his own twin brother Victor!

When you hear that Victor's son has just joined the crew and that other relatives have been in the complement of six, you simply turn away in a glow of admiration and thank the Lord for the continuing quality of those men who go down to the sea in little ships.

In anyone's language they are a truly extraordinary breed.

STILL LIFE IN THE LORDS

"SO they haven't abolished the place?" said the cheerful Cockney cabbie as he drove me into Parliament Square last week in time for lunch at the House of Lords.

"Not yet," I said as we drew alongside the Palace of Westminster and surveyed the sheer magnificence of that historic building.

In the neighbouring Commons, some supporters of Scotland United (no, madam, it's not a football team) were preparing an end-of-term protest and would have joined happily, I'm sure, in any move to abolish the Lords.

But once inside, you wonder if there is any power on earth to do away with this upper chamber. For history is all around you, solid and majestic, from architectural splendour and pompous portraits to the pageant of present incumbents, some shuffling figures from a distant era who raise hairs on the back of your neck because you could have sworn they were long since dead.

In the hush of those hallowed corridors I found myself leaping to safety from the devilish antics of a man in a self-drive wheelchair.

In the face I could see traces of a younger Peter Thorneycroft, dynamic politician dating back to the 1930s. Now in his eighties, the dynamism had been channelled to new purpose.

Soon you are reminded that this is no exclusive haven of the privileged aristocrat and well-connected Tory. The man now being addressed as Baron Mason of Barnsley is quickly identified as Roy, former Labour Minister, down the pits at 14 and proud of it.

Lord Ennals of Norwich is his old colleague and former Minister, David—and there are plenty more of the leftish persuasion who once, you could have sworn, wouldn't be seen dead in a place like this. Most of them, however, can still be classed among the living, if some a little less than others.

One of the membership who is certainly among the living was my lunch companion for the day, that extraordinary Scots lady, Baroness Elliot of Harwood. Her lively conversation is proof of an active mind yet, suddenly, you are aware from the topics that here is living history at the lunch table.

She can tell you, for example, that her Glasgow father was born in 1823, a double lifespan which puts them in the *Guinness Book of Records*.

Lady Elliot herself was visiting 10 Downing Street as far back as 1908, when her older sister, the famous Margot Asquith, was married to the Prime Minister of the day.

Indeed she used to play golf regularly with Mr Asquith, beating him with that skill which took her to a final play-off for the Scottish Ladies' Championship at Muirfield in the late 1920s.

Now in her 90th year, Lady Elliot has known every Prime Minister since Asquith, except John Major, who has still to meet her. Even before she married Walter Elliot, distinguished parliamentarian and former Scottish Secretary, she was on familiar terms with Winston and Ramsay, Ernest and Harold.

Indeed it was Harold Macmillan who introduced women to life peerage—and enabled her to be the first ever woman member to speak in the Lords.

So our conversation ranged over great orators of the century and, much as she disliked Lloyd George, who displaced her beloved Asquith, she graciously conceded that he was probably the greatest of them all.

"I remember once being in the football ground in Cardiff when he was due to address the crowd," she recalls. "The place was packed when out into the centre of the large arena came this small man. Lloyd George was very small and you could hardly see him there. But he started to speak—and suddenly the whole place was electrified. It was a remarkable performance."

At the next table, former Scottish Secretary George Younger was entertaining guests who had come to see him introduced as Lord Younger of Prestwick.

So we adjourned to the chamber in time for a ceremony full of

189

pomp and colour, red robes and ermine. Margaret Thatcher, looking incredibly youthful, slipped into the front bench beside Lord Hailsham and seemed to be following with motherly interest the swearing-in of this man whose fight for Prestwick Airport will live on in his title.

After all, he was one of her boys in those controversial days of Thatcherism which are already taking on the scent of history.

So to question time and the rather inept performance of some wet-eared Government spokesman whose place in a House of Lords defied understanding. It took that old warhorse, Hailsham, to remind him of the answer he should have been giving to a persistent and understandably dissatisfied questioner.

I took one last look at the impressive interior of the House and remembered that on my very first visit to Parliament in the post-war years, the Commons were meeting here while the bomb damage of their own chamber was being repaired.

I could hear the echoes of Churchill and Boothby, Bevan and Morrison. And I knew that the colour of their successors had turned to a faceless shade of grey.

On the way out, adjourning to a more private chamber, I found myself in the next stall to one of his lordships, fumbling under his red robes. Suddenly I was overcome by the humour of this less-than-dignified moment in the life of a peer.

Indeed it gave a whole new slant to the meaning of the word.

WELCOME TO
A FELLOW CALLED FRASER

TO return from an extended session at Babbity Bowster's to find that you have become, prematurely and unexpectedly, a grandfather in your own lunchtime is the quickest route I know to the restoration of an even and sober outlook.

Having taken the telephoned news with guffaws of disbelief that it could be so early, you lean back in your chair and try to envisage the 7lb 1oz bundle of new life kicking his way into the world in faraway Oxford and wonder what heavyweight proportions he would have achieved had he gone the full distance.

Then, putting personal matters aside and keeping abreast of the day's happenings, you tune into the news services and are reminded quite forcibly that your latest grandson has come to inherit a pretty ghastly world.

If, in the years to come, he cares to look back at the newspapers in the week of his birth, he will read an appalling catalogue of man's continuing inhumanity to man.

If he takes to the reading of history, he will be all the more bamboozled to find that the crimes and iniquities of long-gone times are repeated down the generations with sickening regularity.

Who would have believed that, 50 years after confronting the scourge of the Nazis, we would be facing once more the traces of their methods in war-torn Yugoslavia?

Can we look at the pictures of those concentration camps without being rendered speechless at the repetition of history?

Can we possibly hear the sobs and study the bewildered faces of refugees being driven from their homes, some not knowing what has become of their fathers, mothers, sons or daughters, and fail to be haunted by the kind of misery which is bound to attend the rest of their lives?

Can we fully take in the unspeakable evil of Saddam Hussein as he continues, with self-righteous defiance, to impose horrors upon his own people?

And, perhaps worst of all, can we view the obscenity of what is happening in Somalia without realising what an appalling mess the human race has made of this most precious of all blessings, the gift of life?

You would think we would have learned some lessons by now; but we learn very little. And if that depressing view of human behaviour comes mainly from a world outside our own, then the picture on the domestic front is, relatively, little better.

But if Tuesday's child looks back to the day of his birth he will read at least one story which will warm his heart and soften the impression of a bitter and sinister society.

It is the story of 10-year-old Paula Moss who, before dying of a brain tumour, expressed the wish that her organs should be given to others. As a result, a 57-year-old man received her heart, an eight-month-old baby her liver and a teenage boy and girl her kidneys. The corneas of her eyes gave sight to two people.

What an extraordinary gesture from a little child, whose mother was thus suitably comforted by the fact that her own tragic loss had at least given new life to six other human beings.

We have so much to learn from the innocence of childhood before it becomes stained by the corruption of age.

If the royal family still exists in his mature years, Fraser Webster might wonder how it managed to survive the topless romps of a rather silly princess in the week of his birth.

Speaking of which, if he cares to consider that the world is still an ill-divided place, he may be interested to know that, as his mother underwent a long observation in that Oxford hospital, the baby brought in from the next room for inspection was a chap called George.

If that means nothing, it will have to be further explained that wee George was already, at the moment of his arrival, saddled with a grand title—Earl of Sunderland and heir to the £100m fortune which goes with being the son of the Marquis of Blandford and grandson of the Duke of Marlborough.

On the lighter side, too, he might care to cast an eye over the people with whom he shares a birthday and find they are a pretty mixed lot, ranging from novelist Brian Aldiss, film director Roman Polanski and professionally witty Willie Rushton to the former American Secretary of Defence, Caspar Weinberger, actress Shelley Winters and the well-known London-Scottish journalist, Charlie Wilson.

His father, who could deliver a decently fast ball for Clydesdale as a youngster, may not yet have noticed that his new son also shares a birthday with one of his own cricketing heroes, the great Godfrey Evans.

What he and his wife will certainly have noticed is the fact that their son came to intrude on their own third wedding anniversary.

Meanwhile back home in Scotland, the old grandfather, having just been sobered up from a farewell liquid lunch with his office room-mate, Murray Ritchie (off to be our man in Brussels), regarded this colourless condition as no decent way of marking the occasion. So he promptly went back out to celebrate.

THE GENTLE LADY
THAT WAS MISS CATTO

MEMORIES washed over me last week as I watched a fresh crop of five-year-olds, aglow with shiny-faced anticipation, setting out on that very first journey to school.

Despite all the hazards of modern living, an exciting adventure lay ahead; it was a momentous day that would stay with them surely for the rest of their lives.

I could only wish them all the happiness of my own initiation, a day which has stayed with me for all of 56 years and which sprang vividly to mind once more in a week of mixed fortunes.

In that setting of 1936 there had been the rumblings of Hitler outby, while the death of King George V that year would soon bring us the upheaval of his son, the Prince of Wales, falling for an American divorcee in a royal scandal which had no equal until recent times.

But all of that, plus a lingering Depression, provided no more than a distant background to the wonderful world of Miss Catto's infant classroom at Maud School.

Who could forget the smell of Plasticine and fresh exercise books, and the pleasing scent of the little girl across the passage, whose mother had dabbed a hint of perfume on her offspring?

As autumn days blew in, a roaring fire would greet us in that anteroom of life, wet coats and gloves hung up to dry on sturdy guard-rail.

As well as grounding us thoroughly in the basics of education, Miss Catto made cocoa to accompany the lunchtime "piece" of rural bairns, took in the bank money, provided the Friday caramel out of her own pocket—and all on a miserable salary of £130 per year.

194

Her golden hair would glint in the morning sun and the serenity of her manner gave the fledglings of life a soothingly gentle introduction to a world beyond the nest.

Without knowing it, I suppose, we loved Miss Catto dearly and would never forget her. And on Friday afternoons we waved her on to the Aberdeen train as she went home for the weekend to look after a delicate sister.

As the years stretched out and I regained her acquaintance on adult terms, she would tell me tales of the classroom, recalling the day she had asked us what we wanted to be when we grew up and I replied, with deep passion, that I wanted to be "jist like Robbie Burns".

Miss Catto had re-told the story in the staffroom, adding the hope that, in certain respects at least, I wouldn't turn out to be too much like Robbie Burns!

So we laughed over old times and remembered sad times too, the dreaded tuberculosis and diphtheria which stalked the pre-war classroom and would regularly strike us into horrified silence at the passing of a little white coffin.

Only then, in our later meetings, did I discover the full scope of her teaching career. Having been ushered in with the new century, she taught in the coalmining areas of Fife during the poverty-sticken twenties, a harrowing experience which so troubled her compassionate nature that her politics took a turn to the left.

It was in 1926, the year of the General Strike, that she came north to our Buchan village, where she would remain till well through the Second World War. The rest of her working life was spent in the city of Aberdeen and it was there that she was spared for a long and happy retirement.

When I came to write a couple of autobiographical books, there was an obvious and special niche for Miss Catto. And when I turned those books into television films, I dearly wanted to bring her before the camera.

By then she was in her 90th year and the word came back that she was not up to the ordeal. At the last minute, however, there was a change of heart. Having collected her by car in the Seafield

195

district of Aberdeen, I drove her to the Banchory home of her former teaching colleague, Miss Morrison, and together they faced the cameras for the first time in their lives.

In the film *Northern Lights*, the three of us talked over old times and it was clear that, despite her naturally modest disposition, this belated burst of gratitude and public attention had been a welcome boost to morale in her old age.

She said as much in her letters. It had brightened an eventide in which she would quietly confide that the process of growing old was really no fun.

With sturdy independence, however, she maintained her own home until recent times when she moved into accommodation for the elderly.

And there last week at the age of 92, she slept away, as quietly and gently as she had lived. We gathered at Mannofield Church, Aberdeen, to see her on her way, remembering a very special lady who personified that breed of infant mistress whose service to Scottish education could never be suitably rewarded.

And as Miss Catto took her leave of us, amid thanksgiving for a life which had enriched so many others, that new crop of youngsters went happily on its way to school for the first time.

It was the kind of end and beginning which she so readily acknowledged as being the natural order of things.

THE GENIUS OF JOCK STEIN

IT is a perilous business, I know, to put the label of greatness on an individual. But that wouldn't prevent me from nominating Jock Stein among the Great Scots of his time.

Seven years after his sudden death in the heat of a World Cup football match in Wales, I have been thinking more and more about the Big Man in this year which would have marked his 70th birthday.

Even more poignantly, it is the 25th anniversary of the greatest moment in his extraordinary life—the European Cup Final of 1967 when, without the benefit of modern millions, he took a bunch of home-grown boys in the East End of Glasgow and fashioned them into a team of world beaters.

It may have been a story about football, straight from the *Boys' Own* tradition, but it was much more a story of one man's leadership qualities.

Far from the playing fields of Eton, the character of Jock Stein was hewn from the coalfields of Lanarkshire, where sweat ran in black rivulets and boys emerging from the bowels of the earth were glad to exercise leg and lung in the pursuit of a ball under nature's own light.

From such depths of human trial, which at least moulded men of strong mind and will, the prospect of professional football would offer an escape route.

It is a testimony to their breed that, within the same period, the three greatest football managers in Britain came out of the Scottish pits—Jock Stein of Celtic, Matt Busby of Manchester United, and Bill Shankly of Liverpool.

Of the three, Stein was the least performer as a player. Indeed, most of his career was a weekend alternative to digging coal, the modesty of Albion Rovers being finally exchanged for the greater obscurity of Llanelli.

Then fate took a hand. When Celtic needed a stop-gap centre-half because of injury, an old servant of the club, Jimmy Gribben, piped up: "Whit aboot yon fella Stein wha used tae be wi' Albion Rovers?" Few could remember him.

But Jimmy's brainwave not only worked; it brought to Celtic Park the man who turned out to be, in my opinion, the most significant figure in the entire history of Scottish football.

As a natural leader, the stop-gap Stein became captain of a victorious Celtic team. Thereafter, he coached the young boys at the club, went off to prove his managerial prowess with Dunfermline and Hibernian—and was called back to Celtic in 1965. Those youngsters he had groomed were now ready to become his first team.

Within two years he had moulded them into the best in Europe, giving them legendary status as the Lisbon Lions, and not only set new standards of excellence in Scotland but changed the face of European football by turning cynical defence into imaginative attack.

Here was a man of destiny, the Protestant who would bring unimaginable success to the stronghold of Catholicism.

On visits to his office, or his home in Rutherglen or Croftfoot, I tried to get to grips with the personality of Stein, who had developed a hefty frame in middle-age, with a noble head topped off by black, wavy hair.

As he talked, in a slightly hoarse voice, it was fascinating to observe that rare talent which reduces apparently complex matters to simple terms.

He would spill out nuggets of wisdom which suddenly became so obvious that you wondered why nobody had thought of them before. It is the mark of a superior mind.

In fact he was a curious mixture of simplicity and cunning, wit, warmheartedness and quick temper, a brilliant psychologist who knew exactly how to produce reaction in his fellow humans.

The great Jimmy Johnstone was petrified of flying. Before a two-leg European tie with Red Star of Belgrade in 1968, Stein made a deal with the Wee Man, whose book I happened to be "ghosting" at the time.

"If we can build a four-goal lead in Glasgow," he said, "you won't have to go to Belgrade." All fired up, Johnstone laid on Celtic's opening goal. But it was soon cancelled out by Red Star. The little red head went down. But not for long.

Out he went in the second half, scored two brilliant goals himself and laid on two more. At 5-1, the final whistle blew and Johnstone was running around like a man possessed, shouting "I'll no' need tae go!" And he didn't.

In 1975, Stein was seriously injured in a car crash and was never the same man again. He was displaced at Celtic Park but recovered sufficiently to manage the national team.

So much of it comes back with the video called *Jock*, a fitting tribute by Jim Hunter, former head of television at BBC Scotland. Sensibly, Hunter used archive material to let Stein speak largely for himself.

Just what a truly eloquent man he was I had nearly forgotten. I watched it with players from his own day, Sean Fallon and Neil Mochan, and Lisbon Lions like Bill McNeill and Jimmy Johnstone.

Stein's son George flew in from Switzerland. His widow, Jean, watched it privately at her home in Newlands.

The camera zoomed in on the Big Man during that last match in Wales. There he was . . . just minutes before he collapsed and died. The frame was frozen into silence. And so were we grown men blowing their noses and remembering a truly Great Scot.

WHY RABBITS LOVE MY GARDEN

I CAN tell you with some authority that we are right into the season
of the flower show. Not because I know anything about flowers but
because I have been opening so many of these shows this summer—
a situation, I may say, which has generated among my friends such
outbursts of disbelief and uncontrolled hilarity as might have caused
offence if I had been a delicate soul.

But I'm not. I have simply answered the calls dutifully and jour-
neyed as far as the 400-mile round trip to the Moray Firth coast to
deliver a three-minute introduction to some of the most spectacular
displays of nature's bounty you could possibly imagine.

Apart from flowers so scented as to close your eyes in drooling
reveries, I have witnessed carrots, leeks and marrows which have
burgeoned to a size of near-vulgarity.

Old and young, it seems, are growing things with great relish
these days and nothing impressed me more than the magnificent
vegetables of a man who is blind. I overheard someone telling him
how splendid they looked. Not quite satisfied with his entries, however, he replied modestly that they didn't "feel" good enough to
him. His achievements were still remarkable.

In such company there is no point in trying to bluff your way to
some apparent knowledge of the subject. In my opening speeches I
have come clean and confessed that the breadth and depth of my
horticultural ignorance have to be seen to be disbelieved.

The truth is that I am the owner and custodian of one of the last
unspoiled wildernesses in Scotland, well worthy of a commendation
from those ecological freaks who want to preserve nature as it used
to be.

Field mice approaching my territory bring their own periscopes.
And each year I receive an application from the International

Copulation of Rabbits (Strathclyde branch) for permission to hold their convention in my back garden, in the knowledge that their safety is assured since nobody will be able to find them there.

If I exaggerate a little, it is certainly true that I have never been able to tell my geraniums from my pelargoniums and, until I actually saw the word written down, I used to think that "floribunda" was a girl from Clarkston.

The irony of all this is that the garden which now stands as testimony to my horticultural failings was once a showpiece on the South Side of Glasgow. People came from miles around to witness the wonders of Mr Sutherland's enclosure.

He had broken it in, as the first occupant of the house in 1934. There was certainly one owner between Mr Sutherland and myself but if that particular gent happened to learn his gardening skills in the Gobi Desert, turning a floral dream into a nightmare, then I must stand accused of completing the catastrophe.

Mind you, people still come to see this example of what happens when nature rules. But they are generally of that breed which studies the preservation of wilderness in the suburban environment.

They are intrigued to hear about potatoes I once planted which went down in history—as the crop which never came up again, evidently preferring to push their shoots towards the horrors of hell rather than face the impossible struggle of gaining daylight in Webster's wilderness.

I tell them of an early attempt to grow lettuce, dating back to the days when all this worried me considerably. Determined to show that I was not totally useless in a garden, I used to water them under cover of darkness then stand by in semi-religious pose, head bowed, eyes closed, muttering under my breath a mixture which both threatened and beseeched the damned things to grow.

Neighbours who observed this solemn ritual, while peering from behind curtains, would later inquire if I had been trying to put a new slant on the universal phrase "lettuce pray". (Don't some people have a warped sense of humour?)

I have tried examining myself to see not so much where I went wrong but why I didn't come right in the first place. The conclusion is that, if the best farmers make the worst gardeners (and that tends to be true) then the sons of those same best farmers are even worse gardeners than their fathers.

When I first came to Glasgow and acquired a house more than 30 years ago, I also noticed that I was developing an ailment of recurring regularity.

The doctor diagnosed it as myalgia, which a medical friend later confessed was a kind of ragbag term applying to a list of ailments which doctors know nothing about.

They just draw a knowing expression and say "Oh yes, that's myalgia", as if they know all about it and it isn't much to worry you in any case. They send you away with some harmless pill which will keep you quiet until the condition corrects itself, which most illnesses do anyway.

My own particular myalgia took the form of a muscular ache and fatigue but its significance to this article is that it used to happen regularly at the beginning of the gardening season.

I couldn't understand it. My wife didn't believe it. She said it was all psychological. By that, I suspect, she meant that the muscle in need of attention lay somewhere inside my head. And she could have been right.

THE MAJESTY OF WASHINGTON

EVERY now and then it comes upon us—the need to recharge the batteries which keep us going in this troubled world. And for 25 years now I have been heading for the United States, which seems to fulfil that function better than most.

Oh, there is much that is wrong with the United States—but a good deal more that is right. They work hard, tackle their problems head-on. And when it comes to serving the public, they have most other countries beaten hands down.

I suppose our own attitude of a demeaning role is a leftover from the day of downtrodden servants. But the Americans don't see it that way. They are happy to serve with a smile—and even when they trot out the traditional cliché, they sound as if they genuinely want you to have a good day.

So the first stop in this land of doughnuts, pancakes and waffles was Washington where, after recovery from the misdemeanours of British Airways, I went out to rediscover the wonders of the American capital.

I hadn't been here since the country's 200th anniversary in 1976 when, on the morning of the fourth of July, I stood by the Washington Monument, on that broad sweep of the Mall, and tried to absorb the reality of American history.

Its symbols were all around, from the Capitol, at one end of this majestic landscape, to the Lincoln Memorial at the other. Behind lay the Jefferson Memorial and, in front, the gleaming columns of the White House.

I returned to that same reference point last week and have not changed my opinion that Washington, for all its social problems, is one of the world's most truly beautiful cities.

How extraordinary that a nation so geared to the excesses of publicity has not been able to spread the word, with any adequacy, of what a physically spectacular place it is.

So I walked the broad avenues, recalling so much of the Paris on which they were modelled, visited the White House, toured the city by night, and dined in Martin's Tavern in Georgetown, a favourite haunt of John F. Kennedy.

That thought took me once more to Arlington, burial place of the nation's heroes, and there I stood by the eternal flame of President Kennedy's grave and read again his immortal words about asking not what your country could do for you, but what you could do for your country.

In this haven of heroes there was bitter irony in those words which had seemed so impressive at the time. I remembered what his villainous father had done for his country, cheating his way to a massive fortune which financed his obsession to see a Kennedy in the White House.

Well, it worked—but what a price to pay. Even the glamorous President himself has now become such a tainted figure. Thoughts strayed to old mother Rose, still alive, with the debris of her family now scattered as the ashes of ignoble ambition.

I cheered myself up with a drive down the sylvan state of Virginia to Colonial Williamsburg, restored by Rockefeller money and with the utmost in good taste.

No motor traffic here, only horses and carriages and the citizens enacting a living memorial to a bygone age, with craftsmen such as bootmakers creating their wares as you watch, then selling them on a commercial basis.

Such was the peace and tranquillity of Williamsburg that I could have been persuaded to stay there for ever.

Next door at Jamestown, the first English settlement, I ran into a blacksmith who hailed from the Bullers of Buchan, before visiting Carter's Grove, one of the old Virginian plantations.

There I was harangued by the descendant of a slave, now a tour guide, about the conditions of his ancestors—and shown examples of their living quarters. I was tempted to tell the poor fellow that I have known Scots in the twentieth century who lived in worse conditions than that!

But diplomacy reigned and I headed for New York, which remains the living contrast to all I had seen in Williamsburg. Yet who can deny the magnetism of Manhattan?

Spoiling myself in a luxury hotel, I sampled once more the charms of this seductive city, walking through Central Park to Strawberry Fields, just opposite the Dakota Building. It's the former home of John Lennon, which I had first seen in 1980, just days before the Beatle was killed by an assassin on his own doorstep.

And I rounded off the American adventure at the Rainbow Room, on the 65th floor of the Rockefeller Centre. Dining in a small alcove and enjoying the cabaret talents of a favourite singer, Maureen McGovern, I found myself slightly distracted by the man in the next alcove.

He was roughly of my own vintage and an equal admirer of Miss McGovern, as shown in his rhythmic reveries when she gave us songs from the pen of the great Stephen Sondheim.

It was only when she finished and came across to kiss my neighbour that I realised I was sitting side by side with Sondheim. Yes, the man acknowledged as the greatest living songwriter, all the way from *West Side Story* to "Send In The Clowns" was having an evening out.

Needless to say, I didn't pass up the opportunity of conversation which seemed like the perfect way to round off a stimulating trip. The memory of that Manhattan night will linger like a Sondheim song.

FROM MANUEL TO MACLEAN

HEADING for a function in the Burnside district of Glasgow, I deliberately retraced my steps of more than 30 years ago in an attempt to compare the vibrations of totally different periods.

For it was in Burnside that I made my home in those early days of working in the city. After smoke-filled, frenetic nights at the sub-editors' desk, we would walk part of the way home in the hope of clearing head and lungs—a rather ambitious exercise when you recall the smog which blighted Glasgow's atmosphere in days of heavy industry.

Finally, we caught all-night buses to our respective destinations, in my case Stonelaw Road, which ran up from the ancient burgh of Rutherglen to Burnside. From there I walked the final lap along Limeside Avenue to the furnished bungalow at 93 Calderwood Road.

That solitary ritual in the early hours of the morning raised some apprehension in the newcomer to the Glasgow conurbation, who had not only confirmed the history of razor-gangs by reading *No Mean City* but had chanced upon Burnside in the aftermath of Peter Manuel, Scotland's most notorious killer.

His dastardly deeds had included the massacre of the Watt family of Burnside and five other people in the surrounding districts.

Manuel had recently been hanged in Barlinnie but the reek of evil still hung powerfully over Burnside, at least in my imagination as I pulled a collar against the early-morning bite and headed home without delay.

From Limeside Avenue I had a panoramic view of Glasgow by night, heightened by the glow from steelworks chimneys.

Familiarity eventually gave me confidence in Burnside, and affection too. My immediate surroundings lay deep in the pile of Templeton's Carpets, which seemed to own the place. Templeton's playing fields were across the street, along with Templeton's tennis courts and Templeton's bowling club.

Templeton's, with its factory in Bridgeton, had built Limeside Avenue as homes for its managers and key workers. There was a sense of community about the place, even if I did have difficulty with the identity of suburban sprawls, never quite knowing if Burnside was part of the ancient burgh of Rutherglen or more truly a part of Lanarkshire.

Coming from the country, however, I appreciated the fact that Mrs Perratt ran her dairy from the house on the corner, even if my belated sleep was disturbed by the early rattle of bottles.

In time, and rather reluctantly, I came to leave Burnside. But I was far from finished with it.

When publisher Ian Chapman asked me to write the biography of Alistair MacLean, the first researches led me straight back to the streets I knew so well. For MacLean had done all his teaching at Gallowflat School, Rutherglen, and walked along my Calderwood Road to his furnished rooms at 33 Drumsargard Road.

We had missed each other on that route by only a few years. Since he gained fame and fortune with *HMS Ulysses* and *The Guns of Navarone* he had given up teaching in Rutherglen and fled to tax exile in Switzerland.

But it was here that I would find the class of '55 whose pupils, by then in their late 40s, were happy to recall Mr MacLean as a strict but fair teacher who made things interesting, even for those who were not academically inclined.

It was in this neighbourhood that I would find teachers like Dougie Seggie, MacLean's old pal in the staffroom with whom he had bought an old boat and sailed into a near-fatal escapade on the stormy west coast of Scotland.

From those beginnings, my research had taken me from Burnside to Beverly Hills and on to Geneva, Venice, and Dubrovnik, before I could come to grips with the elusive personal story of this Scottish schoolteacher who had escaped the classroom in fairy-tale fashion only to see his dream disintegrate into a nightmare.

Much midnight oil was burned before that book was published

just a year ago. And now that the paperback edition was due to appear, I realised that its publication date coincided with another appointment in my diary.

For the first time in my life I had been invited to a function on that very same evening in, of all places, Burnside. Though Templeton's Carpets had long since vanished from the district, the bowling club had been handed over to its members. Now they were marking a major milestone in their history and I was to join them in the celebration.

I was invited to give them a rundown of my Burnside connection, all the way from Manuel to MacLean. Having come straight from the paperback launching of the author's biography, there I was, standing on his old route to school recalling more innocent days before he set out on the road to triumph and tragedy.

On my way to that function, as I was saying, I retraced my own steps along Limeside Avenue to Calderwood Road and tried to encompass some incredible events of the intervening years.

New housing, where cattle used to graze, now spoils the view over Glasgow and the menace of Manuel has receded into history. But you can still pull a collar against the snell wind and feel perhaps that much remains the same.

Except that the emotional gulf is not for bridging. And that kind of change takes place entirely within your own being.

PERCHANCE TO DREAM

THERE'S a square mile of central London which I can never traverse without thoughts of two contrasting personalities who influenced the emotions of my early life. For very different reasons I have been thinking particularly this week of Winston Churchill and Ivor Novello.

Churchill, of course, because a young academic has reassessed him in the cold light of perspective and concluded that, far from leading us to victory in the Second World War, he really messed the whole thing up.

Evidently, he should have done a deal with Hitler which, among other things, would have saved the Empire. Well, I suppose that is one way to look at it.

Dr John Charmley will no doubt make money from his speculative ramble and heighten his reputation for controversy. But he reckons without the public mood of the time and I have long since discovered that that is a perilous path for any historian.

I clearly remember what the adults were saying about Dr Charmley's appeasing hero, Chamberlain, and can imagine their reaction if we had chummed up with the vile little dictator and shut an eye to his murderous ways.

The author pleads: "Surely the freedom to express one's views is what the last world war was all about." Precisely. And if Churchill had been as big a chump as Charmley, I doubt if the latter would have been enjoying that freedom today.

Old Winston was riddled with human frailty, we know. But what a comfort it was to shelter behind his massive strength when a madman was knocking at the door.

I can still recall the sense that all would be well as long as his fatherly figure protected us. A child's reaction perhaps. But it was

209

the same assurance which steeled my elders to believe we could win that war.

So we idolised him, even if our search for a leftward path was to throw him out of office before the war was properly over. (I can still recall the schoolboy bewilderment that grown-ups could be so ungrateful.)

In the celebration of victory I ran alongside his car and reached out to touch him. "Good old Winnie!" we cried.

My only regret was that I couldn't join the memorable VE night celebrations in that square mile of London where its echoes reverberate with me even to this day.

Someone who did look down on the crowds from his flat that night was my other great hero of the 1940s, Ivor Novello. Earlier that evening, the audience at the London Hippodrome had cheered for half an hour as Novello took the curtain call in his latest musical, *Perchance to Dream*, best remembered for its winning song "We'll Gather Lilacs".

Novello, who sadly needs to be explained to many people today, was the most handsome, magnetic figure on the British stage— Welsh actor, film star, playwright, but most of all composer of lush melodies, from *Glamorous Night* to *The Dancing Years* and *King's Rhapsody*.

As a 21-year-old in 1914 he had written that battle hymn of the First World War, "Keep the Home Fires Burning", and by the second great conflict he was not only the romantic composer who kept us all whistling but the man who saved Drury Lane with that succession of smash-hit musicals.

In the bleakness of the late forties he lightened the austerity and was the only British writer-composer to hold his own with the Irving Berlins and Richard Rodgers who came to dominate our theatres with musicals like *Annie Get Your Gun* and *Oklahoma*.

His successor, I suppose, though in a rather limited way, is Andrew Lloyd Webber. Novello devised, wrote, composed, managed, and starred with spectacular success in his own shows. Not only did the public adore him but, significantly, the whole theatrical fraternity did too.

Lloyd Webber's success does at least tell of a continuing craving for that middle road in music so devastated by the flash-flood of pop in the 1950s.

Long before then I had become a stage-door Johnny, a teenager visiting London to see the stars and to hang around for autographs.

It seemed like my greatest night in the metropolis, in late 1950, when I rose with the audience to acclaim Ivor Novello for his performance in *King's Rhapsody*, later joining the crowd at the stage door of the Palace Theatre. Charisma could have been a word invented for him.

A few weeks later he went home from that same theatre to the famous flat at No. 11 Aldwych, directly above the Strand Theatre, his home for nearly 40 years.

He felt suddenly tired, with pains in his legs, and went to bed. He died in the night, a man still in his fifties.

My own devastation next morning, when the Aberdeen landlady broke the news, gives me some understanding of those who will not let Elvis Presley die.

You don't hear much of Novello these days. Music has become largely polarised, from the classics to pop, with specialist interests like jazz and folk finding their niche. Perhaps he is too unashamedly and unfashionably romantic.

But I never visit that square mile of London without standing by the Aldwych flat, with its narrow doorway and creaky lift. And there I can hear the piano upstairs, leading the strings into the waltz from *Glamorous Night*.

For Ivor Novello was the voice of an age. And it's hard to believe he would have been 100 this week.

THE MAGNIFICENT MAIRS

MY EARLY days in Glasgow were much enriched by the fact that the minister of the South Side parish where I went to live was that gloriously colourful character, Stanley Mair.

Not that I was much of an attender at his church. Indeed, if he had read newspapers as seldom as I was to be found in his pews he would have been a poorly-informed pastor.

But Stanley was up to date with the world, a well-rounded man of brilliance with a theatrical flair for oratory which may have slightly obscured the true depth of his faith.

He originated from one of those Banffshire fishing communities that produce a disproportionate number of fine brains. From there his father, Alex Mair, had gone forth to be a missionary in China, eventually sending his son back home to Fordyce Academy.

From there to Aberdeen University where he met and married a local minister's daughter, Isobel Caldwell, before heading back to the Far East during the Second World War and dropping into the jungle as one of Wingate's legendary Chindits.

He didn't reach his mother's grave by the Yangtse River but he did manage a joyous reunion with his sister and his missionary father, just released from internment.

Back in Scotland, with the air of adventure and a new appreciation of being alive, Stanley Mair settled into the parish of Netherlee and served it with distinction for the next 30 years.

No hour was too late for Stanley to drop in on sinners like me and we would blether beyond midnight, when he would seek to start his old car and cause eyes to peep from behind curtains as he revved her into a sudden burst of life.

Then, winding down the window, he would holler to his anxious host on the doorstep: "Now you know why they call me the Rev!" before disappearing in a cloud of smoke.

Stanley Mair was a delightful human being, the greatest Moderator the Church of Scotland never had. The Kirk hierarchy were much too stuffy to consider him for the ultimate post but, if only they had had the wit to see it, he could have been their finest ambassador. Indeed he was.

His partnership with Isobel, a doctor who has given her life to the welfare of the mentally handicapped, was truly made in heaven. And in those late-night sessions we would hear of the escapades involving their five sons, a bunch of scallywags in the tradition of ministers' children.

On the Sunday after the last boy was born in 1957, the congregation placed a cake of *Five Boys* chocolate in the pulpit. Stanley mounted the steps, appreciated the joke and announced in his Northeast dialect: "Ay—and nae Mair!"

Rory was the last. Whatever would they do with Rory? Whatever would they do with any of them? But the Mair boys buckled down when it mattered. Rory became the youngest chief executive of a local authority in Britain, at Ross and Cromarty.

Graeme became a cancer specialist in London. Ranald looks after welfare care at the List D School at Beith while Colin is a philosophy lecturer at Strathclyde University, also taking care of visiting students.

And the eldest of the family, Michael, is minister of Holburn West in Aberdeen, back in the land of his forebears and filling the pews in much the same way as his father.

Stanley died before his time, slipping quietly away after a cerebral haemorrhage while watching late-night television of the 1976 Olympics. He had suffered blackwater fever from the wartime days.

His old church in Netherlee has undergone refurbishment and for the re-dedication last week his successor, the Rev. David Arnott, made way for Michael Mair to occupy his father's old pulpit.

It was indeed a poignant occasion. The tearaway youngster well remembered by the middle-aged and elderly now mounted those pulpit steps, a grey-haired man of 50, having grown every inch into the stature of his distinguished father.

Michael, too, is of independent mind, having started his ministry at Dumbarton before experiencing disenchantment with the Kirk and putting it all aside for years of social work in Coventry.

But in time he returned to the fold and found his place in Aberdeen, never shirking his duty, whether in pub or pulpit or in releasing his challenging views upon radio and television.

He's his father's own boy all right, a fact soon confirmed by those whose gaze would follow him up those steps at Netherlee last week. For there he preached sublimely and showed the family talent for human contact and understanding, not least among the children, who were entranced. We sang a hymn he composed himself.

The Kirk takes a lot of flak from armchair critics, many of whom have no idea what actually goes on within. Maybe they should try it sometime. For here was a wonderfully warm feeling of fellowship, a sense of the continuing nature of community life.

And sitting in her corner of the back pew was Michael's mother Isobel, a Mother Theresa-like figure now crippled by osteoporosis. Even into her seventies she was still labouring in the villages of Thailand, healing the sick and sometimes getting precious little thanks for it, once cast into jail among junkies and prostitutes for something she didn't do.

But Isobel and Stanley passed on their social conscience. From folks like these . . . can future Moderators now arise?

JOHN BROWN—
AND THE *QUEEN MARY*

IT was one of those precious moments when history comes alive and you can hardly believe the evidence before your eyes.

An audience at Glasgow Royal Concert Hall was savouring a lunchtime talk on the shipbuilding history of the river Clyde, dating back 300 years but capturing public imagination most of all in that glorious period of creating the great *Queens* for Cunard.

Dominating the scene last week were magnificent portraits of those royal ladies, the *Queen Mary* and the *Queen Elizabeth* from the 1930s and their younger sister, the *QE2*, from the 1960s.

With fine dramatic effect, the large video screen was showing the launching of the *Queen Mary* in 1934 when a slight, elderly figure appeared from the wings and made his way to the podium to tell the story.

And who better to tell it than John Brown, now in his nineties, himself a piece of living history as the man whose designing hand gave shape to all three of those famous ships?

His audience listened with rapt attention, well aware of the unique nature of this opportunity to hear it from the man himself (complete with the traditional bowler hat of the industry). To some, it was a surprise that such a figure could still be alive. But John Brown is alive all right, so strong in mind and bright of eye that not only could he marshal his facts with a clear logic but he could read his notes without the benefit of spectacles.

This legendary figure, so little recognised in his own backyard, is not of course the John Brown who gave his name to the famous yard at Clydebank which built those famous ships. It was by a pure coincidence of name that the lad who grew up at 364 Clarkston

215

Road, Glasgow, found his way to an apprenticeship at Clydebank in the immediate aftermath of the First World War.

While working there, he also studied for a B.Sc. at Glasgow University, emerging with distinction in 1923 to apply the theories of naval architecture.

His distinguished boss, Sir James McNeill, spotted the talent and quietly set him down one day in 1926 to design a luxury liner.

With Cunard planning a regular service from Southampton to New York, the prospect of building such a ship was imminent. The Depression was also looming and there were delays before the order was actually placed.

But by the time that luxury liner—the great *Queen Mary*—was launched from Clydebank in September 1934, McNeill had set his young protégé to designing the next development of such a ship.

John Brown beavered away at his drawing board, refining the boilers to a requirement of two funnels instead of the *Queen Mary's* three—and there they had the blueprint for the *Queen Elizabeth*.

She was launched in 1938, in time to join her sister on war service, before attaining her original purpose of taking part in that weekly service between Southampton and New York.

By the time the *Queen Mary* was grinding to her last days in the mid-1960s, John Brown had already become managing director of the Clydebank yard, charged with tendering for her replacement, to become known as the *QE2*.

He did so successfully, set the building in motion and then went quietly into the shadows of retirement. There he has remained for more than a quarter of a century until the curiosity of modern times has brought him back to an unaccustomed limelight.

Because of the very nature of the man, he so constructed his talk last week that he didn't even clarify to his audience that he became the boss of John Brown's shipyard.

But the boss he was. And for those who later wandered into the gallery of the Royal Concert Hall to see a photographic display of nine more great ships of the Clyde, the astonishing truth was that seven of them had been designed under the guidance of John Brown.

For the record, they were the *Arcadia* (1953); the *Carinthia* (1955), now known as *Fair Princess*, cruising along the Mexican coast from Los Angeles; the *Caronia* (1947), shipwrecked at Guam in 1974; the *Ivernia* (1954), later renamed *Franconia* and now operated by the Russians on the Black Sea; the *Rangitane* (1947), broken up in 1976; the *Ruahine* (1950), laid up in 1973, and the *SA Vaal* (1961), sold to the Americans for cruising in the Caribbean and renamed *Festivale*.

Back in that lunchtime gathering, the audience ranged from old men who had worked in the shipyards to schoolchildren who were being given this special privilege of hearing their own history from a man who helped to make it.

For those of us who had sailed the Atlantic on the ships of his creation, and remembered the grace and majesty of those arrivals in the shadows of Manhattan, it was indeed an exquisite experience to hear about the origins.

Besides the partying of high life on the high seas, I could suddenly hear again the silence of the grey ocean on a Sunday morning, when the church bell pealed out eerily across the parish of the Atlantic.

It was one of life's wondrous moments. And when John Brown stepped down from that podium last week, it was the sound of thunderous applause which rang in his ears. Just the heartfelt expression of an appreciative audience which followed him all the way to the exit—and didn't really want to let him go.

NO BOBBY IN MAUD?

AT the very moment when our troubled society is up in arms about rising crime, the powers-that-be have gone and committed a felony of vast and inexcusable proportion. They have shut down the police station at Maud.

You've never heard of Maud? Now I wouldn't go as far as to say you haven't lived if you don't know about Maud. But you certainly haven't been a reader of this column.

For the benefit of the unenlightened, when the Deity created order out of chaos and shaped up His universe, He rounded off the miracle by creating Maud. (That may explain why some uncharitable people have been known to call it the last place on God's earth).

To me, it was the centre of the universe; well . . . *my* universe. For it was the village where I was born and grew up and with which I formed a life-long and loving attachment.

It was the market-place at the heart of the Aberdeenshire cattle country, the railway junction where the northward train from Aberdeen split into two, for Peterhead and Fraserburgh.

So we had a station, a cattle mart, a school, kirk, hospital, village hall, a scattering of shops and a population of a few hundred souls, all woven into the pattern of what used to be known as a community.

And as an indispensable part of that, we had the village bobby. From 1902, there had been a formidable police station at the top end of Maud, giving the resident constable not only a spacious home for his family but a decent view of his domain.

Within the solid granite building there were three sturdy cells, which served the surrounding area. Since Maud itself was rather a douce and docile kind of place, the occupants usually came from neighbouring villages like New Deer and New Pitsligo, which could be counted upon occasionally to produce a drunken rabble.

218

In my childhood home at Park Crescent, directly opposite the police station, I would lie and listen to the howls of a rowdy drunk in the dead of night.

But with that kind of proximity, the bobby was also our nearest neighbour. And with a man like Andra Forbes, who covered a large part of my childhood, he was also our friend, everybody's friend.

Not that men like Andra were soft marks. They simply earned a respect which meant that the folk of Maud had the privilege of living virtually in a crime-free society, with doors unlocked at night and never the thought of an intruder or a mugger or anything more troublesome than a harmless drunk.

Andra Forbes would roll on those old-fashioned leggings, like bandages, and pedal his bicycle to a rendezvous point with Bobbies from the neighbouring villages.

There they exchanged local intelligence, along with any gossip that was a-going, before pedalling back home to keep the lid of the law well in place.

With the tradition of the local bobby came great stories of their eccentricity. In the neighbouring parish of Strichen, there were endless tales of Big Bob, a bull-necked figure with whom it would have been unwise to meddle.

He operated more by instinct than conventional brain-power but that instinct was as sure as the morning light. Give him a few brief facts and he would sniff out the villain in a manner to astonish your highest-flying detective.

In the days when closing-time was 9.30pm, Bob's nose took him along Water Street in Strichen late one night, when he was sure he would come upon a coterie of after-hours boozers in a back room of the Mormond Hotel.

Bursting in upon the illegal scene, he found a group of men, each with a whisky in front of him.

"Is that yours?" he demanded of the first.

No.

"Is that yours?" No.

Along the line, they all denied ownership.

Systematically, Big Bob poured them all into one big tumbler, said: "Well, there's nae damned use in them sittin' here"—and downed the lot, before ushering out the lawbreakers with a stern admonition!

Not only are those days gone but the local bobby is all but gone as well. Big Bob's village of Strichen is among the casualties. So is Maud, where the 90-year reign of the local bobby has just come to an end with the retirement of the last incumbent.

An assistant chief constable of Grampian Police has been doing the rounds to explain to the natives why, in the interests of modern sophistication, it will all now be handled by squad cars from a few centralised points.

Mintlaw will look after New Deer and Maud. And just the other night, the folk of New Deer were sitting respectfully listening to a plausible spiel from the senior cop when . . . what do you think happened?

Thieves were celebrating the prospect of their new-found freedom by breaking into the Newlands Garage 300 yards away.

More seriously, that corner of rural Buchan has just been through two separate murder hunts, after one woman was found dead near Turriff and another in the playground of Mintlaw Academy.

Murder in Buchan? That really is such a telling sign of the times as to make a monumental nonsense of these modern cuts. No bobby in Maud? Andra Forbes will be turning in his grave.

THE GLORY OF GOTHENBURG

Gothenburg, Monday.

IN a lifetime blessed with more highlights than I deserve, there is one occasion in particular which stands beyond all others on the heights of ecstasy.

It was that memorable spring evening of 1983 when the Aberdeen football team I had been following since childhood created a sensation by becoming the cup-winning champions of Europe.

On a dramatic night of thunder and lightning, they came as underdogs to the Ullevi stadium of Gothenburg and outplayed the greatest club name in the world, Real Madrid. It was the story of David and Goliath as applied to football. And it happened exactly 10 years ago tonight.

So I have come back to celebrate at the scene of the triumph, still trying to reconcile myself to the fact that a whole decade of events, joyous and tragic, stands between me and that night when bedlam broke over Gothenburg at the sound of a final whistle. It seems like only yesterday.

And now, on this nostalgic trip, I am accompanied by a camera crew which will put it all on the permanent record of a video film.

This time I am better able to appreciate the attractions of Gothenburg. In the bright sunshine of a late-spring day I have walked the length of the main thoroughfare, known as the Avenue, which gives hint of both Paris and Prague, and absorbed the elegance of the Swedish people as they relax by their sidewalk cafés.

I have regained my bearings and superimposed the memory of 14,000 Aberdonians descending upon this great Scandinavian seaport by car, coach and fishing boat, with the bulk of them arriving in 50 plane-loads.

The ferryboat *St Clair*, which normally plies between Aberdeen and Shetland, had sailed in with 500 supporters to add its own dimension of adventure to an occasion which was already overflowing with drama.

This Red Army of enthusiasm took over the city of Gothenburg and so captured the imagination of local inhabitants that Swedish impartiality was soon giving way to a full-blooded backing of the Scottish invaders.

Apart from the northern European affinity, there was the other consideration that the Spaniards had so regarded the result as a foregone conclusion that fewer than 3000 of their 100,000 supporters had bothered to make the journey.

So perhaps there was an historic inevitability about the outcome. Yet on the great day it seemed as if there might be no match at all. For the rains came down in such torrents that tarpaulins had to protect the stadium from a flooding disaster.

But finally they pulled away the covers and out came the players, and soon we were gripped in the tension of a European final. Only Rangers and Celtic had been this way before.

An early goal by Aberdeen's Eric Black was cancelled out when Real Madrid scored from a penalty. That's how it stood at full time.

So the match went into extra time, with the possibility of a penalty shoot-out if there were still no result. With Eric Black now injured, manager Alex Ferguson brought on the enigmatic John Hewitt, by now famed for arriving as a substitute to perform last-minute acts of heroism.

With just eight minutes to play, Aberdeen attacked down the left wing, the ball passing from Peter Weir to Mark McGhee. When the latter crossed into the goalmouth, Real Madrid's goalkeeper came out to intercept but failed. And who was there to head the ball into an empty net? John Hewitt, of course.

On this anniversary visit I have been sitting in the very seat from which I witnessed that memorable moment, rising instinctively at the recollection of it all to hail the hero of the night.

The manager of Ullevi stadium has been here to heighten the illusion, switching on the illuminated scoreboard in the gathering darkness with the message which could not properly be absorbed on that heady occasion of 10 years ago: Aberdeen FC 2—Real Madrid 1.

Now I was able to believe it and to remember again the scenes of celebration that followed. We lingered with our historic moment till the stewards finally ushered us out around 11 o'clock that May night of 1983.

Back in town, Aberdonians were dancing in the streets, splashing in the fountains, filling pubs and clubs with "The Northern Lights of Old Aberdeen" and leaving very little time for sleep before the great return to the Granite City. It was the first time Gothenburg had hosted a European final and the people still talk of it as a great carnival.

The police chief of the day, Nils Klinteberg, came back from retirement to recall his apprehension about 14,000 British football fans descending on his city. Astonishingly in this day and age, there was not a single arrest throughout the three days of Aberdonian presence.

The local mayor of the time, Gunnar Larsson, came back on his bicycle to recall the joyous nature of the occasion. Out of it came a civic connection between Gothenburg and Aberdeen which survives a decade later.

So I have retraced the steps and relived the memories. And from my hotel window, just a few hundred yards away, I can see the Ullevi stadium standing out against the night sky, its distinctive lines thrown into relief by blue reflected lighting, ghostlike and eerie.

Now it's time to raise a glass in that direction and drink a quiet toast—to the glory of Gothenburg.

OH, WHAT A ROYAL BOOB!

AS the Queen celebrated the fortieth anniversary of her Coronation my generation of journalists was recalling a week of news coverage which was hectic beyond belief.

Apart from the ongoings at Westminster Abbey that June day of 1953, there was the spectacular coincidence of the British expedition conquering Everest for the very first time—and the widespread joy of royal jockey Gordon Richards at long last breaking his Derby jinx and winning the world's greatest flat-race for the one and only time.

My own abiding memory of the Coronation, however, is the weather, the cold, wet, windswept bleakness of a day when June was certainly burstin' out all over. Cloudburstin'.

But as that memory lingered with me 40 years later, little did I know that I was running into another royal incident which would haunt me for the next 40 years if I had that much mileage in my expectations.

As Her Majesty left Balmoral to fly south for her anniversary, I was heading north to an engagement with her youngest son which should have been among the more memorable events in my diary.

Prince Edward is patron of the Haddo Arts Trust, which runs a centre of artistic excellence at the stately Haddo House in the heart of Aberdeenshire, home of June Gordon, the Marchioness of Aberdeen.

In these post-war years, she and her late husband have given Haddo House a reputation for choral, theatrical and operatic performance which is truly international.

I remember, before leaving the North-east, going there to interview the great Benjamin Britten, who was giving a recital. Famous figures like Vaughan Williams were regular participants. Indeed it has been a regret of my exiled years that I lost touch with so much musical activity at a venue which is within cycling distance of my birthplace.

In 40 years, I have been back to Haddo House only once, to deliver an address. So it was with some anticipation that I accepted a recent invitation to return for a major fund-raising dinner, at which Prince Edward would speak and Ronnie Corbett would entertain.

As a writer with local connections, I would sing for my supper by launching a book called *Granny's Wisdom*, compiled by an old friend, Kitty Reid, and given over to the funds of the Haddo Arts Trust.

So come with me on the drive through the wooded grounds of Haddo, crawling with security men, not only for the Prince himself but for the band of the Royal Scots, which would play during dinner.

There I am, resplendent in evening dress, stepping out at the stately home and exploring the vast complex, which includes a magnificent marquee provided by Total Oil for the purposes of this prestigious occasion. In the preamble to dinner a minder has been appointed to see that I am in position to be presented to His Royal Highness, along with the authoress, before stepping forward to address the gathering of 400.

Since my minder has not yet appeared, I assume there is no urgency. But I assume wrongly. Casually crossing the forecourt, I am confronted with a loudspeaker announcement: "Will Jack Webster please take the platform immediately!" Sensing a crisis, I break into a sprint, reach the back of the assembled gathering—and gain the very first hint of my monumental royal gaffe. For there on stage, impossibly out of reach, authoress Kitty Reid has already been introduced to the Prince.

But where is the idiot who should have been standing beside her? With aristocratic aplomb, Rosemary Wolrige Gordon diverts the royal patron to view some nearby exhibits, buying time till her lost speaker shows up.

From the back of the hall, I embark on a dinner-jacket version of a rugby scrummage, elbowing my way to the front with breathless apologies to fashionable ladies.

In a state of flushed disorder, bow-tie birling like something out of an Ealing comedy, I reach the stage and encounter a highly novel version of role-reversal. For there stands the Prince, where I should have been standing, waiting to be presented to his presentee!

His greatest of great-grannies wouldn't have been at all amused. But young Edward takes it with fine good humour, greets me warmly and points me to the microphone.

Now addressing a sea of faces, some of whose ribs I have just bruised on the way past, I throw up my hands in surrender, confess to some confusion and proceed to give one of my lesser performances. At one stage, in fact, my mind goes blank and I struggle to regain composure.

Afterwards, downing a double whisky, I search for consolations and lessons for the future. I must remember to read the small-print of protocol—and never depend on the services of a minder. One day perhaps I'll see the funny side of my royal boob.

Back home, tae aul' claes and parritch, I'm quietly licking the wounds and reading Kitty's splendid book, which is a mixture of recipes and remedies, passed down by a thousand grannies, and graced by the endorsement of the most famous granny of them all, the Queen Mother.

From it, I have learned how to make stovies, mealy puddings and clootie dumplings, and how to cure bites, burns and indigestion.

In this ABC of wisdom, I searched for some other remedies, looking in vain under headings like embarrassment and idiocy. Could they be the starting-point of Kitty Reid's next book?

THE LINGERING GRIEF OF LOCKERBIE

STUDENT graduations can choke me up, almost as much as Saturday's final at Wimbledon, when I would defy all but the totally heartless to have resisted a tear as Jana Novotna cracked up in defeat and was taken into an embrace by that most gracious of royal ladies, the Duchess of Kent.

For those prize-giving days at colleges and universities round off individual stories which may not be the stuff of headlines but are nevertheless a testimony to heroic effort, personal sacrifice, and loving support from within the family.

You catch a glimpse of it in that knowing look between proud parents who may grip hands to confirm that it really has been worth it after all. I saw it again on Friday, which, for two quite disparate reasons, was a day when students were much in my mind.

In the morning I was in that magnificent hall of Glasgow City Chambers, giving the oration to students of North Glasgow College, many of whom were heading out to the real world for the first time. (I was there out of respect for my friend, the late Walter Macphail, who gave so much of himself to this college.)

By late afternoon I was driving south for a rendezvous of a very different nature—one to remind me forcibly of another group of students who were denied the privilege of a graduation day by an evil act which has not yet been settled.

That large contingent from Syracuse University, New York, bright young Americans enjoying a semester in London, would already have graduated but for that bomb which blew apart PanAm flight 103 over Lockerbie in December 1988.

They were going home for Christmas, except that their life's journey was brought to an end at 31,000ft in the ultimate horror of human experience. A total of 259 bodies came tumbling out of the

227

night sky, landing in that quiet corner of south-west Scotland visited by the Queen last week. As the jumbo ploughed into a community it was really the Miracle of Lockerbie that only 11 local people were killed.

Among the Americans here for the royal occasion were Peter and Suse Lowenstein from New Jersey, whose son Alexander came to rest at the farm of Tundergarth Mains. The Lowensteins are frequent visitors, maintaining local friendships and finding their own private solace in the cemetery of Dryfesdale, by the memorial to PanAm victims.

Most of all, perhaps, they find comfort in that field which bears the indentation of Alexander's body, upon which they have erected a cairn to his memory.

I had already met the Lowensteins in America and it was an inspiration to meet them again. They were always substantial citizens but, along with so many others who grieve over Lockerbie, they have expanded to individual greatness, towers of courage who have channelled their devastation into a creative grief. As a united body they stormed their way to the White House to gain meetings with President Bush and are similarly heading towards his successor. As a result of their efforts, America has a new Aviation Security Act and an iron-fisted approach to state-sponsored terrorism.

But people like the Lowensteins will not rest until the two Libyans named in the indictment have been handed over for trial. Both officials of Libyan Arab Airlines, they are said to have been responsible for a suitcase being placed on a plane in Malta, tagged for Frankfurt, London and onwards by PanAm 103 to New York. The suitcase is alleged to have contained a high explosive which detonated as the plane veered over Lockerbie towards the Atlantic.

The attempt to bring them to court, either in Scotland or the United States, is an on-going matter between the UN and Colonel Gaddafi; the relatives are beginning to despair of it ever happening.

Now they are pressing for an oil embargo on Libya (Britain and France are quite disgracefully opposing it for political reasons) and, if that is not achieved, they will ask President Clinton to act on his own.

The Lockerbie relatives had little reason to thank the American State Department, the executives of PanAm or indeed British Ministers like Paul Channon, Cecil Parkinson, or Douglas Hogg.

For them the saving grace has been not only their friendship with the people of Lockerbie but the remarkable operation conducted by Dumfries and Galloway police.

They were the people who pieced together the evidence that fell out of the sky that horrendous night and landed on hundreds of square miles between Lockerbie and Newcastle.

Without that meticulous effort when police crawled on hands and knees in search of particles, there would have been no indictment. One day, no doubt, the whole incredible story will be told, hopefully in court.

Meanwhile, I talked it over with Peter and Suse who, like all the other Americans, have come to regard the Scots as the greatest race on earth. They simply marvel at our integrity.

So they said their goodbyes and made a final call on Chief Constable George Esson, for them the symbol of all they admire in the Scots. Then they flew off to continue their pursuit of justice.

Within themselves at least they feel the better of those visits to Lockerbie. The scars will never disappear. But the peace and warmth in that corner of Scotland which, to them, will be forever America, amount to a balm that makes the heartache of their daily living just that much closer to tolerable.

BUD NEILL REDISCOVERED

WE WERE a motley crew, gathered there in an Edinburgh film studio at the weekend, ranging from artist Emilio Coia to writers like Cliff Hanley, Archie Hind, and W. Gordon Smith and entertainers from Jimmie Macgregor to Russell Hunter and Una McLean.

To pass the time between shots, Coia was sketching Hanley in a big, daft sombrero. For this was the mood of the day.

The object that had brought us all together was the creation of a television film about that extraordinary character, the late Bud Neill, cartoonist, witty writer and, of course, creator of those legends of the Scottish Wild West, Lobey Dosser, Rank Bajin and Co.

Casting an eye over that gathering of people, I mused about the fact that the man himself has become a legend, by the now-familiar process of being discovered by a generation that knew him not.

Our own Tom Shields led the campaign for a memorial sculpture of Lobey and his eccentric cuddy, El Fideldo, which now stands in Woodside Road, Glasgow. A horse race at Hamilton Park next week has been named in their honour.

Young artists like Ranald MacColl, currently writing Bud Neill's biography, have fostered the cult and cannot hear enough from old-stagers like myself who knew Bud Neill and wish we had paid more attention to the details.

Neill's art style, which was idiosyncratic to say the least, has caused many an argument but the genius of the man was surely his ability to ally those daft-like drawings to the inherent wit of western Scotland. His power of observing the subtle details of everyday life was quite brilliant and became the special privilege of *Glasgow Evening Times* readers from 1944 onwards.

Because of that geographic restriction, however, the rest of Scotland was late in catching up with the talents of Bud Neill.

Frankly, I wasn't aware of him till I moved to Glasgow in 1960.

He was born in Partick in 1911 before the family moved to Troon, where his father worked in the chemical industry. After Glasgow School of Art you would find him in a variety of jobs, from salesman to shop assistant.

He once told me the story of how he became a newspaper cartoonist. By then he was driving an Alexander's bus.

"I was on the tea-break in Clyde Street, gnawing away at my cheese sandwich, when I read a letter to an editor deploring the habits of Glasgow bus drivers," he said. "I replied in defence and apparently my pungency took the attention of newspaper editors."

Bud was bothered with verses in the way some people have mice and once he had moulded that talent to the eccentric nature of his art, he was on his way to success.

But Bud was not without his problems. He drank too much and operated on a short fuse, which could land him in sharp conflicts. If he took a dislike to you, it was prudent to take early cover.

For some reason he took a shine to me and would immediately burst into my Buchan dialect on his occasional visits to the office.

He had parted company with a previous employer and was finding his feet on the broader platform of the *Scottish Daily Express* where, incidentally, he was demanding a bigger salary than was paid to its distinguished editor, Ian MacColl.

We seldom saw him. Just as the great Giles lived in Ipswich and sent his cartoons to the *Express* in London by train, Bud Neill lived in Dunfermline and sent his cartoons to the *Express* in Glasgow.

He lived beside a cemetery—his house was called *Dim View!*— but worked from a disused post office outside Dunfermline where he would occasionally be bothered by people peering in. So he drew a blind, on the outside of which he had written: "Budgies repaired Saturdays." That was Bud.

From time to time, however, he would suddenly appear in our Albion Street office, a large angular frame of a man, dressed for his city visit in dark suit, white shirt, and tie.

In sinister-like blue-tinted spectacles and jaw-jutting attitudes, he always reminded me of a security man for the American President.

231

With deadpan expression he would tell you he planned to send all three sons to be chefs, to guarantee himself three square meals in old age. (I'm told all three did start out in the hotel and catering business!)

Alas, there was not to be an old age for Bud. In 1970 the Scottish Arts Council honoured him with an exhibition of his work in Glasgow. As visitors walked quietly round the gallery with smiles on their faces, they didn't realise that the man himself was sitting nearby, answering my questions.

It was one of his rare interviews. He joked about a loss of memory, but as it turned out there was no joke. That Saturday morning he read my article and complained to his wife that it didn't make sense. Words were transposed.

She read the article and could find nothing wrong with it. She called to tell me later it was the first indication they had had of the brain tumour which was soon to end his life.

We never saw or heard of Bud again. He slipped quietly into history . . . until the perspective of time brought him back to a fresh prominence. You will get a clearer idea of what I mean when Murray Grigor's film reaches your screen this autumn.

WHY JOHN EXCELS AS A BOBBY

A DISTINGUISHED chief of police once told me a story which had taught him a salutary lesson. Making the regular assessment, he interviewed one constable who said he had no wish to be a sergeant or an inspector. He was happy where he was.

The boss wrote in his report: "Lacking in ambition." Exercising his right of appeal, the policeman knocked on the chief's door and was invited to make his point.

"I don't think it's true that I am lacking in ambition, sir," he said very politely. "I do have an ambition—to be a very good constable."

Point taken. The chief quickly amended his assessment and took a fresh view of that vast body of police officers who go through their entire service without attaining a stripe.

His story could have applied to the man I would regard as my favourite Glasgow policeman. Though I don't make a point of gaining first-name acquaintance with the men in blue, I do happen to know the name of John Holmes.

I know him because I have long observed what a splendid policeman he is. If you live in Glasgow, the chances are that you know him too, at least by sight.

For he is the bobby on the beat whose patch is George Square, that focal point of daily life in the city.

He is the clean-cut constable, the friendly face, the joker who stands for no nonsense and can defuse a nasty situation in the best possible manner.

The flotsam of life who drift into George Square know and respect him. The drinkers know they will suffer the ultimate agony —watching their cans and bottles being emptied down a drain; the beggars, too, come to acknowledge the rules.

Some would call him a psychologist. He would call it common sense.

For John Holmes knows his parish in that heart of a vibrant city. To the regulars, he is the Big Man, who will give them respect if they deserve it. He knows their names and their backgrounds.

There are the resident working characters, like Tommy the newsvendor at the entrance to Queen Street Station. And Tommy the cleansing man, who sweeps the square.

Among the homeless or aimless you find people like Willie, with his Gabby Hayes hat, a man who could do with an extra bob or two but wouldn't dream of begging. John has been known to send Willie across to Harry in the baker's shop at the corner, with instructions to ask for a carton of soup. It was paid later.

John Holmes has never measured his success by the number of arrests. Instead, he encourages people to avoid trouble and makes them feel better about the quality of local justice. Isn't that what a policeman should do whenever possible?

So what is the background of this humble officer? John is a Springburn man who served his time as a pattern-maker before joining the City of Glasgow Police in 1962.

His beat was around the old Barrowland Ballroom before he joined that special group known as The Untouchables, which operated in jeans and trainer-shoes and had a remarkable success, later to be developed into the support unit.

John Holmes tasted life in the Toronto police but returned in time to know the full reality of what a policeman's lot can mean.

In Bothwell Street one day he apprehended two suspects. Two other men came on the attack and he was slashed with a knife, missing death by a mere half-inch. (The man who did it was fined £60 for breach of the peace!)

In 1978 he stepped out of his patrol car in Sauchiehall Street to talk to a group of youths who were molesting girls. Soon he was felled by a crowd of 20 who gave him a kicking, including a boot in the eye which threatened his sight and put him out of action for six months.

We tend to forget these things when passing judgment on the quality of our lawmen.

It was in the approach to Glasgow's year as European City of Culture that John was given the job of cleaning up the image of George Square. It had not been the most comfortable resting-place for passers-by.

Without throwing his weight about, the new broom made himself known to the "residents", quietly laid down the rules—and proceeded to see they were kept. Sunbathers could lie on the grass but were no longer allowed to loll on the cenotaph. Some decencies had to be observed. Among those who have gained his utmost admiration are the gardeners who tend to the decoration of the square with a touching devotion.

He learned to take royal visits and angry demonstrations in his stride, found time to act as guide to strangers and generally to keep that hub of Glasgow life in good order.

John has not been too well lately and his sick leave has been overtaken by retirement. At 52, he leaves that beat on the square saying: "People feel reassured to see a policeman in the street. If you can communicate with them, it's half the battle. I've enjoyed my job and would do it all over again. All I ever wanted was to be a good street copper."

He was that all right. An unsung hero with a laudable ambition which he fulfilled to the benefit of us all.

LAS VEGAS FOR SURPRISES

THE wide open spaces of America are a paradise for motorists, a kaleidoscope of scenery with such vast expanses as to take your breath away. We used to joke that everything was bigger in America. Well, they weren't boasting. Everything *is* bigger in America. Much bigger.

As the Oldsmobile swept through spectacular valleys and crossed desert scrubland, the city of Las Vegas shimmered in the distance. Last time I was here, in the 1970s, a highlight had been that night at the Desert Inn, when Count Basie led his great orchestra with Tony Bennett in full voice.

This time, driving into the gambling capital of the world, there was an even bigger surprise on the billboards. But then this trip had been so full of surprises it was difficult to keep track of reality.

On that flight from Glasgow to Phoenix, for example, American Airlines finally convinced me that travelling business class is well worth the money. The comfort, food, and attention merely spoil you for anything less.

The states of Arizona and Utah reminded me once more that I breathe so much better in that dry and pleasant heat. So the motoring began, daily dosages of up to 400 miles, covering the same distance from Glasgow to London and feeling very little pain.

Monument Valley conjured memories of film director John Ford, whose arrival in the territory of the Navajo Indians in the 1930s sparked off that series of John Wayne movies which began with *Stagecoach*.

From the motel next morning, we were already on the highway before 6.30, bursting into song with an endorsement of Richard Rodgers: "Oh What a Beautiful Morning" indeed!

I had previously seen the Grand Canyon from the north and

found it, frankly, disappointing. So there were no high expectations as we approached the south rim and drew in to one of the viewing points.

There it was, reaching into the deepest gorge on earth with the breadth of the Colorado River appearing as but a narrow ribbon at the bottom.

I take back all I ever said about the Grand Canyon. It's awesome. Indeed if there is a more spectacular sight on God's earth I haven't heard of it.

Westward to San Francisco, so frequently plagued by fog and rain but coming good for once and giving us the perfect view of the Golden Gate Bridge.

The most haunting memory is the visit to the island of Alcatraz, no longer a prison but once the penitentiary of people like Al Capone and the much-publicised Birdman, Robert Stroud.

Stepping inside their cells offered a chilling impression of that community in all its violence, which existed from 1934 till 1963, when it was closed by Attorney General Robert Kennedy, not long before his brother was assassinated in Dallas.

Surprises all the way. And few more pleasant than the discovery of Carmel, charming little town on the coast between San Francisco and Los Angeles, where their most distinguished local resident, Clint Eastwood, was once the mayor.

So to Las Vegas—and even before we had reached the reception desk of Caesar's Palace, that biggest surprise of all.

In town for a few nights at the Desert Inn, none other than Ole Blue Eyes himself. Yes, Frank Sinatra. Finding tickets would be another matter. But when you are determined enough in this life, the gods have a habit of bestowing favours.

Let's just say my small party had a table within a few feet of the great man.

I last saw Sinatra at Ibrox Park, Glasgow, in the year of culture. People said his days were already over but on that bleak night he gave one of his finest performances. Since then we have heard rumours of senility but the faithful were undeterred. The place was hopping long before curtain-up and burst into waves of ecstasy as

237

the large orchestra, under Frank junior, paved the way for the master himself.

There he was, at 78, belting out songs like "Mack the Knife" with his usual gusto. In softer tones, the notes were no longer there.

But, saddest of all, the memory had gone. Titles and composers eluded him and the promptings of Frank junior alone kept the performance rolling. I was close enough to catch his eye on a number of occasions and it was the eye of an old man whom clarity has deserted.

There was even a fluffed line in "My Way". But he did manage: *And now the end is near—and so I face the final curtain.*

We rose to give him a rousing ovation, realising all too well the poignancy of those words. After all the jokes about his "farewell" performances, surely we were witnessing the very last of Frank Sinatra. Anything more will be a mistake.

Some wept, others just stood and stared at him, trying to freeze the image. He in turn stared back, a little bemused. Was it a counterpoint of this strange symphony that Frank Sinatra was not alone in growing old?

But there was a majesty in the moment. He left us with "New York, New York", sounding as good as ever. And we filtered out to the Strip, thoughtfully, on a night which would surely reach the history books.

GLITTERING NIGHT AT THE
SCOTTISH OSCARS

WHEN a small country like Scotland embarks on its own glittering night of film and television awards, the scene could be set for yet another outburst of that cynicism for which we can claim a native talent.

A Mickey Mouse version of the Hollywood Oscars? Don't you believe it. For this was the night when Scotland put on a parade of entertainment talent out of all proportion to its size.

From the moment you approached the floodlit splendour of the Moat House International there was a sense of occasion which reminded me of some sparkling showbiz nights I've seen at the Beverly Hills Hotel.

The anticipation was more than justified as you joined the 500 guests in the reception area, sipped champagne and began to put names to the faces which would distinguish the night.

For this was, inevitably and unashamedly, a time for star-spotting and name-dropping. But what stars to spot and names to drop!

The sight of so much talent gathered at the Scottish end of Bafta (British Academy of Film and Television Arts) stirred a real pride in our country's achievements.

The Princess Royal was there as president of the academy, alongside David Puttnam, whose Scottish-based *Local Hero* was among his list of distinguished credits.

But it was mainly a night for home-grown Scots, either collecting or presenting bi-annual awards, people like Richard Wilson, Bill Paterson, Brian Cox, Evelyn Glennie. The new Dr Finlay was there in the person of David Rintoul, without his partner, Dr Cameron, only because actor Ian Bannen is recovering from a bout

239

of pneumonia. Dear Janet (Annette Crosbie) was named best television actress for *Dr Finlay* and *One Foot In The Grave*.

Amid the lights and music and buzz of excitement the awards flowed: Peter Capaldi, collecting honours for both writing and acting, acknowledged his debt to David Puttnam, who put the young Scot alongside Burt Lancaster in *Local Hero* all those years ago.

The Bafta Scotland craft award went to that brilliant BBC cameraman, Stuart Wyld, whose work first excited me 23 years ago with his filming of Grassic Gibbon's *Sunset Song*. The two main awards of the night were reserved for one Scot who is already a legend and another who should be. The prize for lifetime achievement went to the incomparable Rikki Fulton, the greatest comedy talent I have seen in 50 years of Scottish entertainment.

The British Academy fellowship went to the less-known name of Professor Colin Young, that outstanding Glaswegian whose work as Director of the National Film and Television School at Beaconsfield, as well as in America, has made him a revered figure in the industry. Happily, honour was going where honour was due.

Gerda Stevenson was named best film actress for *Blue Black Permanent* but threatened us with a political speech about the iniquities of the Government.

It didn't, however, quite produce the anticipated applause from a leftish profession. Rikki Fulton was clearly not alone in his belief that performers should entertain and not turn prize-giving podiums into soapboxes.

Real influence will come more from behind-the-scenes efforts currently being conducted by two other guests of the evening, David Puttnam and Allan Shiach, that remarkable Morayshire man who manages to combine screenwriting in Hollywood with chairmanship of the Macallan malt. On a night given more to celebration than bitterness, it was a pleasure to see John McGrath coming along as best writer (for his drama *The Long Roads*), having so recently been in the grip of serious illness.

Barbara and Murray Grigor were there, fresh from creating their television tribute to cartoonist Bud Neill. And the appearance of Charlie Gormley, maker of films like *Heavenly Pursuits*, was a reminder to the world of what can be done in a small country like Scotland.

My only gripe about the nominations was the absence of Frieda Morrison's outstanding documentary, *Troubled Fields*, which was a winner if ever I saw one. Made for Grampian Television, it perhaps revealed a flaw in the initial voting system of Bafta, whose members are obviously more geared to life in the Central Belt than in rural Aberdeenshire.

With Eddie Mair rounding off the official business, the socialising was soon under way. It was a night for congratulations, some envy and much gossip, whispered conversations, knowing looks and arched eyebrows of surprise.

The appearance of Bill Bryden, BBC Scotland's head of drama, sparked controversy about his successor, Andrea Calderwood, soon to be defended in public by her new boss, the suave Colin Cameron, head of television at BBC Scotland.

Scottish Television's managing director Gus Macdonald was deep in late-night conversation with his departing lieutenant, David Scott. Meanwhile, the latter's successor, Elgin's own Blair Jenkins, was accepting congratulations.

Though her stage show prevented her accepting the award for best light entertainer, the delectable Dorothy Paul turned up in time to dance the night away.

Yes, it was a glamour night in Glasgow right enough. Still hopping at 3am, if I remember clearly.

COURAGE OF LUPINO LANE

THOSE thousands who recently packed the King's Theatre, Glasgow, for the three-week run of *Me and My Girl* will need no reminding that an infectious musical can send you dancing in the aisles no matter your age or theatrical taste.

A box office besieged in advance not only reflected the show's success in London but brought joy and relief to theatre manager David McShane, who knew that productions like *The Sound of Music* and *Aspects of Love* had not exactly taken Glasgow by storm this year.

But a new generation discovered the appeal of a 1930s musical which had its parents and grandparents linking arms in what became the most famous dance in the world: "The Lambeth Walk".

Coinciding with the 1938 Empire Exhibition at Bellahouston Park, Glasgow, it was quickly adopted as the theme tune of that world-class extravaganza, not least on the final night when 365,000 people endured a rainstorm to bring down the curtain not just upon an exhibition but, as it happened, upon the British Empire itself.

As I sat at the King's, tapping toes and marvelling at the star quality of television's Gary Wilmot as the lead, I couldn't help remembering that *Me and My Girl* had a disastrous start in life, not least in Glasgow, threatening bankruptcy for the man behind it all, that legend of British theatre, Lupino Lane. (I hope I'm not alone in remembering Lupino Lane?)

He belonged to the famous Lupino family who came to Britain as political refugees from Italy 350 years ago and used to include in their show the most famous clown of all, Grimaldi.

Lupino Lane was the family star in the first half of this century, taking on the surname of a grand-aunt who had no family of her own and promised her entire estate if the boy would call himself Lane.

The fact that the old soul died before changing her will and that he gained not a penny of her £200,000 fortune was just an early warning of what might be in store for Lupino.

As well as being a superstar of his day, he was a brave investor. Having encouraged Arthur Rose to write this play about the Cockney lad who inherits a title, he asked Noel Gay to write the music.

As Noel strummed a few bars on the piano, Lupino Lane said "We want a slow, cocky sort of march . . . a Cockney walk—the Lambeth Walk!" *Me and My Girl* was up and running, except that he couldn't find the impresario to stage it.

"I'll put the damn thing on myself," said Lane, risking all his savings and heading for Nottingham at the start of a provincial tour in 1937.

That was where his troubles began. As the star himself went down with pneumonia, the cast had to kick its heels, expensively, until the lights went up again: *Me and My Girl*—World Premiere.

Nottingham gave it a reasonable send-off, prompting Lupino Lane to speculate on what might have happened if he had opened in Glasgow instead. Because when the show reached the city, he asked the manager how the theatre was filling up for the first matinee.

"Better see for yersel'," said a long-faced boss. There were seven people in the auditorium. "And they didnae a' pey," said the manager. "Four bodies came wi' complimentaries."

Business improved a little but not enough to raise spirits. When the show reached London, Lane had to settle for the unfashionable Victoria Palace. He offered the female lead to Gracie Fields, Binnie Hale, Vera Pearce, and Frances Day, the leading ladies of the time, but they all turned him down.

Still losing money, Lupino Lane retained his faith in *Me and My Girl* but acknowledged that his savings were running out. In desperation he phoned John Watt, BBC director of variety, and pleaded for an outside broadcast. Watt liked the show but said they could do nothing for seven weeks.

"In seven weeks I'll be out of business," said Lupino Lane.

Surely his luck would turn. Then came a phone call from the

BBC: "Jack Payne wants to cancel a broadcast. It's terribly short notice, I know, but . . ."

Within 48 hours Lupino Lane had it all arranged. The theatre buzzed with excitement that January night of 1938. And when the live broadcast ended with "The Lambeth Walk", the BBC faded on the applause. Within minutes the box office phone began to ring. Next morning they were queuing along the street.

A theatrical disaster had become an overnight triumph, going on to a phenomenal 5000 performances which even broke the record of *Chu Chin Chow*. No wonder we were linking arms in Bellahouston Park, Glasgow, later that year and kicking our legs down Lambeth Way.

Among those who flocked to congratulate Lupino Lane on his bravery were Walt Disney, Stan Laurel, Eddie Cantor, and our own Will Fyffe. Yet my last memory of the man was a farewell night at London's Gaiety Theatre in 1957.

He had tried to save that national institution from its wartime destruction but ran into financial trouble before it could even be restored. Once more, Lupino Lane lost every penny. And today, asking around among younger colleagues, I find they don't even know his name.

SWEET SMELL OF SUCCESS

THERE'S an old adage, significantly popular among doctors' families, about avoiding the surgeon's knife if at all possible. And it is a sentiment to which I have never had any difficulty in subscribing.

So much so that I have managed to separate the two operations of my life by 50 years and to confine myself to just one particular brand of the species, the so-called ENT man.

The tonsils were a necessary removal in childhood and, more recently, a problem in my voice-box was investigated and traced to the nasal regions. It wasn't essential to have the operation but . . . maybe better now than later.

That was how I encountered the jolly figure of the surgeon from Bothwell who conducted his professional examination while I conducted my own devious interview to determine if he could safely be let loose upon my unconscious anatomy.

"Find out a man's hobbies," I always say. And within minutes he was waxing eloquent about his passion for reconstructing old cars. Ah. You mean, putting old wrecks together again? Nothing more had to be said. He was just the man for me.

As I warmed to his sense of fun, I mused that he was the only person I knew who could get up your nose (to use that rather disgusting expression) while still retaining your affection.

On the drive to hospital I was feeling less well disposed towards the radio jerk who was playfully suggesting song titles to unnerve you before an operation. You know the kind of thing: "I've Got You Under My Skin" or "Take All Of Me" (*the very heart and soul of me*).

I ignored such insensitivity, booked into my room and spent the waiting hours pacing the floor like a man about to be hanged. Alternately, I gazed out over the South Side of Glasgow, tried to trace its baffling geography towards my own home (the guiding landmark was the Linn Crematorium!) and contemplated, rather morbidly, that any mishap resulting in my early demise that afternoon would alter the uncaring flow of mankind's routine by not a whit.

Time now for three pills and a wooziness and soon a trolley to the theatre, some vague figures in gowns, an injection in the arm— and nothing more until a blur of semi-consciousness brought the realisation that my nostrils were packed to overflowing and that all breathing for the next few days would be through the mouth only.

Back in bed there was surprisingly little pain, only discomfort. Next day, I was allowed to sit up in a chair when, suddenly, I did something I had never done in my life before. I fainted. And what a peculiar and alarming sensation that is. From a light-headed buzz, you simply fade away as if this might be a gentle route to the Hereafter.

Coming round, I called for help and was soon lying with my feet higher than my head. In a burst of self-pity, I had reached a pretty bleak plain when suddenly the gods came good.

The cheering news arrived with a copy of the *Evening Times*, in which the books page revealed that my latest publication, *Famous Ships of The Clyde*, had gone to the top of the bestseller list within its first week. In doing so (without a single review in any newspaper), it had displaced my colleague Tom Shields whose latest collection of diary pieces had threatened to take root up there.

Still, I don't suppose the editor was objecting when two *Herald* writers were hogging the top slots. What was even more pleasing was that one of the world's biggest-ever blockbusters, *Bridges of Madison County*, was in third place and Michael Dobbs's highly popular television story, *To Play The King*, was relegated to No. 10. My immediate snort of delight put at risk the surgeon's handiwork.

To keep it all in perspective, however, I have to say that neither Tom Shields nor myself is set to make a fortune from our bestselling status. We just happen to have produced titles with a particular appeal to the Scottish market, not least in the run-up to Christmas when such books fall into a useful bracket of gift ideas.

Much as I am delighted to have reached the top spot, I am also bound to say that there is a scarcity of justice when it comes to bestseller lists. On some other books, like the biography of Alistair MacLean, I have travelled thousands of miles and sweated blood to research and write with diligence yet succeeded, only with difficulty, in reaching the top echelons.

I suppose, when you consider that 70,000 new titles are published in Britain alone each year, we should be thankful to get anywhere near the top.

With those *Famous Ships of The Clyde*, I even had the benefit of a researcher, which meant that my writing time was reduced to a few weeks.

Now that the book was launched and had embarked on a voyage of its own I went home to recuperate, grateful that my newspaper nose was now free of its extensive packing—and capable of catching at least a whiff of that sweet smell of success.

MACKENDRICK—LEGEND OF FILMLAND

ONE of the great legends of film-making, Scotland's own Alexander Mackendrick, died in Los Angeles yesterday at the age of 81. Though dogged for many years by emphysema, he could still have passed for a man of 60 and felt his survival was due to the Californian climate.

Until he was overtaken by pneumonia a few weeks ago, he was still imparting his vast knowledge to students at the Californian Institute of Arts, where he used to be dean of the film faculty.

In an extraordinary life story, where his diversion to the academic heights was a result of his disillusion with Hollywood, Mackendrick will be remembered for directing a succession of films which stretched from Ealing classics like *Whisky Galore* and *The Ladykillers* (shown again on television last week) to such Hollywood classics as *The Sweet Smell of Success*.

A man of truly international dimension, handsome, deeply intellectual and quietly articulate, he never compromised on standards, a virtue which nevertheless brought him into conflict with people such as Burt Lancaster and Carl Foreman.

Among last night's tributes, Mr Eddie Dick the new director of the Scottish Film Production Fund who was working on a book with Mackendrick, said: "Consistently from the 1940s to the 1960s, he produced a powerful body of work, with a strong philosophical humour and high moral sense, questioning the relationship between good and evil. *The Sweet Smell of Success* was an under-rated American film."

Professor Colin Young, former director of the National Film and Television School, said: "Mackendrick was my hero, an extraordinarily subtle film-maker, without pretension in his films or himself.

"He then became a great teacher. Some time back he was

runner-up for the post of director at the British Film Institute—and what a loss that we didn't bring him back to this country."

Drama was to follow Mackendrick all the way from his family roots in Glasgow, where his father was a shipyard draughtsman before emigrating to America around 1910. The family settled first in Los Angeles, where he was conceived, and then in Boston, where he was born in 1912.

But his father died in the 'flu epidemic of the First World War and within weeks his father's brother was murdered by a maniac in Los Angeles. With the mother ill-prepared for single parenthood, grandfather Mackendrick, who had also gone to live in America, was so appalled by the fate of his two sons that he brought the child back to Glasgow.

Living at Hamilton Park Terrace, young Sandy went to Hillhead High and later Glasgow School of Art, breaking his course to work for J. Walter Thompson's advertising agency in London.

From there he edged into the film industry, where his talents stretched from making animated cartoons to selling his first screenplay. When the war intervened, he worked for the Foreign Office in psychological warfare during the North African campaign.

Mackendrick resumed screenwriting before becoming a director in time for the famous Ealing comedies of the post-war period.

At his Beverly Hills home he told me of those halcyon days, from 1946 till 1954, when the British film industry could blossom in advance of television. The Ealing of Michael Balcon was making four or five films a year, always inside the studio.

Someone struck on what was then the novel idea of making a whole film on location and Mackendrick was given his break as a director, charged with turning Compton Mackenzie's latest book into a movie.

Taking a film unit of 60 people to the island of Barra in miserable weather seemed a foolhardy venture. In the absence of hotels, actors accustomed to West End comfort found themselves living with the crofters whose lives they portrayed.

But people like Gordon Jackson, John Gregson, and Joan Greenwood fell in love with Barra. Compton Mackenzie, who made a personal appearance, was still adding refinements as they were filming.

What was intended as a second feature was suddenly promoted when the main production failed and *Whisky Galore* became an unexpected legend of the cinema.

Alexander Mackendrick's career soared through titles like *The Maggie*, *The Man in The White Suit*, and *The Ladykillers* (introducing a new talent called Peter Sellers). Whisked off to Hollywood, he was to make a significant start with *The Sweet Smell of Success* in 1956.

As the first of the big stars to finance his own productions, Burt Lancaster engaged the Scot to prepare for Shaw's *The Devil's Disciple*. But that was shelved and the two men parted company.

Lancaster later assured me he had never lost his belief in Mackendrick's genius but claimed that his pursuit of perfection simply proved too costly for his paymaster.

Uncomfortable with Hollywood, he came back to Britain, by which time the industry was in decline. The situation was little better in Los Angeles, when he returned to direct major movies for 20th Century Fox.

Once again, his independence of mind ran him into conflict, this time with big-time producer Carl Foreman, who had engaged him to direct Alistair MacLean's blockbuster, *The Guns of Navarone*. It would have been a happy coincidence, with MacLean and Mackendrick both former pupils of Glasgow's Hillhead High School.

After six months of planning in places such as Cyprus and Rhodesia, however, Foreman and Mackendrick couldn't agree on direction and the latter was sacked, to be replaced by another director of Scottish background, J. Lee Thompson, who picked up the threads of one of the greatest action films of all time.

Mackendrick veered more and more to the academic world, revered by everyone from Steven Spielberg to our own Bill Forsyth but leaving a sense that we had somehow failed to reap the full benefit of a cinematic genius. The consolation is that he inspired a new generation of actors and directors.

His latter days were blighted by yet another family tragedy, involving his beloved grand-daughter, Merry Mackendrick from Lochwinnoch. Newly qualified as a doctor two years ago, she was travelling with her boyfriend in Africa, helping villagers with medical advice, when they were set upon and murdered by bandits.

Alexander Mackendrick's first wife, who later married Fleet Street editor Hugh Cudlipp, was the mother of their son Kerry, an executive with the *Daily Record*.

Apart from Kerry, he is survived by his second wife Hilary and their two sons, John and Matthew.

THE DIGNITY OF MATT BUSBY

TRIUMPH and tragedy were the dominant elements which went to make up the legend of Matt Busby, that extraordinary human being who died yesterday at 84. The heights he would attain with Manchester United were beyond the dreams of the little lad who grew up amid the coal mines of Bellshill in Lanarkshire, from which his father departed to the First World War and didn't come back.

That family tragedy gave the young Matt a taste of responsibility which, in the strange ways of fate, was to equip him for the greatness that lay ahead.

I remember seeing his substantial frame playing for the British Army in Aberdeen during the war. His moderate career as a player had been spent with Manchester City and Liverpool but it was at the end of that war that he began the climb to real prominence.

He became manager of Manchester United in 1945, won the FA Cup in 1948, followed by the League Championship, and was building what was generally accepted to be one of the greatest club sides of all time in the 1950s.

The forecast of 1958 was that his so-called Busby Babes would carry off the European Cup, as the first British club to do so. Then tragedy struck. Returning from Yugoslavia in the latter stages of that competition, the plane carrying the Manchester party crashed at Munich and the bulk of his wonderful team was wiped out. Young stars like Duncan Edwards and Tommy Taylor were among the dead, who also included journalists like Henry Rose, and Frank Swift, that greatest of all goalkeepers.

Matt Busby himself was so badly injured that hourly bulletins assured us that he was still alive. The nation was shocked beyond belief.

252

It took years to put aside the Munich Disaster, as it was called, but Busby fought his way back to reasonable health and, within 10 years, was poised for the triumph which had been snatched from his grasp in 1958.

By now Celtic had become the first British team to win the European Cup but Manchester United were heading that way in 1968, now with new names like Denis Law, George Best and Bobby Charlton, who had been a young survivor of the air disaster.

I'll never forget that night at Wembley Stadium when Busby led out his men to meet Benfica of Portugal, which had in its ranks the great Eusebio. Manchester United survived the 90 minutes, won in extra time—and Wembley went mad for Matt.

What followed was one of the most moving experiences I have known. Leaving the grandstand, I ran into a little woman whom I knew to be Matt Busby's mother. Rescuing her from the general melée, I took her to where she wanted to be—with her boy. When we reached the dressing room of Wembley Matt came out, stood and looked at her, then grasped her in his arms and they both wept.

It was not hard to guess what was going through their minds. Busby had done it for his dad and he had done it for his hard-working mother, who was only 17 when he was born. And of course he had done it for his Busby Babes.

Before that night was out, we were all back for the celebration at the Russell Hotel in London, where Joe Loss and his band played for the massive gathering.

Through in a private room, however, Matt Busby was holding a more private party. In the course of that evening he made a quietly dignified speech to confirm that this was without doubt the greatest night of his life. He just wanted to thank his friends for all they had done to make it possible.

Poignantly, there were absent friends whose fate had taken him to the brink of despair. He was remembering them most of all that night.

That quiet dignity was the hallmark of Busby's career. In time he stepped up to the board and became himself the great legend of Old Trafford. His counsel was there for all his successors, including Alex

Ferguson, who is shaping Matt Busby's club once more towards the greatness of another day.

Football has lost one of its greatest ever figures—a gentleman whose standards were an example to us all.

THE MYSTERY MAN OF
QUEEN STREET STATION

LONG before homelessness became the Big Issue on every street corner, I had seen the vexed problem personified in the shuffling figure of the man I knew only as Frank.

You would see him wandering between Argyle Street and George Square, Glasgow, a tall, red-haired and bearded man who seemed to find the setting of Queen Street station as the safest haven of all in which to play out the musings of his distant and private world.

People like that stir your curiosity. What is their background? Are they down-and-out through drink or mental illness? Are there relatives who care at all about what has happened to them? What guides the random movement of their aimless days—and where do they spend the night?

Suddenly homelessness became a clearer issue, given voice in fact by a fortnightly publication called *The Big Issue*, which confronts you a dozen times on a short walk through our city centres.

The vendors are the homeless themselves, varying in their sales approach from the shy and modest to the slightly pushy, whose impassioned pleas to "Help the homeless!" are hard to ignore if you wish to live with your conscience. Personally, I tend to bypass the more aggressive, who could surely find a commercial role in this age of the hard sell, and buy my copy from those who are clearly ill at ease with their lot.

The definition of homelessness, I have to say, has bothered me since I watched one of those investigative television documentaries, which took you under the arches of London's down-and-out land, cardboard boxes and all, and spoke to an assortment of human

255

flotsam who, like southern trade union spokesmen, seemed to come almost exclusively from Scotland.

A policeman who saw the same programme, and who was well acquainted with the floating population of central Glasgow, told me he had identified one after another of those London "homeless" who had perfectly good homes to go to in their own city.

They had merely joined the boxcar trek to the metropolis, drifters who found, for a time at least, a certain glamour in the notion of sleeping rough in the wider world.

Such programmes distort the issue of homelessness, which is real enough without exaggeration and is said to involve more than 40,000 people in Scotland alone.

Some of those who were begging on the streets not so long ago have now found a more self-respecting role as vendors for *The Big Issue*, an American idea brought to this country by Scotland's Gordon Roddick, chairman of the Body Shop. They keep 30p of the 50p selling price, gaining a sense of doing something for their money.

The fact that it is a kind of halfway-house to rehabilitation is confirmed by the magazine's director Tricia Hughes, who says: "Many of our original vendors have changed out of all recognition and some have gone on to find permanent accommodation and work." That's great.

The magazine itself deals not only with the problems of the homeless but extends to some interesting general features. Reaching Dundee for the first time this month, the latest issue has a very professional interview with that city's most famous actor, Brian Cox, back home with a production of Ibsen's *The Master Builder*.

I also learned that Scotland's best-known, privately-owned doss-house, Glasgow's Great Eastern Hotel in Duke Street, has been housing the homeless since 1907 and charges £54 a week for bed and breakfast. One lodger has been there for 30 years.

In the current issue there is even a defence of Jimmy Hill, the sports commentator most Scots love to hate. Writer Simon Pia points out very properly how often Jimmy the Chin's criticisms have proved to be justified.

In conversations with the magazine's vendors, I have found a recurring explanation of why they were homeless. Their parents had thrown them out. But there must have been a reason. Eventually we get to the heart of the matter: drugs. So once more this modern evil is playing havoc with the social structure and creating problems well beyond its own immediate misery.

But to get back to Frank, the lonely wanderer of Queen Street station . . . come to think of it I haven't seen him for months. And the reason, I now discover, is that poor Frank died recently of pneumonia. He was 45. Frank Tinney was his name, believed by some to have been a professional man for whom the world went wrong.

Contrary to appearances he was not an alcoholic but he was a schizophrenic. He did have a family, who had done their best for him, and they were there at the funeral along with friends from the Talbot Centre, where Frank would find shelter of a night.

He was a quiet and popular man, a lost soul in a troubled world. I had always intended to speak to him and feel sorry now that I didn't. I'm told that one man who did was artist John Kilmartin, who went one step further and actually painted his portrait not long before he died.

So the image of Frank Tinney will live on when others are long forgotten, a strangely haunting face giving hint of a potential which, by the pattern of his destiny, was not to be fulfilled.

STRANGE CALL ABOUT THE DAFFODILS

A READER called me the other day to tell of a wonderful display of daffodils on Great Western Road, Glasgow.

He could see it from his window and this symbol of spring had so stirred his feelings that he wanted to tell the world about it. Why didn't I come and see for myself—and write a column on it?

It is impossible to respond to the many suggestions which come this way but, for some strange reason, I lingered with the man and his eloquence, even though I was just leaving to catch a flight to London.

The view, he said, was all the more meaningful to him because he was suffering from cancer—did I know that the daffodil was also the emblem of the Marie Curie organisation for cancer care?—and suddenly the world had become an even more beautiful place.

All right, I said, when I get back from London I'll make a detour by Great Western Road and share this host of golden daffodils. He left his name and address: Bryce Morrison of Ascot Court.

In London I was reminded of my caller as I walked through Hyde Park on one of the most heavenly days of spring I have ever known. Yes, the daffodils were in full bloom and London was looking its seductive best. (For all its flaws I'm still inclined to agree with Dr Johnson that he who tires of London tires of life.)

That evening I went to the Prince Edward Theatre to hear Gershwin's music in *Crazy For You* and ended up in an Italian restaurant in Old Compton Street, gazing out on the Soho scene and thinking not only of Bryce Morrison's daffodils but of the spring-time of my own life.

It was 45 years ago that I first came to this great city and sampled the excitement of the bright lights. Yet it seemed like only yesterday that I trod those same streets of Soho, absorbing the magic of theatreland.

I used to stay with two grand-aunts in Stanmore, Middlesex, Sophie and Babs, Aberdeenshire ladies who followed the southward trail to serve in the stately homes of England.

In the early part of the century they cooked for King Edward VII and later worked for the King of Egypt in his London home.

Dear old Sophie had the impossible task of exercising control over the prince who became King Farouk and would tell of the randy young devil chasing housemaids round the table.

On those memorable visits of my early years I would take the grand-aunts to a West End show, to see Noel Coward or Ivor Novello, and there we gathered lilacs in the spring again.

And now, from the window of the Italian restaurant, I could see a very different Soho, reflecting the changes of my own lifetime.

A scattering of skinheads, loud in their vulgarity; couples passing by the window, the homosexual pairings now outnumbering the heteros.

I was out of tune with so much of this modern world yet there was a reassuring continuity in the music of George Gershwin which was echoing in my head from an hour ago, just as it had done more than 40 years earlier when I saw the first London production of *Porgy and Bess*, which didn't reach these shores till 17 years after Gershwin wrote it.

So I headed back to Scotland, clearer in my memory of life's early season, appreciating afresh the daffodils of spring.

Next day I opened *The Herald* and glanced as always at the death announcements. "After a long illness, fought with tremendous courage and determination, Bryce Lindsay Morrison . . ."

The poignancy of his phone call came clearer when I spoke to his stepson, Bill, a research scientist who had flown home from New York.

It transpired that Bryce Morrison, the man I had never met, had called to tell me about those daffodils just as he was taking his very last look at them. I sensed there was something special about his call but I couldn't have guessed that on that very same evening, he would be taken to the Western Infirmary to enter the closing hours of his life.

259

On the phone that morning he was so full of an infectious enthusiasm and vitality. Yet by then, I'm told, he had lost the power of his arms.

The call, however, did not surprise his family and friends.

For this, apparently, was Bryce Morrison, a former senior executive with British Telecom who was still only 56 when he died.

He was a popular man who spread warmth and joy, a deep thinker and keen traveller who would turn up at Bill's home in New York en route to a Bermudan cruise on the *QE2*.

The greater significance of the daffodils emerged when I learned that Mr Morrison was still mourning his wife, who died of cancer in the Marie Curie home at Huntershill, Glasgow.

Yes, the daffodil was the emblem of Marie Curie, as he had reminded me.

And that was his last thought as he prepared to fold over the petals of his existence and drift away with a fragrance that would linger for ever.

THE BEACHES OF NORMANDY—
50 YEARS ON

THERE was something inevitable in what I did last week. After all, how could I forget that June morning of 1944 when I heard the news of the D-Day landings on my way to school?

On the threshold of teenage, there was a sense of missing out on what would soon emerge as the most dramatic military operation in all history. Perhaps it was the early journalistic instinct which prompted me to feel I should have been there. I was missing the story.

In time, our village lads came home with tales of the Normandy landings. In time, bedraggled Germans arrived at the nearby prisoner-of-war camp at Stuartfield. They worked on local farms and my mother would invite young Werner Hoffmann for tea on Sundays. He was far from home, she said—and he was somebody's boy.

So the legend of D-Day has hovered with me ever since. If I had missed the actual event, perhaps I could catch the echoes half a century later.

And that was what took me on a plane to Paris and a train to Caen, focal point of the German defence, where I arrived on the eve of the anniversary. The town, now tastefully restored from wartime devastation, was buzzing with busloads of veterans pouring in with accompanying wives and middle-aged children.

The Normandy landings of 1994 were properly under way. With the heads of state arriving, roads were already being closed as I drove down the dozen miles from Caen past the historic Pegasus Bridge, towards the sea at Ouistreham where the royal yacht was berthing.

From there it was westward to the famous beaches, a chain of villages which could have been the Ayrshire coast or my own native corner of Aberdeenshire. Places much smaller than Troon or Fraserburgh were now immortal on the maps of history.

So I walked along Sword Beach, where the British forces had landed 50 years ago, and tried to visualise what had been happening here that June morning as I made my way to school in distant Scotland.

At the village of Courseulles I paused by the stone which tells you it was here Charles de Gaulle stepped back on French soil eight days after D-Day. (Here too that men like Lord Campbell of Croy stormed ashore with the 15th Scottish Division to punch the first break-out corridor.)

At Arromanches the pipes and drums were already stirring the air with "Scotland the Brave", amphibious vehicles were bobbing their way ashore in a reconstruction of history—and a carnival atmosphere was developing at promenade cafés.

The seascape running on to flat stretches of beach and hinterland (except at the notorious Omaha) seemed the perfect setting for history's biggest invasion. Yet it was hard to imagine.

I walked to a place of peace and watched the shallow waves as they broke upon those sands where once young footsteps had little further to go. And suddenly, that air of quiet which had tested the imagination was rent apart by wave upon wave of wartime aeroplanes, bursting on the scene with dramatic effect.

Now you were there, on D-Day, vividly aware of the noise, the action, the mixed emotion of fear, excitement, anticipation. Poised on the razor's edge, this might be the day when you would die.

For the first time I could sense the heady cocktail and begin to understand the veterans' assertion that, for all its potential as a gateway to heaven or hell, this was without doubt the most memorable day of their lives.

I stood and watched *them*—as they stood and watched and remembered. Darken a grey strand and strip away a pot belly or a plastic hip and you had young heroes of 50 years ago. Wives who had heard the stories told and retold to the point of tedium now granted them proper respect.

For they were true after all; and many a female hand clasped a husband's arm as they wept in the silence of their hearts.

The Queen and President Clinton took their respective places. Before them all now, the sea of little stones and crosses told its own heart-rending tale, each one a wasted life, a memory, a heartache that would never go away—young men who indeed would grow not old as those who were left had now grown old.

But they were here today, those men who fell in France, in spiritual greeting to those comrades who had come back—and would never forget.

At the going down of the sun I boarded the Paris train and warmed to the sight of American youngsters unashamedly telling a delightful old veteran from Frank Sinatra's home town of Hoboken that they had come away with a whole new appreciation of what they owed him. He beamed.

Back home, a letter from Germany reminded me that Hitler's victims lay on both sides. Werner Hoffmann, our prisoner friend, was thinking of my mother's kindness and recalling that he was just 18 when wounded at Normandy. Now a retired businessman, he wrote beautifully about the healing wounds and the grass and the sand which now covered the blood and tears of 1944.

To gain the full perspective, I knew I simply had to be on the beaches last week.

THANKS FOR THE MEMORY

IN Scotland last week we took our farewell of Bob Hope and were glad of the chance to say "Thanks for the memory". His appearance at the Glasgow Royal Concert Hall was a nostalgic celebration of a star who has performed in every decade of this century.

Most of us this side of the Atlantic remember him best through the *Road* films, in which he was accompanied by Bing Crosby and Dorothy Lamour on the various routes to Rio, Bali, Singapore, or Morocco.

This time Bob Hope was back in his native Britain for the D-Day concert aboard the *QE2*. And when that was over, he made a single appearance at the Royal Albert Hall in London and agreed to one more engagement.

Cameron McNicol brought off a coup for his Glasgow venue by offering the Hollywood star the irresistible bait of the Road to Gleneagles, with a professional detour by the Royal Concert Hall.

For so many wealthy Americans Gleneagles means peace and pampered living in the glorious heart of Perthshire. It also means golf in the land where it began.

Mr Hope, of course, is an addicted golfer so it was no surprise that he was still out on the course when I arrived for our rendez-vous.

Back in the cocktail bar, it was plain that his hearing was none too good and that he wasn't exactly the razor-sharp figure I had met in that same haven 20 years ago. But what could I expect? He is, after all, into his 92nd year.

Happily, that didn't stop him bursting into song at every opportunity, especially with Vera Lynn's wartime favourite "We'll Meet Again". They had met up on the *QE2* and it was one of those songs he couldn't get out of his head.

264

There was then a touching moment as he went in for dinner at Gleneagles. Cutlery fell silent as diners broke into spontaneous applause and the pianist struck up "Thanks for the Memory", his long-established theme song. The timing was perfect as ever and Bob waved his acknowledgment all the way to the table.

After dinner we repaired to the luxurious suite accompanied by his charming wife Dolores, a greatly under-rated singing talent, as we would discover at the concert hall on the following evening.

And there it was time for nostalgia, from that early childhood in Eltham with his stonemason father and Welsh singing mother, who uptailed from England in 1907 and took their seven sons to live in America.

"We sang all the time," Hope was recalling. "And if you were singing, my mother was happy. She wanted me to succeed and I remember once we went to see a top entertainer, when suddenly she turned to me and said in a loud voice: 'He's not half as good as you!' "

The chances are she was right. For, as we all know, Bob Hope went on to become one of the world's leading entertainers, teaming up with great names like Judy Garland, Jane Russell, Ethel Merman, Jimmy Durante, as well as Bing Crosby and Dorothy Lamour.

"Yes, Bing was one of my great friends," he says. "So were Pat O'Brien, George Murphy, and Ray Milland. I still see Dorothy. She came to my 90th birthday party and was in great shape."

Bob and Dolores, who have been married for 60 years, were first in Scotland in 1939 and were on their way back to New York on the *Queen Mary* when the Second World War was declared.

A lifelong Republican, Hope was once courted to stand for President ("Dolores didn't want to move to a smaller house!") and has known every occupant of the White House since Franklin D. Roosevelt. Bill Clinton sent him a birthday greeting last week.

By now it was well past midnight and I was privately wondering how he would cope with a Glasgow audience later that day. I left him to his sleep.

In the dead of night, however, the fire alarms broke the peace of Gleneagles and guests were outside in their dressing-gowns, though there was no reported sighting of the man from Hollywood.

By evening, as the concert hall buzzed with anticipation, I was still apprehensive about how Bob Hope would cope with the confusion of lights, music, audience, and a memory that wasn't what it used to be.

I reckoned without the delightful Dolores, now in her mid-eighties but a lady with such a true and attractive voice that I'm sure she would have been a star in her own right if she hadn't given her life to her husband's career.

She is a dignified lady, deeply hurt by recent revelations of Bob's earlier life, but there she was on stage, guiding him through his routine, along with their brilliant musical director Nick Perito, and charming an audience which wondered why it had not been more aware of such a talent.

They sang "We'll Meet Again", I suspect more in hope than expectation. And we responded with "Thanks for the Memory". It was another of those very special nights when a legend gave us a wave which had about it the look of finality.

THE ARTISTIC FRAME OF LIFE

ALTHOUGH I know very little about art, it is one of the pleasures of my advancing years that I am beginning to see life itself as something of an artistic adventure.

It is not too difficult to turn the window-frame of the bus or the train or the restaurant into the frame of a picture, containing a canvas of nature which we would rave about if some mortal creature had painted it.

Nor is it too hard to turn that still picture into a moving one, in which the scenes of daily life become a kind of kaleidoscope of colour and motion. Set to the music and natural rhythms which space out our existence, it all adds up to an artistic experience which enables you to see the apparently drab and mundane in a very different light.

From time to time I make a conscious effort in this direction, as I did on that springtime day a few weeks ago when I was heading off to London and received that curious phone call from the gentleman called Bryce Morrison, who told me about the host of golden daffodils he could see from his window.

What I didn't know was that he was taking in his very last view before he died. So again last week, as I travelled to London at the height of the heatwave, I was remembering Bryce Morrison and looking once more for what was best in nature's picture.

I think it was Oscar Wilde who taught me to seek out this view of life. By coincidence, my visit to London would include a rendezvous with Wilde's only grandchild so the senses were especially sharpened.

For all that people say about large conurbations, London remains for me one of the most fascinating cities in the world. The first picture I observed last week was through the window-frame of the Shuttle flight from Glasgow, circling over Tower Bridge and Buckingham Palace before coming in to land at Heathrow. What a view it was.

On the Underground into town I studied that collection of travelling faces, each with its own thoughts, no doubt with its own dreams. Where were they all going? Was their journey really necessary? Were they as lifeless as they looked or might conversation bring forth an unexpected burst of animation and radiance? Perhaps they were looking at me with similar thoughts.

As I moved about London my eyes fixed on three sights which, together, used to represent to my child mind the stability of Great Britain during the Second World War.

In Parliament Square I could see two of those symbols, Big Ben and the hunched mass of Winston Churchill, while further uptown just beyond Oxford Street, the rounded bow of Broadcasting House came sailing down Portland Place towards me.

All vocal communication during the war had come to us from its lofty transmitter—the good news and the bad, Chamberlain's declaration of war, Churchill's speeches, those ENSA concerts and *Music While You Work*.

Just across the street from Broadcasting House, the pianist in the lounge of the Langham Hilton was syncopating in the manner of the thirties. At an even earlier stage, in Victorian times, this same Langham was the rendezvous of the Prince of Wales and his various mistresses.

All very private, discreet, and uninvestigated of course, arousing some envy, one would imagine, in his successor of four generations later who, this very week, would be exposing himself to the scrutiny and prying eyes of a nosy-parker world.

So I meandered through Mayfair towards Green Park and found myself a deck-chair in the heat of high summer. Young couples frolicked on the grass, elderly ladies with poodles sheltered under the trees, groups of foreign visitors drifted past and an Italian businessman took a phone call on his portable.

Showered in the cool of evening, I dined alone but found conversation with the American couple at the next table, who were

268

appreciating the joys of London and reiterating their admiration for Churchill while apologising for the calibre of their current President. Only when the gentleman laid down his card on leaving did I realise that I had been in the company of a Los Angeles vice cop and his wife.

Ending the day at the rooftop bar of the Park Lane Hilton brought another of those artistic adventures—the view of a handsome city by night, the diamond-and-ruby patterns of traffic circulating by Hyde Park Corner below and filtering off to radial arteries. Two Russians beside me were finding it no less entrancing.

Next day, as the crowds streamed towards Wimbledon, I peeled off to a neighbouring district and kept that appointment with Oscar Wilde's grandson, a subject to which I shall return in a forthcoming Weekender.

Then it was back home to Scotland, to a howling wind which could have belonged to early winter—and to that television programme about which the nation would inevitably divide itself. When it was finished I merely asked myself one simple question: Did I feel better or worse about Prince Charles? And I was in no doubt that I felt better.

The whole programme, I thought, was an interesting insight into the royal routine. Within the frame of the small screen, it was another artistic experience in itself.

THE WINDOWS OF TIME

PAUSING by a shop window in central Glasgow I caught a reflection which pulled me up in my tracks. It could have been my late father. Instead, as composure was regained, I realised it was myself, confirming a belief that the older we grow the more we resemble the parent of our own gender.

Indeed my Aberdonian father, with his shrewd observation of the human species and his rugged sense of humour, used to caution young men in search of a wife: "Tak a damned gweed look at her mither!"

That incident by Waterstone's bookshop window took on a deeper significance, however, since I was looking, with undisguised satisfaction, at a display of books which trace a fair part of my personal history.

One of them, bringing my autobiography back into print, carries a front-cover picture of the teenage Webster, complete with tartan bow tie and checked bunnet and thinking he is fair Airchie, on a 1940s visit to the Longchamps racecourse in Paris.

There I was at the very beginning of a career which seemed as if it might stretch to infinity. But another birthday at the weekend made plain the truth of that infinity. It's finite!

At the other end of life's scale, I have gained a pleasurable rapport with a new audience in the centrefold of *The Herald* and that liaison should have some mileage in it yet.

For that reason, I parried a publisher's suggestion that he should bring a selection of these columns into book form. It was an appealing idea but one which could wait, in the hope that there will be other candidates for the best-of-Tuesdays.

Instead he has turned his attention to an earlier decade of my career, when I was in my thirties, arriving in Glasgow and discovering the joys of being a feature writer on a national daily paper.

I don't know if it captures anything of the essence of its time but I have merely gathered together 100 of the articles I was writing back in that curious period around the Swinging Sixties, showing at least some of the topics to which I was turning my attention 30 years ago.

Interesting people who were still around to be interviewed included Compton Mackenzie, Robert Boothby, Richard Rodgers, Bing Crosby, Robert Graves, Barnes Wallis, Bud Neill, and Lex McLean.

I was writing about disasters like Ibrox and Clarkston and the James Watt Street fire as well as the sensational murder of Northeast farmer Maxwell Garvie. I was flying in the very first Concorde, making forays into the troubles in Northern Ireland, and managing to raise a cheer as I watched the English football team winning the World Cup at Wembley in 1966.

I went from the Berlin Wall to the heights of Hong Kong and, in lighter vein, sought names for a new-born son, sampled the joys of long johns and examined the allure of the miniskirt.

From a professional point of view it is interesting to look back and gauge any development of style. Many of those articles were written on the day, often cooked up in the course of the forenoon and delivered by teatime. Sometimes the haste shows through; at other times the urgency of the moment stirred the brain cells to a phrase you might not have hit upon given more time to think about it.

If there are subtle changes of topic, style and presentation, there is a massive difference in how it is all produced. Those 100 articles were battered out to the clack of the old standard typewriter, with carbons to retain a copy, sub-edited by people with pencils and put into type as large slabs of hot lead which would have lasted till Doomsday if they had not been melted down for reuse in the following day's paper.

Now newspaper offices are havens of carpeted calm, quiet keyboards and hypnotic screens which seem to replace human contact with a form of video game. It comes to us all in time, I suppose, to say that things ain't what they used to be.

As I looked in that shop window and saw myself as a young man in Paris—and again as a top-hatted scribbler at Princess Anne's 1974 wedding—I was lost in a bygone age, adjusting to the reflection in the glass and thinking it not too inappropriate that I was looking more and more like my father.

He thoroughly disapproved when I forsook the land for journalism, which he assessed with characteristic bluntness as "a tippence-ha'penny bugger o' a job". But that did not prevent me from paying him a warm tribute when he retired from his auctioneering job in 1970. It goes without saying that John Webster takes his place in my latest volume.

There is a Glasgow launching at Waterstone's on Thursday and anyone who has had the grace and intelligence to reach this far is welcome to join me in an early evening glass of wine.

THE WONDERS OF PARIS

STROLLING along the boulevards of Paris recently I found myself marvelling once again at the sheer grandeur of that magnificent city. I had been here as an impressionable youth in the 1940s but it was reassuring to find that I could still be stirred by its aura of glamour and romance five decades later.

As a country boy with an enthusiasm for big cities I had, in the years between, left my heart not only in San Francisco but in such a diverse range as New York, Cairo, Hong Kong, Bangkok, Singapore, even London.

A special warmth for Washington may arise from the fact that it was modelled, to a considerable extent, on Baron Haussman's master plan of Paris. But a return to the French capital itself was a reminder that there is perhaps no more stunningly attractive city in the world.

Standing at the Arc de Triomphe and casting around those avenues which peel away in radial splendour, the Champs Elysées proceeding with dignity towards Place de la Concorde, the Eiffel Tower rising as the symbol of a nation, you know there is probably nowhere else on earth to stimulate you so.

Five decades bring their own inevitable change but how easily I could transport myself to that very first visit, so soon after the Second World War, when I started out by train from Aberdeen, passed through London (I didn't see it till later), crossed from Folkstone to Boulogne, and finally spotted the Eiffel Tower on the train's approach to Paris.

I still have those snapshots of distant youth, the would-be man-about-town watching the Grand Prix de Paris at the Longchamps racecourse and running into Prince Aly Khan and the glamorous Rita Hayworth, the very first encounter with a Hollywood star.

I revelled in the extravaganzas of Bal Tabarin, the Moulin Rouge, and the Folies Bergère, where I was lucky enough to catch that legendary entertainer, Josephine Baker, and roamed the shady, mysterious back-streets of Pigalle and Montmartre.

My clear memory of Paris in that immediate post-war period is of a city not much removed from the steamy, seductive days of Toulouse Lautrec. Certainly there was still that pre-war whiff of perfume and prostitutes, mature ladies of the night wrapped in fur stoles and beckoning from every second doorway.

By the time I returned in that Coronation year of 1953, Paris seemed to have escaped the timewarp and faced up to a very different world.

Looking back on that visit of the late forties, I had not appreciated just how recently those Nazi jackboots had strutted down the Champs Elysées. It was no time at all since General de Gaulle had followed that same route in a triumphal march of liberation.

And it was only yesterday—in fact it was 50 years ago this week—that Ernest Hemingway walked into the famous Ritz Hotel, complete with war correspondent's uniform and sten-gun in hand, announced that he had come personally to liberate the Ritz—and ordered a dry Martini! Needless to say, he did not stop there, for the retreating Germans had left behind a fair old selection of wines and spirits.

Paris is celebrating half a century of freedom this week. They will light up the skyline with fireworks and re-run De Gaulle's liberation speech for all to hear.

And, as I walked around those streets which still pulsate with memory, I came upon the exclusive Hotel Maurice near Place de la Concorde and remembered that that was where the German army set up its headquarters during the occupation.

From there I crossed the Seine to Napoleon's Tomb, where history comes at you in waves, and strode on again towards the Eiffel Tower, a feat of engineering which, at the close quarters of walking up its stairway, defies all imagination.

Regaining breath on the second platform, I gazed out over Paris and wondered why I had been so long in coming back. It must have been 20 years since my last visit. And how lucky are the French, I was thinking to myself, in their geographic situation, so central to the continent. Puir Aul' Scotia, on the other hand, labours away as the Cape Wrath of Europe, taking the brunt of the worst Atlantic weather and having so far to travel to its markets.

It was a cue for a drink. So I wheeled towards the Champs Elysées once more and found solace at the famous George V Hotel. But, in casual clothes and trainer shoes, was I dressed for the occasion? Ah well, they could only throw me out.

I found the cocktail bar, all plush and dignified, and no-one seemed to notice my lack of suitable attire. I certainly couldn't hide in the crowd for, apart from a small group of wealthy foreigners lining up women for the night, there was no-one to be seen. I could soon understand why.

At £10 for a gin and tonic, they were no doubt glad to serve anyone, even a Scottish sucker in sannies. It's the price you pay for a city like Paris. And, considering its irresistible charms, I didn't grudge a penny of it.

TO NEW YORK ON THE *QE2*

ANY fear that Scotland may have lost her love of great ships was surely dispelled by the tumultuous reception accorded to the *QE2* on the recent return to her cradle on Clydeside.

It was only the second time she had seen the river of her birth since sailing away on that memorable day of 1969, to replace her sisters at Cunard, the *Queen Mary* and the *Queen Elizabeth*.

For her silver-anniversary cruising the *QE2* was taking in Greenock as an extended point of embarkation for the normal crossing of Southampton to New York, giving Scots the rare opportunity to sail from their own land.

How they grabbed that opportunity! And what a send-off they were given, by a crowd which was estimated at 150,000, as that sleek creation of Clydebank craftsmanship sailed down the sunset of a glorious late summer evening.

Even young people were suddenly caught up in the mixed emotion of a pride in this small nation's achievements and a deep regret that we ever let slip our reputation as the greatest shipbuilding race on earth.

By the time she headed out into the Atlantic the *QE2* was buzzing with the assorted accents of the world.

The Scots were there in such numbers as to raise the question of who could possibly be left in such small communities as Skelmorlie. Mind you, not so many were left standing when a fierce storm in the North Atlantic sent the *QE2* veering to a southward course.

My own queasiness was compounded by the thought that I was due to give a talk about those Clydebank ships. How could I face an audience—if there was an audience left to face? The answer was to be found in a most effective injection which can now remove all fear of seasickness.

With the sea rolling heavily—and 130 brave souls staggering towards the theatre—I was now doubly convinced of the public's fascination with ships. What an intriguing hour we had. There was the Scot who had sailed on the *Queen Mary* during the war and wanted to tell of his experience. But he choked up emotionally.

There were Americans wanting to know more about our Scottish *Queens*; and Scots, like Willie Chestnut, who had helped to build them. I could spot familiar faces like George Wyllie, the sculptor who once built a full-size paper boat, and Bill McMurdo, agent for the stars, currently embroiled in controversy over sculpture of another sort—the Argyll sex picture.

Yet another familiar face came by, later revealed when he took the stage himself and showed why the name of Neil Sedaka reached the heights of showbiz fame. Life on the *QE2* is full of surprises.

By now the sea had calmed and I was exercising on deck, listening to Mozart in the Queen's Room, learning to jive, sunbathing, browsing in the bookshop—and signing 100 copies of one of my books.

Always, on board ship, it is time to eat. You dress for dinner and enjoy an aperitif in the Midships Bar, soothed into the mellow mood of evening by the pianist playing Gershwin and Cole Porter. After dinner it's cabaret in the Grand Lounge and dancing the night away, strolling on deck with a sense of nature's power around you—and reaching the early hours in the Yacht Club, where Mr Sedaka doesn't object to the fact that the pianist is playing and singing *his* songs.

Last time I crossed by sea, in the 1960s, the *Queen Mary* was taking me on that very first visit to the United States. Wondering if this arrival might prove an anti-climax, I was up in good time to find out.

But I need have had no fears. There is an enduring magic in that Manhattan skyline which draws you to its bosom as you pass the welcoming arm of Liberty's statue on the port side and turn to starboard for one of the greatest sights on God's earth. It stuns you into a thoughtful silence. For this is America.

A taxi to the New York Palace and soon I'm sauntering on Fifth Avenue, rediscovering one of my favourite cities. At night it's the

Shubert Theatre and Gershwin's *Crazy For You*, spilling into Times Square and mingling with other theatre-goers, all fresh from the exhilaration of Broadway.

Even for a mince and-tatties man like me, there is no missing the Sunday brunch at the Plaza Hotel, which has to be consumed to be believed. (There's a choice of everything, except mince and tatties!)

I never miss a sentimental visit to the Waldorf Astoria, running my fingers over the keys of the piano on which Cole Porter composed his evergreen melodies. Porter lived in a private apartment at the hotel for 25 years.

After all that luxury, it seems almost obscene to say that the homeward flight was by Concorde. But three hours after leaving Kennedy Airport we were approaching Heathrow, a novel if rather expensive way of defeating jet-lag.

The *QE2* is coming to Greenock and Invergordon on a round-Britain cruise next year. But Cunard must surely consider turning Greenock-New York into an annual crossing. Those 150,000 people who turned out, fascinated and envious, are the basis of a whole new market for a great Scottish ship.

DIAMOND DAY FOR THE *MARY*

Los Angeles, Tuesday.

A BOTTLE of champagne smashed across her bow to celebrate the diamond jubilee of the great *Queen Mary*, launched at Clydebank in September 1934 and now a floating hotel and holiday attraction at Long Beach, California.

Fire boats spurted fountains of salute and Prince Michael of Kent repeated, symbolically, the words of his grandmother as she stepped forward at John Brown's yard and said: "I am happy to name this ship *Queen Mary*. I wish success to her and to all who sail in her."

In a deeply moving ceremony the great ship blasted her horn as if about to sail and gave notice that there's life in the old girl yet.

Among those who witnessed the Long Beach ceremony was John Templeman from Muirend, Glasgow, winner of *The Herald* competition for stories about the *Queen Mary*, who was flown out for the occasion by British Airways.

Indeed, the American audience listened in fascination as John read his winning essay, recalling that day in 1943 when, as a young airman about to train as a pilot in Canada, he joined the *Queen Mary* at Greenock and realised that a VIP was coming up the gangway. It was none other than Winston Churchill, heading for the famous Quebec Conference to meet President Roosevelt. In the course of that voyage Churchill was presented with the plans for the D-Day invasion of 1944.

This was living history. And to add to that sense of listening to the witnesses of a disappearing age, 77-year-old George Kean from Clydebank told the company of his part as an apprentice shipwright at Clydebank, working on the building of the *Queen Mary* in the 1930s.

The work had been suspended during the Depression and the ship lay still for two years and three months before the government of the day decided to support her completion, not just for commercial reasons, but to boost the morale of the nation.

As thousands of unemployed flocked back to work, "my mother didn't cry any more," said George Kean, who was given the task of walking across a carpet of dust to clear the portholes.

On that launching day of 60 years ago he was underneath the hull, waiting for Queen Mary to christen the liner before he helped to knock away the final blocks of support and run for safety.

Completed in 1936, the *Mary* sailed away to carry the rich and the famous between Southampton and New York. A troopship during the war, she resumed her transatlantic role with her sister, the *Queen Elizabeth*, which had been launched from Clydebank in 1938.

By the 1960s, however, jet travel was threatening the viability of great ocean liners and the *Queen Mary* was sold off to the city of Long Beach, where she has lived ever since.

The Disney organisation ran her for a time, but two years ago she was under threat of the scrapyard. There was a public outcry and the old lady survived through the affection of the American people.

On her diamond jubilee, chief executive Joseph Prevratil was announcing that, despite the commercial problems of keeping her alive, the *Queen Mary* had now turned the corner towards profitability.

The signs were encouraging. In a weekend of hectic activity, there were five weddings taking place on board the *Queen Mary*. Hollywood people come down to make films there. Former GIs and their wartime brides were trooping on board to dance to the big band sound—and what an advertisement they were for the spirit of survival and eternal youth.

Crowds flocked to see the great ship on her birthday and to meet Prince Michael. Former boss of Scottish Opera, Peter Hemmings, now director of the Los Angeles Opera, was there with his wife. Paul Brown, a Clydebank lad who runs his own video business in California, came along to record it all on film.

Former well-known Scottish cyclist Jack Madden, who worked as a draughtsman at the Albion Works in Scotstoun but emigrated in 1949, drove up in his gleaming Rolls-Royce, proving that the New World had not exactly impoverished him.

At a champagne reception they watched the film *John Brown: The Man Who Drew a Legend* and marvelled at the fact that Dr John Brown, the naval architect who drew the first outline of the *Queen Mary* in 1926, is still with us at the age of 93. The man whose designing hand had touched the *Queen Elizabeth* and the *QE2* as well as the *Queen Mary* was attending a celebration dinner in the Cunarder home port of Southampton, but his name was very much the toast of Long Beach.

And as the birthday morning broke, Provost Jack McAllister of Clydebank was among those who rode in horse-drawn carriages to the quayside by the bow of the ship. He was here, not only as the bearer of Scottish greetings and Scottish pride, but as a man in search of economic ties between Scotland and California.

In that respect he had common purpose with the British Consul-General Merrick Baker-Bates, who has been beavering away at economic ties between Glasgow and Phoenix, Arizona. Prince Michael himself was in Arizona at the weekend playing his own part in fostering those links.

As one of the world's largest ports, Long Beach is a vital gateway for trade between Britain and the United States. But on diamond jubilee day it was the romance of the *Queen Mary* which was uppermost in people's minds—a ship which somehow wormed its way into the public's affection with a reputation as the finest ship that ever sailed the seas.

Prince Michael quoted the words of his grandfather, King George V, on the *Queen Mary's* launching day: "She has been built in friendship among ourselves. May her life among the great waters spread friendship among the nations."

She has indeed become a symbol of the relationship between Great Britain and the United States and there she lay on her sixtieth birthday, floating gently in shallow waters, bearing her incredible size and scope with immense dignity.

You look along the corridors and decks, long avenues of splendid wood-panelling, and marvel at the courage of those who believed that you could build a ship of this size. As we suffer the indignity of a lost industry, the *Queen Mary* stands proud at Long Beach, her three magnificent funnels reminding us that Scotland was once the greatest shipbuilding nation in the world. They remind us, too, of what can be achieved when vision and imagination are given full rein.

THE FLYING SCOTS

THEY WERE once the Brylcreem Boys, dashing young airmen of the Second World War, but now the hair had turned to grey and the step had lost its spring as they came together in warm reunion at the weekend.

There were legends of the air, like Bill Reid, the Glasgow lad who won the Victoria Cross for his bravery as a bomber pilot; Eric Starling, that colourful character who pioneered Scottish air routes in the 1930s; Raymond Baxter, famous BBC commentator and a Spitfire pilot with the City of Glasgow Squadron during the war—and his wee pal from Rutherglen, Tommy "Cupid" Love, with whom he flew in comradeship but hadn't seen for 50 years.

In a sense I brought them all together as a result of having delved into the story of aviation in Scotland at the request of Glasgow Royal Concert Hall, which wanted to produce a book in line with its current theme of trains, boats, and planes.

Frankly I hadn't been aware of Scotland's part in the history of aviation. But I was soon finding out. In fact it is just on 100 years since a young naval architect called Percy Pilcher built his first glider at his lodgings in Byres Road, Glasgow. He was ages with the American brothers Orville and Wilbur Wright but several stages ahead of them in reaching for the skies.

So as not to disappoint a crowd that had come to see his glider, he took off in bad weather one day in 1899 and crashed to his death. The Wrights marched on to a place in history four years later and poor Percy Pilcher, who would almost certainly have gained their glory, has been totally forgotten.

My enthusiasm thus fired, I followed the trail of plane-building in Scotland and found that William Beardmore of the Parkhead Forge built no fewer than 487 aeroplanes for the First World War.

Across Glasgow the well-known engineering firm, Weir's of Cathcart, was responsible for 1100 planes for that same war (it refused to take a profit for its efforts) before moving into the development of the autogyro and the helicopter.

But all the technology had to make way for the stories of human ingenuity and courage.

In that age when people were still getting used to the motor car, young David McIntyre from Prestwick and his friend, the future Duke of Hamilton, were creating history in 1933 as the first to fly over Mount Everest. They came home as heroes, determined to open an airfield—and that was the starting-point of all that has happened at Prestwick.

The Second World War turned weekend flyers into the daring pilots of the Battle of Britain, men like Archie McKellar and Sandy Johnstone, whose escapades are the stuff of gripping drama.

Into that war, too, went Bill Reid, the blacksmith's son from Baillieston who took off on a bombing raid one night in 1943, came under attack, suffered head wounds but kept going towards Dusseldorf, memorising his route because most of his crew lay dead behind him.

He completed his mission and somehow managed to reach British soil, landing his plane as he slumped unconscious over the controls. That earned him a Victoria Cross at 21. Bill was back on another raid when a bomb from one of our own planes struck him on the way down. He managed to bale out but fell into the hands of the Nazis.

On the way to the prison camp he came upon his wrecked aircraft. The bodies of his dead colleagues lay inside. That was the kind of traumatic experience which young lads barely into their twenties had to endure.

By coincidence I had met Bill Reid after the war when, as a returning hero, he was working for Lady MacRobert at Douneside in Aberdeenshire. Therein lay another remarkable tale.

For that brave lady lost all three sons in the air and made her own reply to Hitler by paying for new aeroplanes. She also provided careers on her estate for young men like Bill Reid, who became her substitute sons.

284

So the stories came rolling. There was the mystery of Hitler's deputy, Rudolf Hess, and his wartime flight to Scotland. My childhood stories had also included the romance of Amy Johnson, who flew solo to Australia. I knew vaguely that she married another great flyer, Jim Mollison, but I had no idea he was a Glasgow man.

Well, I ken noo. And, as we all gathered for the launch of *The Flying Scots*, Tommy Love, the Rutherglen man, recalled the day he was down in the "drink", desperately looking up from his dinghy— and there was a plane circling round and round. Yes, it was his old pal Raymond Baxter, frantically trying to spot his wee Glasgow mate in the water.

Raymond Baxter had come north to launch my book and revelled in the story of Eric Starling, training as a pilot at Croydon in 1933 when he lost his bearings in the dark and came down in a street— in Calais! He has dined out on that story for 60 years.

We laughed at it afresh over lunch as the years rolled back and the scent of Brylcreem seemed to waft over the table. We were, indeed, toasting a century of aviation in Scotland.

MARCHING WITH MY HEROES

Flushing, Holland, Sunday.

AMID tearful scenes of joyous emotion, the Scottish soldiers who came to liberate Holland exactly 50 years ago returned to a heroes' welcome along the streets of this picturesque town on the estuary of the River Scheldt.

Queen Beatrix set the royal seal on the scenes by attending a memorial service in St Jacob's Church and a grateful nation lined the streets in tens of thousands to say: "Thank you for our liberation".

They burst into rounds of spontaneous applause as the pipes and drums of the King's Own Scottish Borderers headed towards Uncle Beach—the landing point 50 years ago—followed by veterans of their own regiment, along with those of the Royal Scots, the Glasgow Highlanders, and the Commandos.

My own involvement dates back to wartime when the men of the 4th Battalion of the KOSB came to our village of Maud in Aberdeenshire to train for the day when they would invade the Continent and help to drive Hitler to his destruction.

They taught me to play the pipes, adopted me as their unofficial mascot, and were tolerant as the 11-year-old boy insisted on marching alongside them. On the day they began to move south for the battles ahead, I marched alongside them once more, out of the village.

At the first rest point, Captain Frank Coutts came back to say: "You had better go home now son. Your mother will be worried about you." So I stood and wept and waved and wished I had been old enough to go.

Fifty years later, on hearing that they were returning to the scene of the invasion, I phoned the same Frank Coutts, now a retired brigadier of 76, and said: "Can I come this time?"

And so it was that he welcomed me into the fold of the Old Comrades of the 4th KOSB and today the "wee loon fae Maud" marched beside him as he led his men past their memorial near Uncle Beach where they had stormed ashore that November morning in 1944. We had come to honour those 10 lads of the battalion who fell here at Flushing, as well as the many others who were to die in the battles ahead.

It had all begun when we joined a bus in Edinburgh and collected Old Comrades through Galashiels, Selkirk, and Hawick before driving to Hull and crossing on the ferry to Rotterdam.

The route in 1944 had been rather different. These Scottish soldiers were standing by as a back-up to the Arnhem assault but, when that ended in disaster, the plans were changed. Instead, they crossed from Southampton to Ostend and drove north to the port of Breskens on the estuary of the River Scheldt.

The Allies needed to gain the port of Antwerp but first had to drive the Germans out of the Dutch island of Walcheren. That would entail a two-mile crossing of the estuary from Breskens to Flushing. And here we were back at the scene of that raging battle.

Waiting to greet us was Adri van Wyngen, a courageous member of the Resistance who had provided the Scottish soldiers with so much assistance

There too was Hans Tuynman, a Dutch schoolmaster exactly the same age as myself. Just as I had seen the KOSB on their way, Hans was there to witness their arrival.

"We were hiding in the cellar of our house as the battle raged above," he told me. "Then I heard the skirl of bagpipes and thought it was very funny. When I looked out and saw men wearing skirts, I said: 'They will never beat the Germans.'"

But they did—and to celebrate the victory 50 years later the Scots were entertained to a civic reception at the Britannia Hotel, a highly poignant venue, particularly for the Royal Scots.

The Britannia, now rebuilt, was the German headquarters and the men of the Edinburgh Regiment had to wade through water from the burst dykes to launch the attack which successfully drove the Nazis from their base.

Now there were only the Scottish veterans, marching in to the thunderous applause of the Dutch, celebrating together in style and hearing the local mayor saying: "You did not just liberate the people who were living here in 1944. You also liberated those who came after, right up to the current generation, even if they have no memory of the atrocities. Those generations also say 'Thank you'."

The Flushing pipe band, which is affiliated to the KOSB, struck up "Flower of Scotland" and there was not a dry eye in the house.

So to the church, where the pipe band of the Calgary Highlanders repeated "Flower of Scotland" and the congregation rose to applaud the arrival of Queen Beatrix.

Later in that same church Brigadier Coutts provided a special moment. On the eve of the Flushing invasion, he told the congregation, the KOSB's padre, the Rev. Frank Findlay, held a service of communion for the whole battalion. His widow, Muriel, had presented that communion cup to the battalion and now, 50 years later, they were presenting it to the church where the service of thanksgiving had been held after the Battle of Flushing.

We sang "Abide With Me" and then came the parade to Uncle Beach for the laying of wreaths. The Dutch cheered and applauded, threw flowers and wanted to thank us all for their freedom.

Old Davie Paterson, a Glasgow Highlander from Bishopbriggs who lost an arm in the battle, was wheeled through the town, smiling and waving to the crowds and quipping: "I've come to look for my arm!" Women embraced him.

Jock McCallie from Dunbar had brought his grandsons, Jonathan, 22, and Timothy, 19, to see it all for themselves and they were deeply moved.

So I marched once more with my heroes. The flags of the nations were raised, wreaths were laid, and the band of the Royal Marines played Elgar's "Nimrod". This was a day for living heroes.

But, at the going down of the sun tonight, they are laying wreaths to their dead comrades at the cemetery of Bergen-op-Zoom. And in the morning—and for ever—they will remember them.

THE TOWER OF EMPIRE

I CAN still close my eyes and recall a particular sensation from the Empire Exhibition of 1938 which has lived with me ever since. Within the framework of that magical event—the largest and most impressive spectacle Scotland has ever seen—it was the Tower of Empire which so mesmerised the country schoolboy as to fire my imagination and enrich the intervening years.

That exhibition ran from May till October and brought the world to Glasgow's doorstep—a total of 13.5 million people, who thronged to Bellahouston Park and marvelled at those magnificent pavilions on broad avenues, the Billy Butlin funfair, the Clachan, the spectacular restaurant built into the hillside as a ship's bow by the Anchor Line, where the King and Queen had lunch on opening day.

But above all the tower, sometimes known as Tait's Tower, after the Paisley-born architect who dreamed up the shape and style of the entire exhibition.

It began 150ft up the Bellahouston hill and rose a further 300ft piercing the night sky in floodlit splendour, with waterfalls tumbling down the hillside and the crowds singing and dancing the song of the moment, "The Lambeth Walk", from the show of the moment, Noel Gay's *Me and My Girl*.

On that last night, in spite of a deluge, no fewer than 365,000 people were linking arms inside Bellahouston, watching the lights go down for the last time. Symbolically, though they did not realise it, they were watching the lights go down on an empire.

Chamberlain came back from Munich that month and the rest, very definitely, is history.

Twenty-five years later I was back in Glasgow, working as a journalist, wandering nostalgically in Bellahouston Park one day, seeing and hearing it all inside me, when I felt compelled to rush to my typewriter.

That day in 1963 I wrote a column suggesting it was time to do it all over again. What an inspiration for another generation of youngsters! Remembering what that tower had done to my emotions, I suppose I wanted my own children to share the experience.

Nobody, I have to say, paid a blind bit of attention. Another 25 years passed by before we came up with any kind of exhibition, the Garden Festival of 1988, a brave enough attempt but pale by comparison.

Mercifully, perhaps, nothing is forever. As we embark upon the countdown to another century, Glasgow prepares to be UK City of Architecture and Design in 1999 and all manner of plans are afoot to celebrate the occasion.

Towers are back in favour. And yes . . . there are those who share my vision of rebuilding Tait's Tower at Bellahouston Park. Why did they ever pull it down? Where Paris has its Eiffel Tower, Sydney its harbour bridge and opera house, San Francisco its Golden Gate and New York its Statue of Liberty, Glasgow could have had its own symbol of international status.

Could it still happen? To save old men being accused of nostalgic ravings, I'm glad to leave it to a bright young architectural historian who is far advanced with a plan which, I believe, would finally establish Glasgow on the global map.

A Lenzie lad, Neil Baxter, was so fascinated by the Empire Exhibition that it became the thesis of his honours degree at Glasgow University in the early 1980s. Now, at 34, he runs his own business with a team of architects, masterminding major events.

Central to his current ambition is the rebuilding of Tait's Tower on a permanent basis. The models are all there. The 3500 tons of concrete foundation are still there. And according to Mr Baxter, that tower could be restored to Bellahouston hill for a remarkably modest £3m.

His total vision would cost around £10m. That would also restore the only remaining building to its glory of 1938. The Palace of Arts, like Bellahouston Park itself, is under-used.

Baxter's idea is to turn it into an interpretation centre for Glasgow. Having learned how the city came together, visitors would then be whisked up the hill by funicular railway to the base of the tower, a winged structure with restaurant facilities.

And from there they would be spirited to the top of the tower, with its three viewing platforms and a vision spread below them in reality, of what had just been learned at the Palace of Arts. It is an exciting prospect which, I understand, has already stirred the imagination of leading Glaswegians.

For one very special lady it stirs vivid memories. I called the other day on Margaret Brodie of Beith, the only woman in the 17-strong technical team of 1938.

She was the young Glasgow architect who went to London to work for Thomas Tait in time for his Empire Exhibition project. She was not only given the task of designing the Women of Empire pavilion but was sent north as the first on-site architect at Bellahouston.

A charming lady of 87, she told me of the giants who surrounded her—names like Basil Spence, Jack Coia and Alistair MacDonald (son of Prime Minister Ramsay MacDonald). Above all, Thomas Tait, the Paisley Buddy with London overtones.

In Miss Brodie I found reassurance that my boyhood enthusiasm was well justified. Could we possibly be at the beginning of something which would fire imagination for children of the millennium?

THE STRANGE FATE OF
GEORGE GERSHWIN

THE magic of George Gershwin has fascinated me since boyhood, those haunting melodies evoking the spirit of New York City in particular as no other composer has managed to achieve.

The fact that in my own youth an old friend of our family used to tell us about visiting the Gershwin home in the early part of the century added a personal poignancy to the story of a man who changed the face of music before his tragic end at the age of 38.

So wherever I hear the hint of a Gershwin melody, from "Rhapsody in Blue" to "Porgy and Bess", I become a willing victim. It was the bait which took me to the Theatre Royal in Glasgow the other evening for one of those "Thank You, Mr Gershwin" programmes which, too often these days, leave you wondering why they bothered to thank Mr Gershwin.

When some of those jazz ensembles get together they have an irritating habit of disappearing up the aperture of their own ego, so indulging themselves in fancy improvisation that you are hard put to recognise what it is you have come to hear.

Mike Pyne's Manhattan Club Trio had its moments and Elaine Delmar possessed all the vocal requirements of the composer's repertoire. But during a quite dexterous keyboard version of a Gershwin Rhapsody, my fairly keen musical ear was much more aware of Mr Pyne than Mr Gershwin.

Similarly, as I anticipated one of my favourite songs, "The Man I Love", at its best in a lazy velvet, I couldn't believe the high-speed rhythmic race which turned it into farce for people like me.

To crown all, there was this infuriating practice of mutual admiration, where the musicians point at each other to solicit applause for solo performance, rather like they used to do in the circus when the seals had done their bit.

So my mind wandered to happier thoughts of George Gershwin, whose music took on that added dimension in our rural home with the periodic visits of Bertie Forbes from New York.

Bertie had gone forth from our Aberdeenshire parish at the turn of the century, a poor country lad who nevertheless founded the most prestigious financial journal in America, *Forbes Magazine*. Back home every two years, he would play Saturday night card games with my parents, breaking off to tell us of his acquaintances in New York.

The names Rockefeller and Woolworth cropped up frequently. And so did Mrs Gershwin, with whom Bertie joined in Saturday night card games like this. So I would sit spellbound as he regaled me with tales of her sons, George and Ira, when they were just boys about the house and long before the world would savour their genius as composer and lyricist.

They were native New Yorkers, of Russian stock, but the call of Hollywood compelled the Gershwin brothers to move to California, where they established a quite palatial home at No. 1019 North Roxbury Drive, just a couple of leafy streets away from the Beverly Hills Hotel.

When I eventually made it to that seductive corner of the Los Angeles conurbation, I began paying homage outside No. 1019, by then occupied by singer Rosemary Clooney. (Ira had moved next door to No. 1021 by the time I saw the inside of a Gershwin home.)

And there I would stand with my thoughts, trying to fit the musical genius of George Gershwin into a particular villa in Beverly Hills, where he would sit at the piano, forging his harmonic patterns and surprising even himself with the originality of phrase.

In 1935 he had seen the birth of his folk opera, *Porgy and Bess*, which didn't reach Britain for another 17 years. I remember the excitement of going to London in 1952 when it opened at the old Stoll Theatre, which was due to be pulled down when the run finished.

Standing outside his old home, I remembered how George Gershwin disliked the Hollywood scene. And something else was troubling him: his bald patch. Seeking a solution, he invested in a contraption as big as a washing machine, which sucked blood to a stimulated scalp. But was that all?

As I stood by the sidewalk of North Roxbury Drive, I was recalling the night George arrived home from a Sam Goldwyn party and didn't make it into the house. He sat down on this very kerb, trying to contain an unbearable headache which had been alternating with bouts of depression.

There were tests and reassurances but finally the emergency of an operation. He did indeed have a brain tumour, which turned out to be inoperable.

George Gershwin died in July 1937, still just 38, with so much achieved but surely so much more to come. They took him by train to his beloved New York, for which he never ceased to pine.

And there the crowds gathered for his funeral service at the Temple on Fifth Avenue, brother Ira so devastated that his exquisite talent as a lyricist refused to function for quite some time afterwards.

Passing the Beverly Hills house even now I could swear there's a piano playing inside, reaching for that opening ascent of "Rhapsody in Blue" with echoes that will last for ever. Bertie Forbes could never have guessed that Mrs Gershwin's little boy was heading for immortality.

HOW WE WRAPPED UP THE
SECOND WORLD WAR

WITH Scotland rounding off the Victory-in-Europe celebrations at Perth on Saturday, I suppose we more or less laid the Second World War to rest. The magic milestone of 50 years, raised in 1989 to mark the outbreak of Hitler's war, has since reappeared at appropriate anniversaries, through the D-Day events of last year to the final Victory in Europe which, for most of us on this side of the world, spelled the end of the war.

That war, with all its triumphs and tragedies and mixture of strangely haunting memories, will now recede into a settled place in the panorama of history, re-emerging with the maturity of time to take prominence on a distant horizon as the most awful human conflict the world has known.

The numbers who actually remember it will inevitably diminish till there is not a living witness left. Yet how well I recall from my childhood that there were still those who remembered Crimea and large numbers who saw the Boer War.

Survivors from 1914-18—it was then commonly known as the Great War—were still in the prime of life as we faced the prospect of something even more ghastly.

Now it is all behind us, by half a century of as much world peace as we can expect, and what a cause for rejoicing that is. As a passing thought, however—and considering how thoroughly history used to be taught—I'm surprised to find how little the younger generation knows about the Second World War.

"Oh, that was before my time" is the modern way of flippantly excusing ignorance. But we need to know the context of events because conflict will lurk for as long as we enjoy the freedom of two points of view.

It is in the very nature of things, to be found in the simplicity of a nest with two hens. Remove one straw and there's trouble. So we are strange creatures but at least we have the choice.

For my part, one choice I'm glad I made was to be in London for the VE-Day celebrations. It was a truly memorable Monday. As planned, it started at the Langham Hilton, directly opposite Broadcasting House, that wartime hub of all information.

Crossing Oxford Circus, I hoofed it down Regent Street, skirted Berkeley Square, where the nightingales sang, and descended on the Mall, with its magnificent sweep towards Buckingham Palace. For that was the focal point of the day, large crowds already converging on the Victoria Memorial and stretching back towards Admiralty Arch.

It was still mid-morning, with two hours of waiting, but quarter of a million of us stood patiently for the chance to recreate those scenes outside the palace of 50 years ago.

There was time to look around, to study the sea of faces, gauge the generations and to wonder what this could mean to different people. In the buzz of anticipation we were suddenly talking to one another, strangers all but breaking down the barriers in the manner of wartime.

There was matiness and good humour as we exchanged tales of this day 50 years ago, making allowances for the fact that even the grey-haired in their mid-fifties (the Beatles generation) were just too young to remember!

The military band played in the palace forecourt, then one old chap bedecked in medals broke into "Tipperary" and suddenly we were all in song. Eastenders led us in "Maybe It's Because I'm a Londoner" and a tide of warmth broke over the crowd.

It was a British crowd, waiting to be patriotic and conjuring memories of an age of innocence, recognisable families as they used to be before the social revolution put that unit out of fashion.

With not a yob in sight, the Union Jack was restored to a place of decency, instead of being the hijacked tool of modern fascism, an irony if ever there was one for a flag which symbolised the demolition of Hitler.

296

Then the balcony windows opened and out came the Queen Mother with her daughters, the three survivors of that same scene of 50 years ago. It was not too hard mentally to sketch in the missing members—King George VI, who survived the war by seven years, and Winston Churchill, who managed 20.

The only jarring note of the day was the incongruous presence of Cliff Richard. Pop stars have their place but this was not one of them. Mercifully, Vera Lynn restored the mood and led us all the way from those other Cliffs (of Dover) to that "Land of Hope and Glory".

But it was mainly the Queen Mother's day, smiling and serene at 94, withdrawing but returning for yet another encore. And you knew she was taking one last look at a scene she would never know again.

So we wrapped up history and turned to a very different future. As the sun went down on that 50th anniversary I dined on the rooftop of the Park Lane Hilton, with its bird's-eye view of the closing ceremonial in Hyde Park. We rose for the two-minute silence, saw the Queen light the beacon and watched the fireworks break upon the evening sky.

The laser beams might as well have been searchlights. Except that there was not an enemy bomber in sight.

THE WRITING MORRISONS

THE only regret about my recent visit to India was that I missed the Royal Lyceum Theatre's production of *The Gowk Storm*, adapted from the novel by Nancy Brysson Morrison, the Glasgow lady whose name raised such a flurry of interest in this column just over a year ago.

Nancy was one of a remarkable family of five from High Burnside, on the edge of Glasgow, who all grew up to be distinguished writers in one genre or another.

Brother Tom, for example, who started as a reporter on *The Herald*, was a considerable novelist but became best known as leading screenwriter at Elstree Studios, with films like *Ice Cold in Alex* to his credit.

Sister Peggy gained fame in America under her pen-name of March Cost, while Mary's forte was the short story. Indeed, the three sisters tempted description as a Scottish version of the Brontes, who were the subject of one of Nancy's books.

But "the writing Morrisons", as they were known, had gone so far out of public focus that a whole generation had never heard of them. Yet the moment I mentioned the name last year there was a whole gowk storm of reaction, ranging from those who knew that Nancy Brysson Morrison was a brilliant novelist to those who re-membered the family from pre-war days, sitting in the front of the gallery at Carmunnock Church.

One lady who knew their old home in High Burnside went to the trouble of going along the street to take a snapshot for me!

I raised the name in the first place because Scottish playwright Colin MacDonald, browsing in a bookshop, had come across *The Gowk Storm*, the story of three sisters brought up in a Scottish manse, and found himself quite entranced by what he read.

The book had actually brought Miss Morrison an international reputation after she wrote it in 1933. Now MacDonald felt compelled to turn it into a stage play but faced the problem of securing permission. Was there any family left? Who was the executor?

Well, the readers of this column provided all the answers. Within hours we had pieced the story together. A certain Dr Michie, a lecturer at Aberdeen University, had befriended Nancy Brysson Morrison and become her literary executor.

But the novelist died in 1986 at the age of 83, and Dr Michie died soon afterwards. It was his widow, also Dr Michie, who took over the responsibility and when I phoned her at home in Hull she was delighted to give the copyright clearance.

So Colin MacDonald completed his play and, during my recent absence, it ran for two weeks at the Royal Lyceum in Edinburgh where, despite mixed reviews, it ended up with a succession of full houses—and a profit.

The bandwagon was rolling. After that first article I had a call from Dr Marjory Palmer McCulloch, a literary lady who had been asked to contribute to a forthcoming book on Scottish women writers, dealing particularly with fiction around that 1920s and 1930s period.

Dr McCulloch knew well of a Scottish renaissance at that time, with men like Neil Gunn and Lewis Grassic Gibbon. But, much to her delight, she discovered there were more distinguished women of that period than she had imagined.

She was planning to write about women like Catherine Carswell, Dot Allan, and Catherine Gavin. But by sheer chance, she too had just discovered the name of Nancy Brysson Morrison. Captivated by *The Gowk Storm*, she went on to other gems like her first novel, *Breakers*, and was inclined to agree with Hugh Walpole's verdict that "She writes like a poet".

Now, with *The Herald's* revival of interest, she wanted to know more. Dr McCulloch tells me that the book on Scotland's women writers is due from Edinburgh University Press in the coming months. She also plans to give more exposure to the Morrison texts.

I suspect the fates are behind many a so-called coincidence. That copy of *The Gowk Storm* which Colin MacDonald spotted in the bookshop was a reprint edition which was lying there in a state of modesty.

That was what, unwittingly, sparked off the renaissance of Nancy Brysson Morrison. Now Canongate, the Edinburgh publishers who had the wit to bring it out, tell me that *The Gowk Storm*, dating back more than 60 years, has not only been appearing on the list of Top Ten bestsellers but is now at the point of another reprint because of the upsurge of enthusiasm.

Nancy, a lady of that First World War generation who remained unmarried, would be astonished and quietly delighted that her tale of passion had found a new audience in the 1990s.

She and sister Mary lived in Hillhead and then Kilmacolm, and were familiar figures at Glasgow theatres in the early and middle parts of the century. They were good friends of the Queen's physician on Deeside, Sir George Middleton, and developed such a love of that idyllic corner that Mary chose to be buried there.

Nancy passed away without notice in 1986, except for a simple death announcement in *The Times*. No obituary. Nothing. In her time she had a strong fascination with the spiritual boundaries of life and death. However that was resolved, her ashes followed Mary to that simple grave at Ballater, where they now rest together in peace.

MY RUSSIAN RHAPSODY

BIRTHDAY celebrations, I had come to the conclusion, are for the very young and the very old, with perhaps a few exceptional milestones along the way, like the 21st and the 40th.

Personally, I can remember very few. But the fact that I have just had one of the most memorable of all birthdays would suggest that the advancing years are beginning to tell me something. Mind you, the circumstances were rather special.

There I was, up by 6am, striding the deck of the luxury liner *Royal Princess* as she sailed up the sunrise of a glorious morning, out of the Baltic and into the safety of St Petersburg harbour.

This city of stunning beauty, which used to be Leningrad, was strangely deserted this Saturday morning, its long, broad avenues opening out to spectacular squares and breathtaking buildings like the Winter Palace, a reminder of the style in which the Czars of Russia used to live.

In the lazy atmosphere of a week's end—and with cruise-line passengers spilling on to the streets of the city—the irony of it was that there were more Americans than Russians to be seen in the heart of St Petersburg.

So, in temperatures reaching for the 90s, I took in the marvels of the Winter Palace, overflowing with some of the greatest art treasures from Rembrandt to Picasso, and eventually found my way to a birthday lunch at the city's Moscow Hotel.

In the vast dining-room, you could have believed that they had laid on a special event for the birthday boy. There was champagne on the table, a full orchestra, and a floor show which featured all that balletic beauty at which Russian dancers excel.

As I sat with a largely American clientele, I couldn't help remembering the days of 25 years back, when I found myself visiting both the United States and the Soviet Union—warming to both sets of people and wondering how they could possibly be at each other's throats in the dark suspicion of a Cold War.

The privilege of journalism enabled me to raise such a question. But surely, I had said, it would be different if the people themselves could meet. Given the understandable human frailty of suspecting the unknown, the plain fact of those days was that very few Americans had ever seen a Russian, and vice versa; except that American life itself had been so enriched by the immigrants from that distant land.

In one area alone, where would the great American musical have been without men like George Gershwin, Irving Berlin, and Richard Rodgers?

But if the Soviet bloc of 25 years ago had seemed such an impenetrable fortress of totalitarianism, the astonishing events of the 1980s would show that the age of miracles was still with us.

Now that the frontiers are open and the Americans are flooding in, there is willing acknowledgement that there are no horns or hidden tails in the Russian citizenry. They are just people like themselves, in some ways very like themselves.

So the lunchtime cabaret swirled to a climax and the Americans gave the Russian entertainers a thunderous ovation. People from the two most powerful nations on earth had found each other at last, warm, friendly, appreciative.

But if the stifling nature of totalitarianism has been replaced by the greater freedom of the market economy, there is a certain price to pay. The waiters serving our lunch delayed the pudding and the coffee for a purpose more pressing in their priorities. They were trying to sell us their souvenirs!

This was capitalist opportunism run riot, rather sad in its clumsiness. No thanks; no crystal goblets today. But, if you don't mind, I would rather like my ice-cream.

Out from the cabaret and champagne, I sought a quieter, more private rendezvous with one of my great heroes, Piotr Ilyich Tchaikovsky. I found him in a corner of the quaint little Tikhvin churchyard, where his remains lie beneath a life-like bust of the great man.

I sat down to look at him and caught the eye of a rather melancholy, troubled human being, as if he had just become resigned to the fate that was in store—the suicide which was pressed upon him in 1893 by a so-called court-of-honour at the Conservatory when they discovered his relationship with a male aristocrat. The poor genius was hounded to his death at the age of 53.

With Borodin lying a few feet away and Rimsky-Korsakov just round the corner, what a wealth of melodic splendour to thrill the ghosts of the night. Inside the adjoining church, the choir sang softly and I could hear again the wonder of Tchaikovsky; so much so that I went back and sat by his grave and found it hard to pull myself away.

Back on board the *Royal Princess* there was dinner and more champagne, a birthday cake and a card from the captain. We all danced the night away till I wandered out on deck to discover that the big red sun was still hovering on the rim of the horizon at 11.15pm.

It seemed like the glorious backcloth to a spectacular Russian ballet. Goodnight St Petersburg. Goodbye to another year. Time now for a swelling overture from the soul of Tchaikovsky.

THE MAN WHO WAS HITLER'S MENTOR

THOSE ceremonies which rounded off half a century since the end of the Second World War reminded me of a question I'm often asked: Of all the people you have interviewed, does any one stand out in your memory above all?

You can rake over formidable characters like Paul Getty, Robert Boothby, Margaret Thatcher, Ian Paisley, Mohammed Ali or film stars like Charlie Chaplin, Bing Crosby, Bob Hope, Sophia Loren, Elizabeth Taylor.

But when you put them into the perspective of powerful personalities and intriguing life-story, the name which shoots to the top will be unknown to most.

Yet the considerable anonymity which surrounded Dr Ernst Hanfstaengl was in contrast to the enormity of the role he played in history, taking us back to that ghastly war and the monster who started it.

Adolf Hitler would no doubt have emerged in time as the fiend he was. But how much easier the route when he crossed the path of the large, genial semi-aristocrat known as Putzi Hanfstaengl, respected historian, magnificent pianist, and charismatic figure of Munich society.

I caught up with Hanfstaengl in the post-war privacy of that same Munich villa where, without enough thought for what he was doing, he played host to the gangsters who were planning to rule the world.

The scene was unchanged: That was Hitler's chair, he said. Eva Braun sat here; Goering, Goebbels, Hess over there. In this cluttered study, the grand piano was still in the corner and there were pictures to show the whole gang around Hanfstaengl at the keyboard.

So how did it all happen? Putzi Hanfstaengl was born in 1887 of a German father and American mother and sent to Harvard, where he befriended Franklin D. Roosevelt. The Hanfstaengls were well-known in the art reproduction world, with shops in Munich and New York.

After college, Putzi stayed on to run the family business on Fifth Avenue, gaining friends like William Randolph Hearst, T. S. Eliot, and Walter Lippmann. Returning to Munich in 1921, he was asked by the American Embassy in Berlin to check out a would-be politician who was due to speak in a beer-hall.

Hanfstaengl knew everybody who mattered in Munich but queried the name of Adolf Hitler. He had never heard of him. At the Kindlkeller beer-hall that night he listened and introduced himself. If he didn't know Hitler's name, Hitler certainly knew his.

The Hanfstaengl home was the society hub to which he needed an entrée. He couldn't believe his luck. Promptly accepting an invitation, he would soon meet that spectrum of infuential people so vital to his political ambitions.

Two years older than Hitler, Hanfstaengl became his mentor on everything from international affairs to the social graces, occupying a unique position which raised jealousy in the rest of the pack.

The beautiful Mrs Hanfstaengl was having to fight off Hitler's attentions, revealing to her husband that the little man was really a neuter, suffering a complex about the syphilis he caught in Vienna in 1908.

Hanfstaengl told me of having studied his speaking technique and concluded that the last few minutes were really an orgasm in words.

But one of his stories intrigued me more than most. Hanfstaengl had befriended the Churchill family and, one night in the early 1930s, was due to dine with them at the Hotel Continental in Munich. He was asked to bring the Nazi leader with him but Hitler refused.

Over dinner he realised how vital it could be to bring together those two men who had never met. Excusing himself to see if he could make one last plea by phone, he reached the foyer—to find the man himself taking his farewell of a Dutch financier.

Surely this was it. Hitler in the foyer, Winston Churchill a few yards away in the dining-room. In the dirty white overcoat and green hat, Hitler said he was unshaven and in any case had too much to do. Who knows if they actually caught sight of each other? It was the closest they would ever come—and we are left to ponder what might have happened to the shape of twentieth-century history.

Hanfstaengl accompanied Hitler to Berlin when the Nazis took power in 1933 and was regularly on call when the Führer couldn't sleep. Taught by a pupil of Liszt, he sat down and gave me a demonstration of how he used to play a lullaby for the monster. Hitler's favourite late-night music? Irving Berlin's "Russian Lullaby"!

Increasingly concerned about the course of events in Germany, Hanfstaengl eventually fell foul of his old friend and fled to Britain in 1937. With the war, he was sent to Canada but managed to contact his other old friend, President Roosevelt, at the White House. And that was where he landed—as the President's adviser on political and psychological warfare against Hitler!

Back in his Munich home, we would sit far into the night and dispose of a few bottles of wine, discussing this little-known chapter in the creation of Adolf Hitler. Hanfstaengl and I became friends and it was an incomparable kind of history lesson when I took my three sons to visit him in that house of ghosts.

It all came back last week, as we laid the Second World War to rest.

NEW YORK, NEW YORK!

YELLOW cabs blared down the canyons of concrete and glass, horse-drawn carriages ambled through the falling leaves of Central Park, Broadway buzzed and, in the warmth of an October day, I knew from the spring in my step that I was back in a favourite city.

New York, New York—so good they could have named it a thousand times. Of course it is also the paradox which can stir such dislike in many a civilised soul that they cannot escape its confines soon enough. I just happen to be a sucker for its charm.

And charm tells you everything about the University Club of New York, one of the city's most fabulous listed buildings, all wood panelling and marble pillars reaching to heavenly heights, with a library of breathtaking proportions.

In the spacious drawing-room, gentlemen read their *Wall Street Journal*, fully approving a notice which says "Quiet please!"—as they look out on Fifth Avenue, one of the world's noisiest thoroughfares! New York keeps its sense of humour.

My engagement at the University Club (it welcomes graduates from all over the world) was to address the American-Scottish Foundation, an interesting body which not only promotes good relations between our countries but offers practical support to ventures this side of the ocean.

Alan Bain is its president, an influential lawyer-cum-businessman with his base on Madison Avenue, a Dundee jute man's son who read law at Cambridge where he became a firm friend of Calum Bannerman, son of that great Scot, John M.

In the audience that evening was a fascinating cross-section of those who fly the Saltire across the States. People like Deirdre Livingstone from Argyll, combining a professional post of encouraging travel to Scotland with a passionate desire to help her homeland.

Deirdre, incidentally, is writing a book about her grandfather, a relative of David Livingstone, who went to Africa to run the estate of the explorer's daughter and ended up by being murdered.

The spectre of assassination was closer at hand as I returned to the Plaza Hotel to find it crawling with security men. Had I forgotten that New York was playing host to the biggest-ever collection of world leaders, gathered to mark the 50th anniversary of the United Nations? With no embassies in New York, four main hotels were helping to house the dignitaries, who ranged from Bill Clinton and Boris Yeltsin to Fidel Castro and Yasser Arafat.

The King of Morocco was sleeping two floors below my room, having taken over a considerable part of the hotel. With gun-totin' guards at every bend of the corridors, it seemed there were security men to watch security men.

No chances were being taken with revolutionary groups, including Algerians, who had threatened trouble.

Down at the Palace Hotel on Madison you found yourself pursued by sniffer dogs preparing for the world's richest man, the Sultan of Brunei, who also happened to own the place.

Back at the Plaza (Donald Trump's former pride and joy), my lady companions came upon Queen Noor of Jordan having her hair done. Then, as we walked into the evening air, along Central Park South, a familiar frame ambled across the sidewalk from his hotel door to a stretch limousine, easing himself into the luxurious seat with some difficulty.

"Luciano!" we exclaimed in unison. Yes, it was indeed Pavarotti, who acknowledged the spontaneous greeting. New York is just that kind of town, stirring the adrenalin as no other place I know; a name-droppers' dream—but oh, what names to drop.

Down Broadway the lights were dancing their way to Times Square, proclaiming a revival of Jerome Kern's *Showboat* and yet another revival of Jerry Herman's *Hello Dolly*, this time starring Carol Channing.

Now it was time to hurry back to the hotel for a face-to-face interview with Mary Ryan of Cable Television, a 30-minute programme which went out last Tuesday night.

New York, in all its sultry attraction, leaves you pleasantly breathless with excitement. Before leaving for home, however, there is one sombre call I always try to make. It takes me up the west side of Central Park to that block of luxury apartments known as the Dakota Building.

It was there I passed, out of curiosity, one early winter's day of 1980, having gone to America for the presidential election which put Ronald Reagan into the White House. That curiosity was to see the home of John Lennon, who had found such peace, privacy, and apparent safety in the bustle of New York.

I was scarcely home when I heard the newsflash which shocked the world. Lennon had been shot dead by a young fan at that very entrance where I had stood so recently.

Last week I stood again on that sidewalk spot from which the assassin fired the gun, and tried to reconstruct those ghastly moments which ended Lennon's life.

Across the street, in Central Park, they have laid out a garden of peace, appropriately named Strawberry Fields, through which the people pass in respectful silence, pausing to glance at the memorial plaque.

I remembered my favourite Beatles tune, "The Long and Winding Road"—and prepared to take it, homeward to Scotland. But knowing always that I would be returning at the first opportunity to this city which John Lennon, and so many more of us, had come to love.

LAND OF THE WRIGHT BROTHERS

I WAS on my way to a wedding in America last month, flying high over the Atlantic and marvelling at the technology which kept us in the air, when my thoughts turned to Percy Pilcher, the Glasgow naval architect who should have had his place in history.

It must have been an association of ideas. For the wedding destination was North Carolina, where the famous Wright brothers became the first men to fly. And it was Percy Pilcher, who worked at the Fairfield and John Brown shipyards, who would almost certainly have stolen their thunder if the fates had not intervened.

Exactly the same age as Wilbur Wright, the Scots lad was four years ahead of the Americans in his development of powered flight, having built his first glider at his digs in Byres Road, Glasgow.

After trials on farmland at Cardross, Percy was due to give a demonstration in Kent on a day of foul weather. Not wishing to disappoint the large crowd, he went ahead—and crashed. Percy was dead at 32. The Wrights followed his course of development and gained their immortal place in aviation history.

There is no place in life for runners-up, I was thinking to myself as the plane touched down and my party of Scottish friends prepared to meet the American relatives for the first time.

Weddings may be much the same the world over but the Americans can add a charm to an occasion which I find appealing. Their customs are also rather different.

For example, the sit-down meal takes place not on the wedding day, as in Scotland, but on the previous evening, when it is hosted by the bridegroom's parents under the name of the Rehearsal Dinner.

On this pleasant occasion the groom's widowed mother, Ayliffe Macphail from Glasgow, welcomed her American guests with true

310

Scottish hospitality (it included a taste of the Macphail whisky from Elgin) and looked forward to seeing them all again next day.

Before then, however, there would be a Wedding Day Brunch for ladies only, at which the beautiful bride, Winborne Thorn, introduced her bridesmaids and explained how she came to know them.

It was a longish story. For, while it wasn't exactly a case of Seven Brides for Seven Brothers, it was certainly Seven Bridesmaids for Seven Groomsmen. Meanwhile, it was a different story for the bridegroom, Cameron Macphail, former assistant at Drumpellier, who went to America as a professional golfer and now mixes in the company of the Tom Watsons and Fuzzy Zoellers.

Cameron spent his wedding morning at golf, with a stunning victory over one of his distinguished groomsmen, Forrest Fezler, the man once pipped at the post by Hale Irwin for the US Open.

With the preliminaries over, we turned up at the Methodist Church in the village of Duck, a charming resort on the Atlantic coast, where they are not unfamiliar with Scottish culture.

For it was to this corner of America that our heroine, Flora Macdonald, emigrated after serving her term in the Tower of London for aiding the escape of Bonnie Prince Charlie after Culloden. There are still Macdonalds everywhere, as can be seen at their massive Highland games.

Appropriately, this Scots-American wedding was another tartan occasion, with both the groom and his lawyer brother, Roderick, resplendent in kilt, and the bagpipes played by a gigantic American Highlander.

The organ was augmented by trumpet and flute, and the beautiful soprano of Deborah Kasten gave us a memorable rendering of the Lord's Prayer.

After a sermon of fire and brimstone, we repaired to the magnificent beach house of the bride's parents, Bill and Marion Thorn, where they entertained 200 guests to a sumptuous reception. The Scots and Americans were on such instant and gloriously good terms as to prove not only the strength of old bonds but the potential of human beings, given half a chance, to foster good relations.

So we sang and danced and strolled on the balconies, the heady champagne tempered by warm sea breezes which rose from the golden beach below. If this was not heaven, it was the nearest that some of us will see.

And, on a new day, I was driving nearby when I realised I was in Kittyhawk. Yes, this was where those Wright brothers wrote their names into history.

So I pulled into the memorial field, where they had carried out the same experiments as Percy Pilcher at Cardross. In the visitors' centre I joined the audience to hear the full story of how the Americans had shown the way to the stars.

As the enthusiastic presenter came close to arousing a patriotic cheer, I bit my tongue—and then decided to ask him a question: Have you ever heard of a man called Percy Pilcher?

Unsure of what I might reveal next, he blushed a little and assured me that he knew all about Percy Pilcher from Scotland. Yes, he conceded, it was indeed Percy who was four years ahead of the game. Yes, he might well have replaced the Wright brothers in aviation history. But he was killed, wasn't he?

Yes, Percy was killed. But in the home of the Wright brothers, whose names will live for a thousand years, it brought some satisfaction to know that they at least recognise a great Scotsman who missed out on immortality by the narrowest thread of mischance.

TEARS OF FAREWELL FOR
SCOTLAND THE WHAT?

THAT Was A Good Week To Be An Aberdonian That Was. After too many years in the wilderness, the football team from Pittodrie went to Hampden Park last Sunday and won the Coca-Cola Cup, reviving memories of life as it used to be.

It might not have been the vintage champagne of Gothenburg (1983), when the Dons were masters of Europe, but the softest of drinks is a gift from above when your throat is parched and your soul is weary.

But in terms of Aberdonianism, I have to say, the memorable nature of last week did not depend upon football alone. Given my devotion to the round-ball game, it tells you something when I say there was an experience even more exquisite than the cup final.

I went back to the Granite City for the farewell performance of Scotland The What?, that unique trio of bow-tie entertainers who have been together for close on 40 years. And what a night it was!

It had all begun in the magnificence of His Majesty's in Aberdeen—and that was where it ended, in one of the most emotional nights ever seen in a British theatre. After a month-long run in their native city, Buff Hardie, Steve Robertson and George Donald came out to yet another remarkable house, packed from stalls through dress circle and upper circle to the utmost rafter of the gods.

They aroused tears of laughter before taking us, with a parody of Rod Stewart's "We Are Sailing", to the humorous but deeply touching conclusion that "We Are Failing".

The audience was in a mood to call its denial of lines like "We're a hat-trick . . . of geriatrics" but not to deny the brilliance of Buff Hardie's lyrics, which are worthy of a public far beyond Scotland.

313

And when that dreaded final curtain prepared to drop, the reticence of the Aberdonian race fell apart in a display of affection which would not have been matched for the great Harry Gordon of a previous generation.

For Scotland The What?, still fresh-looking men but now touching the sixties, had become legends well inside their own lifetime, blending talents of comic genius with the brilliance of George Donald at the piano.

So the audience got to its feet—and stood for a good 10 minutes of unashamed adulation. Buff, Steve, and George seemed bewildered by the demonstration and then, with a kind of old-fashioned courtesy, they turned towards each other and exchanged handshakes.

Evidently, throughout their career, this has been a ritual in the wings before they took the stage. But it was the first time the audience had seen it—and there wasn't a dry eye in the house.

When we finally let them go, the audience hung around the bars and the foyer in a last gesture of savouring a memorable night. For an occasion like this becomes a milestone in your own life. And it was certainly a milestone in mine.

Back at the farewell party in Poldino's, when asked to round it off with a few words, I recalled that I had first met up with Buff Hardie, the writing brain of the team, when we were 12-year-olds at Gordon's College, Aberdeen.

From football in the playground, we graduated to the school play called *The Auld Hoose*, the story of Robert Gordon, in which Buff and I played out a scene together. The poignancy of all this was that I had witnessed his very first appearance on a stage—and now I had witnessed his farewell 50 years later.

A brilliant academic, Buff Hardie went on to Cambridge University but continued to write the students' shows back home in Aberdeen. In the mid-1950s he teamed up with Steve Robertson, a leading light of student comedy, and then with George Donald, whose music added another dimension.

After university they became the Aberdeen Revue Group but, as professional men with other careers, decided to call it a day in 1969, with a farewell show at the Edinburgh Festival.

By then a feature writer on the *Daily Express*, I suggested to my colleague, Neville Garden, that he might want to review it.

Neville went—and wrote that this was the funniest show of the Fringe. From then on it was packed out, with such an overwhelming reaction that the three Aberdonians had to rethink their future.

The result was that the "end" of Scotland The What? became, in fact, just the real beginning, destined to run for another 26 years, for part of that time in tandem with their own careers. Buff was chief executive of Grampian Health Board, Steve was an Aberdeen lawyer and George was deputy rector of Perth Academy.

The rest is theatrical history, already matured into legend. On that farewell night they looked too youthful to go. There will still be an occasional appearance in the North-east but the touring days are finally over.

Proposing that farewell toast the other evening, I knew we were saying goodbye to three men who had done more than anyone to stem the decline of that North-east tongue which is sometimes called the Doric. It will be the poorer for the parting.

Now, with honorary degrees from Aberdeen University already bestowed, Buff, Steve and George will go to Buckingham Palace on December 12th to collect their MBEs. That honour has never been more deserved.

NEW YEAR NIGGLES

WE HAD the last of the light at Turnberry on Christmas Day, an unforgettable spectacle as Ailsa Craig stood high in the bold silhouette of a glorious sunset and mighty Arran brooded nearby.

Kintyre went almost as far as the clear air would take you and the distant horizon was surely Northern Ireland.

In the course of the year I had sampled hotels from London to Delhi, awarding a raspberry rating to the New York Plaza which was a big disappointment. For customer service and courtesy it could learn from our own Turnberry, on the Ayrshire coast, which takes its place among the truly great hotels of the world—with ease. Scotland doesn't make enough of its own.

So, as the fading glow of a winter's night finally dipped to darkness, we dined on Christmas evening in an ambience of warmth and quiet cheerfulness dictated by the mellow tones of an unobstrusive pianist.

And in the morning, last night's sun came up over the rim to turn its silhouette of dusk into the detailed picture of dawn. With the crispness of snow reaching to the sand dunes of Turnberry it was time to don the warm clothing and scamper across the frozen golf course towards the sea.

There, below the dunes, the deserted beach was an invitation to go bounding, with child-like glee, along the sands towards that lighthouse so familiar on television when the Open golf is here.

In that bracing walk of Boxing Day, little did we know that another sunset would bring the coldest night on record. But there was always Hogmanay Night to come, a chance to thaw out, albeit with the prospect of a bleary-eyed morning with which to welcome this New Year's Day.

So here we are in 1996, careering towards a new millennium

which will be upon us in no time. In the dying embers of the century, it seems to me that change speaks louder than progress. (It's a sure sign of advancing years when you shake your head and wonder where it will all end.)

But it is too early this New Year's morning to face the bigger issues of life. I'll settle for airing a few smaller niggles which test my patience—and maybe yours too.

On the entertainment front, for example, whereas I would like to see more of Rory Bremner, Rikki Fulton and Gary Wilmot in 1996, I could do with a great deal less of Esther Rantzen, Paul Gascoigne, the royal battlers and that abominable Australian character Dame Edna whatever. (Can someone tell me what's so funny?)

Speaking of England's outstanding footballer, my own profession has much to answer for in turning him into the headline brevity of "Gazza". What is this fascination with *za*? No sooner have we Gazza than we turn his girlfriend into Shezza. Obsessed by this childish diversion, we then transform a potential Prime Minister from Heseltine into Hezza.

But the tabloids don't leave it at Gazza. Carried away by this matiness with footballers, they manage to turn his Rangers colleague Ally McCoist into the slickness of "Coisty". Speaking of the ever-smiling Ally, darling of the media, isn't it time we gave him a break from over-exposure to the limelight? It's bad for your skin.

I could also do with less of the Cockney contraction. What is so marvellous about reproducing Terry as "Tel"? And actually lengthening Derek into "Del Boy"!

So to some of the daily words and phrases which have been . . . no, I detest the phrase, *getting up my nose*.

Much of it dates back to the sixties, when a deliberate policy of pointing two fingers at the rules of language produced ill-informed children who have grown into teachers. (I'm told there are some who don't even recognise an infinitive, never mind a split one.)

So we descend into a slither of verbal slovenliness, acknowledging words such as *alright* when they don't even exist.

I'm getting accustomed to *disadvantaged*, clumsy though it is, but there's a vulgarity about turning words like *rubbish* into a verb and

317

an appalling snobbishness in making an adjective out of *designer*, meant to cover anything from a suit to a few days' absence from a razor.

I can just about come to terms with *the bottom line*, which has some logic, but I rail against the sheer ugliness of slang-words like *scam*, which seems to mean some kind of nasty rip-off, and *folded* when it means apparently that the company has collapsed or simply closed down.

And what are we supposed to make of business phrases like *Give me a ball-park figure*? It suggests an Americanism which needs a nasal delivery. Or southern English usages such as *I doubt he can do it*? (On the broader question of sounds, I would gladly ban those car stereos which thump out their moronic beat.)

In the dawn of a New Year, therefore, is it too much to hope that we will regain a proper respect for language? That is, along with a proper respect for our fellow-citizens, controlling those excesses of violence, vulgarity and downright nastiness which seem to be taking possession of the human soul?

Having given vent to my spleen, can I now wish you a safe and contented New Year, in the long-held belief that contentment is the closest we ever come to true happiness?

SOLVING THE MYSTERY OF
THE *LUSITANIA*

FOR 80 years now, rumour and mystery have surrounded the fate
of that great creation of Clydebank, the *Lusitania*, torpedoed by a
German submarine on May 7th, 1915, as she skirted the south of
Ireland on her way from New York to Liverpool. Nearly 1200 of
the 1959 people on board died.

With even a hint of mystery, it never takes long for someone to
generate thoughts of conspiracy and cover-up. The modern world is
obsessed with it.

The rumours at the time raised questions of whether the *Lusitania*,
launched from John Brown's yard in 1906, was carrying munitions
for the British war effort of the time. Why was there a second explosion, after the torpedo struck?

More intriguingly, did Winston Churchill, then First Lord of the
Admiralty, engineer the whole atrocity in the hope that the sinking
of a civilian passenger ship would bring America into the First World
War and unite the neutrals against Germany? There were people
prepared to believe the worst.

In 1993, Dr Robert Ballard, a leading American marine explorer,
set out with an expedition in search of answers. He had first surveyed the scene from the southern Irish coast—from the same
viewpoint as a family who had been picnicking there in 1915 when
the four famous funnels of the world's largest, fastest and most
luxurious liner came into sight.

Within a horrifying few moments, that family had seen the *Lusitania*
struck by a German torpedo and sink in less than 20 minutes.

Ballard was just the man to lead the investigation. He had
already gained fame as the person who made the 1985 discovery of

319

the most famous shipwreck of them all, the *Titanic*, and for his exploration of the *Bismarck*. His conclusions on the *Lusitania* are contained in a fascinating book which he has written with the Canadian author, Spencer Dunmore.

Before the great Cunarder left New York on that fateful voyage of 1915, however, there were one or two shivers of apprehension. On the same page of the New York newspaper in which Cunard announced the *Lusitania's* scheduled departure, the German Embassy in Washington inserted a notice, warning the public that ships sailing the British flag or those of her allies were at risk of being destroyed in British waters.

More personally for the stokers on board the ship, their black cat deserted ship at the last minute.

Nevertheless, the *Lusitania* sailed and the book contains pictures of her departure, with the Manhattan skyline receding into the background.

On the day before the *Lusitania* left New York, a submarine slipped quietly out of the German port of Emden, headed round the north of Scotland, between Orkney and Shetland, and down towards Ireland.

The *U-20* was slinking around British waters in search of prey that day when the great liner came in sight. It was a deckhand who suddenly spotted something streaking along just under the surface of the water.

Torpedoes were notoriously inefficient at that time but this one did its job. All hell broke out on the *Lusitania* as she listed and sank, with passengers and crew making for the lifeboats. Only one in three made it.

The master of the German submarine, Walter Schwieger, wrote in his log that he had not known the identity of his victim until he spotted the name on the ship's bow as she went down.

So Ballard has sifted all the theories, as well as taking his team to that part of the Irish coast and examining the wreck, with a small submarine and remotely-controlled camera vehicles. The quality of their pictures is remarkable.

His conclusions? Ballard convincingly manages to dismiss the sinister theory of conspiracy, which would certainly have been an appalling reflection on Churchill.

As to the explosion itself, he found no evidence on the wreck that any munitions on board had exploded, or that the boiler had blown up, which was another theory. Suddenly he and his team realised that the real evidence lay all around them. It lay in the chunks of coal. Towards the end of that voyage from New York, the supply of a highly combustible coal was so low that layers of coal-dust formed thick carpets on either side of the boiler-room.

It needed only the detonation of the torpedo to turn it into a highly volatile mixture, force-fed with oxygen. The result would be a massive, uncontrollable explosion.

There will no doubt be those who seek to sustain the mystery. But Ballard's diligent exploration may well, at long last, have laid the ghost of the *Lusitania*.

WHEN JACKS ARE ALL THE RAGE

SUDDENLY—and almost certainly for the first time in my life—I seem to be in fashion.

For the latest statistics show that, of the 578,000 babies born in Britain last year, the most popular boy's name was Jack.

Why this should be I don't begin to understand, unless it follows the kind of perverseness which turned some of the dreaded girls' names of my childhood, like Annie, Lizzie, Maggie, and Kirsty into the trendies of a later day.

I was aware of an increase in my namesakes but I didn't think we had so taken over the moniker market as to establish ourselves at the top of the pile.

In my own generation we were mostly christened "John" and became Jack merely to save our fathers becoming "old John". I had come from a line which was long on Johns, if short on originality. In fact seven of my direct ancestors are buried in one North-east kirkyard, every one of them a John Webster.

The name continues as an option for my eldest son and eldest grandson, though the latter promptly became Jack. Come to think of it, maybe we started this fashion five years ago!

Poor old John, which used to lead the field in British names, tumbled to thirty-ninth place in 1995 and has been overtaken, would you believe it, by Mohammed.

So Jack's the Lad for the Nineties but by the time this lot reach school in the year 2000, the place will be so jam-packed with jumping Jacks that it will surely fall out of favour pretty quickly.

Frankly, it is not a name with which I have ever been comfortable. It suggests a slickness, a weakness, a lack of weight and gravitas. It can surely be no coincidence that certain names conjure up a profile which is universally recognised.

So we have Jack-in-the-box and I'm all right, Jack, and a string of nursery rhymes which don't exactly enhance the reputation.

I mean, what kind of prat was Jack Spratt, who would eat no fat and would marry a wife so far out of culinary fashion that she would eat no lean? They were an odd pair.

And what about that other little horror, Jack Horner, who sat in a corner, eating his pudding and pie; he put in his thumb and pulled out a plum and said "What a good boy am I!" Now you couldn't produce such nonsense if the little bleeder had carried the strength of a name like Robert or Edward or James, could you?

According to Dr Johnson, Jack arose as the diminutive of John, just as Eddie is the cheaper version of the powerful Edward. (Can we really take seriously, as the head of the Bank of England, a man with the name of Eddie George?)

The proof of Jack Horner's pudding lies in the fact that, as soon as men reach positions of power and responsibility, they quickly seek to shed their dodgy handle.

One of Scotland's great industrialists, Jack Toothill, who master-minded the Ferranti operation, had no sooner gained the tip of the sword from Her Majesty than he re-dubbed himself Sir John Toothill.

In America, Jack Kennedy was quite happy to conduct his rakish existence at the lower levels with his early label. But as soon as he assumed office at the White House, he transformed himself into John F. Kennedy.

Mind you, not even that change of image would have saved his bacon if he had lived to face the music.

In my own youthful days, I had good forewarning of what my name would look like as a newspaper byline. In those days, another journalist called Jack Webster was regularly in print as the Vancouver correspondent of Kemsley Newspapers, which included the *Aberdeen Press and Journal*, where I worked.

It was much later before I discovered he was an exiled Scot, on his way to becoming a hell-raising legend as a broadcaster in Canada, the man who invented the phone-in.

This Jack Webster was a Glasgow journalist of the 1930s who

returned after the war and helped to set up Scottish Television, before heading off to fame and fortune in Canada.

We eventually met up in Glasgow (by chance, I was staying in digs in the very Battlefield Avenue where he grew up) and he invited me to Vancouver to appear on British Columbia TV, where I took the chance to tell his legion of viewers that I was the real Jack Webster and that this guy was just a blustering imposter.

In the strange ways of fate no sooner had I started to write this article than a Canadian magazine dropped on my desk. The cover-story is all about . . . yes, the same Jack Webster, now well through his seventies but still ruffling feathers, gruff and gravelly but extremely likeable—and now being lined up to appear in films.

Canadians love him as a kind of card-carrying curmudgeon, a rather weighty and exceptional character to have a name like Jack.

In time, I managed to put my byline alongside his (mercifully in different papers) and there it has stayed for 48 years. I may not have been too comfortable with the name I was given. But one thing is certain: It's much too late to change it now.

THE TRIALS OF A STAMMER

AN EVENT which put me on the news pages last week was a poignant reminder of a life-long struggle with the faculty of speech. That stammer had dogged me from the first faltering syllables of childhood, an embarrassment which affected every aspect of daily life, shaped every spoken sentence which might include a bogey word.

So I was taken on the rounds of speech therapists, child psychologists, and quacks, who could offer a variety of advice, ranging from "Take a grip of yourself!" to a contradictory "Relax!"

"You'll grow out of it by your teens," said some. But I didn't. I stuttered on through that verbal minefield, blocking up in embarrassment, whether in classroom or in those first uncertain steps towards romance. The longer it goes on, you feel, the longer it is likely to go on.

The strange thing was that, while good speech has much to do with rhythm, I was not at all short of that quality in my own body. Indeed, as an eight-year-old at the beginning of the war, I was spotted by a distinguished eurhythmics teacher who wanted to turn me into a dancer.

But the rhythm of speech remained elusive. Come to think of it, a psychologist examining that early desire to become a journalist might well think I was channelling the frustration into the greater safety of the written word.

If that were so, I had not reckoned with the need to talk to people, to conduct interviews, to use the phone. Sometimes it was a nightmare, to be postponed to the last possible minute. Maybe I should have been a Jack Buchanan after all!

Looking back, it is surprising that I view my career in journalism with such warmth and joy. For it was not unusual to hear the stifled giggles of some telephonist as I tried to reach her boss. It was not so much a rat-at-at stutter as a strangulated, agonised groan.

Interviewees, on the whole, were understanding and helpful. Indeed one editor thought my stammer had the advantage of encouraging people to say more than they might have done. The more they talked, the less they were subjected to my painful efforts! But it wasn't an advantage I appreciated.

There was one particularly bad experience with the famous country-and-western singer Johnny Cash. At an interview in England, he expanded on his great compassion for human frailty, the man who liked to sing in penitentiaries and such places.

Immediately afterwards, I was sitting in the hotel foyer checking my notes, when I overheard him, behind a big marble pillar, give a colleague an impersonation of my stammer. From a man of compassion, it was not the kindest cut I had ever heard.

I showed face round the pillar, to let him know I had heard. And the best I can say for Johnny Cash is that he had the grace to blush. But I have never forgotten him.

So I struggled with the affliction right into middle age, when two significant things happened. First, I encountered that amazing device, the Edinburgh Masker, invented by Scottish speech therapist Ann Dewar and her medical husband. I had always known I could fare better when I stuck fingers in my ears to cut out my own embarrassment.

Apparently there was a scientific explanation for this. And what the Dewars did with their apparatus was to break the faulty circuit of speech by separating the stammerer from the sound of his own voice. (This is more a *his* than a *hers* problem.) I was astonished by the improvement.

Around the same time, I suggested to the BBC a documentary film which they, in turn, asked me to write and present. Present? How could I? Well . . . at the age of 54, it was maybe time I tried. Now, on most days at least, I was managing to channel that rhythm of the body towards the betterment of speech. With a new-found freedom, I could even accept engagements to speak in public, more as a novelty than as a belief that I was any good at it.

As it happened, the audiences included members of the Association of Speakers Clubs, a nationwide organisation which not only seeks to improve standards but chooses an annual Speaker of the Year, someone involved in verbal communication.

It seemed like a tender gesture when a lady from East Kilbride phoned to ask if they could put forward my name for 1996. Oh yes. Why not? The list of previous winners would indicate my chances. They included Peter Ustinov, Sir John Harvey Jones, Terry Waite, Edwina Currie, Kate Adie, and Betty Boothroyd!

This year's nominations included Tony Benn, Trevor McDonald, and John Prescott.

Well, to say the least, the news of last week was surprising. Speaker of the Year 1996? Whereas the Scots flocked south to Betty Boothroyd's presentation dinner in London last year, the English will have to come to Glasgow this time.

In accepting the award at a gala dinner in the autumn, I'll be expected to vindicate those who voted for me. If, in the process, this becomes an encouragement to those countless thousands out there who have shared my agonies over the years, then I'll be delighted.

And I'll promise to say so . . . without hesitation!

THE MASSACRE OF DUNBLANE

THERE is one topic only—and if it tells us about anything at all, apart from the power of evil and the inadequacy of words, it is the depth of human decency and the basic need we have for one another. What a pity it takes a tragedy like this to bring it out.

We tuned into the Commons, that frustrating chamber of petty bickering, and saw a human face as we have never seen it there before. Suddenly, all the posturing and pathetic point-scoring didn't matter a fig. In fact nothing at all seemed to matter on that unbearable day.

It was personified in the brave but quivering figure of George Robertson, a decent man always, now speaking for the community in which he lives, a man who had argued in his own home with Thomas Hamilton but who knew, in this age when personal freedom seems to be paramount, that nothing much could have been done in advance to thwart this mass murderer. It is the price we pay for an open society.

So far it has been superfluous to mention the name of Dunblane, that charming little town with its cathedral, its hydropathic hotel on the hill, and the splendour of its marvellous school for Servicemen's children.

The only problem with Dunblane used to be its bottleneck of traffic, until they built a fine motorway which now bypasses the town and takes you streaking towards Perth.

But Dunblane will be bypassed no more. For the worst possible reasons it will take its place alongside Lockerbie as the town whose very nameplate sends a shudder down your spine.

Together they will even take their place alongside the assassination of President Kennedy for that rarity in human experience of remembering exactly where you were when first you heard the news.

On this dire day we sought the precise minute of evil and tried to pinpoint what we were doing. What were we doing five minutes earlier, when those children had a lifetime ahead of them? All then was normal. How could we know that hell was only minutes away?

We gathered in huddles, talked with disbelief and fell silent. Suddenly I remembered neighbours whose grandchildren lived near Dunblane. Frantic phone calls. Yes, they had dashed to be with their daughter and, yes, the children were in the school. But they were safe. I gathered that the boy saw the gunman passing his classroom on the way to the gym.

In a massacre like this we are ill-equipped to handle our emotions. In some ways the human psyche prefers a living murderer upon whom to vent its anger. For sure we all need an outlet for that uncontainable flood of feeling.

We need scapegoats. No matter what the nature of the tragedy, there must always be someone to blame. At the very least we need constructive grief—pursuing a campaign, seeking to change the law, as happened with American parents after Lockerbie when they took their case about aviation security to the White House and achieved results.

Yet, apart from some change in gun laws, the inescapable if unpalatable truth is that nothing, absolutely nothing, was likely to have prevented the massacre of Dunblane. If, for example, the police had gained a conviction on their suspicions about Thomas Hamilton, the certainty is that he would have been out of jail in due course, ranting all the more about society's rejection, still hell-bent on evening the score.

As it was, not only were the police cautious in their deliberations but there were scores of people—no doubt some calling for action today—who actually signed petitions in support of Hamilton when he was refused permission to run his dubious boys' clubs in public halls. We cannot have it all ways.

Yet people, in their natural desire to vent feeling, do expostulate in a manner which owes more to gesture than substance. Plainly, short of an armed guard on every school in the land—and what kind of an unnerving nonsense for children would that be?—there is no defence against a madman.

So we return our thoughts to Dunblane, afraid of our own subconscious reconstructions: Hamilton setting out from his home, a cheery wave to a neighbour, no doubt planning to go out in a blaze of suicidal drama.

There was once a faith to cushion us from the unbearable but, by and large, that has gone. Now we are on our own, seeking the hands of one another. Maybe this has changed us all a little, at least for a time. Yet before long the families will hear distant laughter on the wing of an April evening and wonder how that emotion can be stirred so soon.

The world will have turned its grief to a memory, leaving only the nearest and dearest to that increasing ache of loneliness. If and when they do find the heart to laugh again, it will take them to the brink of that well from which all tears are drawn, where the dividing line is hard to find.

The fact is that the antics of an evil creature have virtually ended all prospect of a happy life for hundreds of people. They will find a new level of existence of course. But the massacre is much more widespread than we know.

AN HISTORIC DAY IN MAUD

WHEN I left our village school in 1943 I couldn't have foreseen, even in my wildest dreams, the panoply of memorable moments which would lighten the journey ahead.

But, for all the wonderful days gathered into my experience, I doubt if there has been one to compare with last Sunday. The day itself may have been bleak but for me the sun was shining and my heart was dancing to the rhythms of childhood.

I was back at Maud School, 100 years to the day since it opened, unveiling the centenary plaque and addressing a large gathering in the playground of our youth.

Resplendent in Victorian garb, the children of today—exactly 100 on the roll—had paraded from that earlier school in the Low Village, just as they had done in 1896, and were sitting respectfully as their headmistress, Mrs Howlett, called on me to speak. As I scanned that gathering, from youngest child to 92-year-old Mrs Ann Duncan, the pageant of childhood unfolded before my disbelieving eyes with an impact which deepened as the day wore on.

From my own class alone, I could pick out nine of us who came here that April day of 1936, even now under the watchful eye of three of our teachers, Miss Morrison, Miss Duffus, and Miss Hunter, whose married names peeled away.

I recalled an infant classroom with roaring fire, where we had arrived during the brief reign of Edward VIII, clutching glossy picture books of the king who would never be crowned. Then came the Coronation of his brother in 1937 and soon the crisis of Munich and Hitler's war.

Village life had revolved around the railway junction and I re-called that 1939 day when trainloads of evacuees came thundering north from Glasgow to double the roll of rural schools.

331

And there, suddenly, I caught sight of two of those evacuees who had come back for this day, Margaret and Renee Rankin, once of Vine Street, Partick.

Those war years, with soldiers billeted in village halls and homes, had given Maud the peak point of its social history. It was now a very different place, without a station, a policeman, and soon without the weekly cattle mart, once the biggest in Britain.

So-called progress had strangled rural life but Maud would survive no doubt. And I told the children about a brush with history which intrigued them. As a boy in the 1940s, having already decided to be a journalist, I started a magazine called the *Maud Review* and went to talk to the very first headmaster, John Law. By then retired to a house overlooking the playground where we now stood, Mr Law had told me about that opening day of 1896. And now, nearly 50 years later, I was telling the children.

So history was not some dull and dreary subject but a living fascination which we were making that very moment. They would hold another day like this in the year 2096, looking back on today in the same way as we were looking back to 1896. To that end, I then helped to bury a time capsule, to be dug up by future generations.

As a child in the Maud I loved, I had once thought we were perhaps a backwater, speaking in a local tongue which might be a disadvantage in that wider world beyond. But I had discovered that a Scottish rural education was far superior to most—and that my plain, Buchan tongue turned out to be as rich an asset as I possessed.

Nor was it a coincidence that so much of my writing, in journalism, books, and television films over the years, had been about this locality which shaped my life. So we moved inside a school bedecked with memorabilia, including the pupil register for 100 years. Spot the year and you spotted the name: John Barron Webster.

They served lentil soup and sausage-rolls and tea, and that kaleidoscope of childhood kept moving before eyes that were entranced: Sandy Dyer, who ran my mother's messages, was there to recall how he used to play speed-cars with my pram (with petrified me inside).

Margaret Cassie turned up, as fine a ballroom dancer as ever you saw, and we remembered our youthful partnership, in dancing as well as in love. My school pal, Norman Rothney, is long since gone but his family was there to stir silent thoughts of a deeply innocent friendship.

We hung about in joyous recollection, unwilling to part with this day, suspecting no doubt that we would never see its like again.

Finally, with a last, nostalgic look, I drove off south, a thousand echoes in my head, the adrenalin flooding every inch of my being. Of all the great days in my life, there had never been one just quite like this.

AN ODD TALE ABOUT
THE DUCHESS OF WINDSOR

FOR years I have dined out on a piece of gossip about the late Duchess of Windsor which was so outrageous that mouths fell open in amazement, before the table companions would dismiss it on the grounds that, surely, it could not be true.

Though I began to doubt it myself, I never forgot the circumstances in which I gathered this sensational story.

Researching the biography of Scots novelist Alistair MacLean, I was staying with Count Giovanni Volpi at his palace on the Grand Canal of Venice, trying to find out why he had owned the film rights of *HMS Ulysses* for more than 20 years without making the film.

That was a story in itself. But as we discussed it in the study of the man whose father founded the Venice Film Festival in 1932, the rather brusque Count Volpi suddenly announced that we were due for cocktails at a friend's place.

He wasn't the kind of man to furnish you with advance information. I simply followed him to the palace doors, from which his speedboat whisked us up the canal to some narrow back-streets which opened out to a grand square.

Approaching the large door of what looked like a cathedral, Count Volpi and I were received by a flunkey who led us up the broad stone staircase, complete with its red carpet.

Still baffled by the grandeur, I came to realise that this was no more than a dwelling-house, albeit the grand home of one of the Merchants of Venice (yes, they still exist), and that our hostess was just having a few guests for supper.

More at home in the farmyards of Aberdeenshire, I set about the cultural adjustment and tried to figure out this cosmopolitan gathering. There was a hard core of Venetian wealth, the inevitable German professor—and the obligatory visiting lady from America.

After a few glasses of Italy's best, it was this last-mentioned whose nasal drawl suddenly quietened to the confidential as she unfolded, for my personal benefit, the strange story about the Duchess of Windsor.

The American had a lady friend who was driving on the outskirts of Paris one night, not far from the Windsor home, when she came upon an older woman in some distress because her car had broken down.

She stopped to help and was showered with such gratitude that she accepted an invitation back to the house.

The lady in distress turned out to have been a nurse to the Duchess of Windsor and the substance of her remarkable claim, given in confidence of course, was that the Duchess was really a *man*.

Never! Yes. In the later years, it had been the lady's regular task to bath the Duchess and, without being too specific, she was certainly not a woman. This poor dear was tired of bottling up the information.

Well, that was the story I carried for years, good enough for the dinner-table but not the kind of intelligence to spread too widely without more evidence.

Matters changed the other day, however, when Michael Bloch brought out his book, *The Duchess of Windsor*, in which he presents a strong case for the fact that, because of physical peculiarities, the former Wallis Simpson was incapable of sexual intercourse and may well have died a virgin.

Far from being a sensation-seeker, Mr Bloch is in fact the man engaged by the Duchess's lawyers in Paris to edit the Windsor papers. As he approached the task, he was evidently told by the late Dr John Randell, consultant psychiatrist at Charing Cross Hospital and an authority on sexual matters, to keep in mind that Wallis Simpson was really a man. Dr Randell was given the details by a colleague who examined her.

Bloch's subsequent inquiries revealed that her likely condition was Androgen Insensitivity Syndrome, commonly known as AIS, though he doesn't claim independent proof of it. Roughly speaking, AIS children are born genetically male but develop outwardly as female.

Though they can be sexually attractive—their number includes fashion models—the reproductive organs don't exist. (Some historians now believe Queen Elizabeth I was the same.)

It would explain a lot about the Duke and Duchess of Windsor, whose romance of 60 years ago rocked the monarchy and led to the Duke's abdication after he succeeded his father as King Edward VIII in 1936.

He always denied indignantly that the American Wallis Simpson was his mistress before marriage. It now seems possible there wasn't intercourse even after marriage.

For a start, she was named Wallis after her father, indicating some confusion at birth.

Another recent book, *Dynasty* by Donald Spoto, reported that, on the eve of her wedding to the Duke, the Duchess told her closest male friend, Herman Rogers, that she had never had intercourse with either of her first two husbands.

Her French lady lawyer, Suzanne Blum, was also convinced that her client remained a virgin. And her lifelong butler believed her intimacies did not go beyond an embrace.

As for the Duke of Windsor, it would seem that, for his own peculiar reasons, he loved the idea of her dominant role.

So my tale from the home of a Merchant of Venice seems to have credibility after all. It's not the kind of story you might normally expect of a Monday morning but I thought you might be interested. Shakespeare certainly would have been.

COLUMNIST OF THE YEAR?
I EAT MY WORDS

IT all came back to haunt me—and I suppose it really served me right. It was many years ago that I attended the ceremony of presenting awards to Scottish journalists and found myself in rather heated discussion with one of the judges.

He had asked, in the course of lunch, if I had entered the competition, to which I replied that I hadn't; and, what's more, I wasn't greatly impressed by such occasions, nor by the method of choosing the winners.

To my surprise, he thought that was an arrogant view. Personally, I thought the opposite, believing that the winners should be chosen from afar, without the prerequisite of submitting their own entries.

Well, in my 49th year of writing columns of one kind or another, embarking with a sports column on the *Turriff Advertiser*, the powers of resistance were clearly not what they used to be.

Having been prevailed upon to enter the Bank of Scotland annual awards—there were 365 entrants in all—I found myself on this year's short leet for Columnist of the Year, due to attend the ceremony at the Edinburgh Conference Centre.

I was due in Southampton that night, for the Jubilee Dinner of the *Queen Mary's* maiden voyage, so this would mean a later plane south. With the results of the press awards a well-kept secret, we had to be there for the moment of truth.

At the door of the *Herald* office we bundled into a private coach, like a group of readers en route to one of the paper's foreign tours. Together with partners, the nominees of both *The Herald* and *Evening Times* were on their way, harbouring hopes of taking the capital by storm.

337

On occasions like these you sense a nervousness. Everyone pretends it's just for fun; they are here only for the beer or champagne or whatever it is. Yet inside, you know that everyone wants to win. It is only human nature.

So we tore along the M8 towards the capital and were particularly glad to have the editor on board. As an Edinburgh man, he was a useful guide to the bus driver who didn't know where to find the new conference centre. It turned out to be beside the Sheraton Hotel.

At last we were there, milling with the crowds in the foyer and gaining our various directions in a most impressive venue. The awards and speeches would take place in the auditorium before lunch, which could then be enjoyed without the tension of uncertainty.

So the lights were lowered, Kay Adams took her place as presenter and the decisions of Lord McCluskey and his fellow judges were about to unfold.

The Herald was doing exceedingly well. Alf Young was Financial-Business Writer of the Year in a field where he dominates; Michael Tumelty was best critic, Jill Crawshaw was the best specialist writer and the up-and-coming Stephen McGinty the Young Journalist of the Year.

I could feel a pounding in the heart, pleased that *The Herald* was doing so well but now convinced that this run of success could not be maintained.

Sitting beside me, God's own John Macleod showed real Christian spirit when a rival beat him to the feature-writing award. Magnanimously, he led the applause and called his approval.

The screen above now showed the nominees for Columnist of the Year. Kay Adams was reading the four names and giving the judges' verdict on the winner. He was evidently a craftsman with words, who wrote a column which was both unique and personal.

That couldn't be me. But it was. In the mental confusion, I rose from my seat—then wondered if I had misheard! Was it wishful thinking? I continued towards the rostrum, hoping I hadn't got it wrong, and received a glass engraving with a substantial cheque for good measure.

338

There was a lump in my throat, I have to confess, so it was just as well no speeches were expected from the winners. I suppose I was thinking about my longstanding stammer and mediocre school record and here I was, collecting a national writing award, with a speaking one to follow later in the year.

It proved, if nothing else, that in this weird and wonderful life of ours all things are possible. And for that I was truly grateful.

So *The Herald* swept the board and now we could relax and enjoy a splendid lunch. Everybody was congratulating everybody else in an atmosphere of warm fellowship.

Even the judge with whom I had crossed verbal swords all those years ago came over to say his piece. I don't know if he remembered the incident and I wasn't going to remind him.

I had eaten not only my lunch but my words and was prepared to acknowledge that this day had been one of the best I could remember.

In mellow mood, we piled into the *Herald* bus and headed home to Albion Street. I was just in time to dash home, change clothes and reach for Glasgow Airport, en route to Southampton.

And there I enjoyed a celebratory dram with my good friend John Brown, who drew the first outline of the *Queen Mary* in 1926 and was still here, aged 95, to make a splendid speech about her maiden voyage.

Now there, if ever there was one, is a man who deserves an award.

AMAZING GRACE
IN AN ENGLISH MINSTER

THE more you travel around, the more you realise how little you know your own land, a thought which persisted last week as I crossed the Border and began to pick my way towards Dorset. The motorway network merely makes it all the more disastrous if you miss your exit.

On the way, I would call on a son who lives near Oxford. But Oxford was not where I thought it was. I could have sworn it was away to the south-west of Birmingham. In fact, checking the map more carefully, I realised it had moved rather perceptibly towards the *south-east* of Birmingham.

With that lesson under my seat-belt, I then drove towards Southampton and pondered upon the coincidence that, having seen that city only rarely in my lifetime, I was now within sight of it for the second time in a week.

A few days ago I had been here for the diamond jubilee of the *Queen Mary's* maiden voyage. Now I was back in the southern counties on a mission more personal.

For the last leg of the journey I was veering towards Thomas Hardy country, absorbing England's green and pleasant land and catching sight of the historic Wimborne Minster, which would be the centre of our attention next day.

Before the wedding, however, there was the final destination of Blandford Forum, a charming little Dorset town in which the Crown Hotel would host the reception and house the guests.

The motorcade from Scotland was arriving with that sense of adventure which used to accompany the football drive to Wembley in the days, before lager-loutishness, when people knew how to behave themselves.

So we generated anticipation and, in the morning light, lingered over a late breakfast before the 10-mile drive to Wimborne. Like back home, the English were bemoaning the wintry weather which had extended through May. But suddenly on this June morning the summer of 1996 arrived—and kilted Scots were given credit for having brought it with them. We turned up at Wimborne Minster, causing a bit of a local stir with the swirl of tartan and skirl of the pipes.

Inside the Minster, that piper stood beyond the altar of this vast church and struck up a harmony with the mighty organ as together they raised the hairs on the back of your neck with a memorable "Amazing Grace".

It was stirring stuff, bringing a tear even to many an English eye. And there at the altar, awaiting his Tracey, was my youngest lad, Martin, a journalist and newsreader with the BBC in Southampton, resplendent in Highland outfit.

A thousand thoughts run through your mind at a moment like that: the childhood of your chicks, the schooldays, the ups and downs.

I remembered the day he was rushed to hospital with a toy ring stuck up his nose. (They never did find it.) I remembered the day he finished his Highers because it landed on the eve of Gothenburg. (For the uninitiated, that means the European Cup Winners' Cup Final of 1983, when Aberdeen Football Club claimed its greatest moment by beating the legendary Real Madrid.)

Having been long indoctrinated to the support of Aberdeen, on a simple but effective diet of no-Dons-no-food, Martin dashed out of school that Tuesday afternoon, ran to catch a bus to Aberdeen and arrived in Sweden by the very last of the 50 charter planes which took 12,000 people to the match.

Memories are made of stuff like that. After school he became a copy-boy on *The Herald*, having already claimed the distinction of being the youngest person ever to work for the much-lamented *Sunday Standard*.

Following father and brothers into journalism (it's either in the blood or they lack originality), he trained at the Lancashire

Polytechnic in Preston, gaining a reporter's job on *The Burnley Express* and an English award as Young Journalist of the Year.

So, in an historic pattern which hardly changes, our offspring make their way in the world, leading to marriage and children, and we move along our advancing positions on the conveyor-belt of life. Two grandchildren were there in attendance to prove the point.

Outside the Minster the bells chimed in celebration as we posed for photographs in glorious sunshine. So it was back to Blandford Forum, to champagne on the lawn and a mixing of the Scots and English cultures as we prepared for the meal.

Unaccustomed as most people are to public speaking, they generally come good on a day like this, when plain sincerity shines through and brevity becomes the soul of being a hit.

Getting to know your own children takes time. But if I didn't know the inner Martin before his wedding, I discovered it on the day. For he got up and made a brave speech, acknowledging the absence of his mother and paying her a deeply moving tribute.

It was not something I could have tackled with any hope of composure. Martin knew the risk. But he took it—and succeeded with taste and dignity.

So after a night to remember, we headed north once more, glad of the summer suns and the clear blue sky and the warmth of fellowship and the privilege of being around to touch the wonders of a world which offers more than we probably deserve.

SO TODAY I'M 65 . . .

AT the breakfast hour this July morning, I'll watch the hands of the clock as they reach a quarter to nine and try to come to terms with the fact that I have been on this earth for exactly 65 years.

It is that watershed of life which somehow became the point of retirement (in this case I linger until the end of the month) and the official date of entry to the realms of old-age.

At first you cannot believe it, summoning up every known cliché about the passage of time, which seems like no time at all. The boy who stirs eternally within you denies every shred of evidence which says you have been around for so long.

Yet one look in the shaving-mirror tells another story of wear-and-tear which cannot be denied; and in all truth, you wouldn't wish it to be otherwise. For those lines of age and experience are drawn from a long and winding road of adventure on which you have tasted everything from quiet melancholy to the heights of ecstasy.

My life has been lived pretty much to the full, leaving such an appreciation of the good things that I am forever grateful for the sheer privilege of survival.

I first saw the light of day in that Aberdeenshire village of Maud which has remained central to my being. On my 50th birthday, armed with a bottle of champagne, I went back to those two rooms at Fedderate Cottages and stood in the corner where first I picked up the rhythm of breathing. The occupants, Bill and Isobel Clark, were most understanding.

A check on events of that July day in 1931 shows that King George V was holding a glittering reception at the Palace of Holyroodhouse, Oswald Mosley was leading his New Party of five into the Commons, to the jeers of the ruling socialists from whom he had just departed.

That great comedian Tommy Lorne was appearing at His Majesty's Theatre, Aberdeen, while Harry Gordon was entertaining at the city's Beach Pavilion, with supporting acts which included Flanagan and Allen. On the National Radio, Henry Hall's Gleneagles Band was filling the airwaves from 11pm till midnight.

That period of the 1930s, which left a childhood impression of a golden era, is one I would have wished to know with greater maturity. As opposed to the raucous blasts of today, I would like to have been a teenager when the dominant music of popular taste lay in the mellow tones of Lew Stone and Roy Fox—the heyday of gliding around a ballroom with a sense of ecstasy which owed nothing to a pill. I just caught the tail-end of that period which spilled over to the post-war years.

I would have revelled in a New York scene which could boast an array of popular composers like Cole Porter, Irving Berlin, George Gershwin, Richard Rodgers and Jerome Kern—all in full melodic flight at the same time, without a deafening amplifier in sight.

But to have enjoyed all that I would now be celebrating my 80th birthday! So I'll settle for the fact that I was born a little after my time—and try to take stock of what I was given.

That precious childhood of the 1930s was interrupted by the Second World War, so that I didn't know where to stop blaming the war for all that had changed and start acknowledging that childhood was slipping away in any case.

I did not regard teenage as a happy part of life. Nor do I hold fond memories of the twenties, an unsettled time of adapting to the calls of adulthood.

I was into my thirties before I began to taste the greater calm of maturity, a joy which increased with the succeeding decades, as you searched for that optimum but elusive point where experience and energy complement each other before that latter commodity begins to diminish.

Of the tasks facing medical science, one of my priorities would be to see them stretch that optimum point, delaying the onset of the downward curve so that more of us might see a century on earth. My only complaint with old age is that it doesn't last long enough!

For the moment, however, I'll settle for the fact that I have come thus far, counting my luck in a family with mixed fortunes when it comes to lifespan. Of three male cousins, I'm the only one to have passed 45.

Yet even this extended run hardly seems long enough to achieve what you would wish from this, as far as we know the only adventure we are likely to have on earth.

It puts into perspective the achievements of so many people who have had little more than half my lifespan. They range from Robert Burns in poetry to George Gershwin in music.

The lesson must be to appreciate our days, make the most of our time. It is a discipline I have tried to follow—and I will continue to do so as future milestones beckon from the horizons of time.

So I intend to enjoy this day when I become an old-age pensioner (let's forget this "senior citizen" nonsense). Facts are chiels that winna ding—and we had better face up to them. Which reminds me: What did I do with the pension book?